365

Fascinating

FACTS

about

JESUS

365

Fascinating

FACTS

about

JESUS

Robert Strand

New Leaf Press

First printing: March 2000
Third printing: February 2006

ISBN-13: 978-0-89221-488-4
ISBN-10: 0-89221-488-0
Library of Congress Catalog Number: 99-069282

Cover by Farewell Communications

Printed in the United States of America

WHAT ARE THE ODDS?

1

THERE are approximately 250 biblical prophecies about the birth and life of Jesus Christ which were written *before* He was born! The mathematical odds against this many events being fulfilled in a single person have been calculated to be about 1/ 1,000,000,000,000,000,000,000,000,000,000,000,000,000,000,000, 000,000,000,000,000,000,000,000,000,000,000,000,000,000,000!! AWESOME! If you didn't take the time to count them — these odds are 1 out of 1 followed by 90 zeroes!

Here is a very small listing of some of those prophecies.

JESUS WAS:
> Born of a virgin
> Born of the seed of Abraham
> Born of the tribe of Judah
> Born of the lineage of David
> Born at Bethlehem

The proof that Jesus is the Messiah is awesome — absolutely overwhelming! And perhaps the best proof of all is that He is alive today!

THE BIRTH OF DATES

2

THERE is one birth that is absolutely unique in all human history! Should it not also follow that any person knowing the unique circumstances of this birth would also expect an extraordinary life of accomplishments?! That's exactly what happened.

The precise date is not known but the date is generally considered to be 4 B.C. This birth was immersed in a miracle, clothed in mystery, and surrounded by the extraordinary.

This birth of Jesus Christ of Nazareth set the time boundaries and datelines of history. The Greeks attempted to date all other world events from their original Olympiad but were largely ignored. Rome attempted to measure history from the date of the founding of the Roman Empire and failed, too. Frenchmen revolted in the 18th century and attempted to label their revolution as the start of a new era and new calendar, but couldn't even convince the majority of the French people.

What the Greeks, Romans, and French have failed to do, Jesus Christ has accomplished. His arrival on earth in human form became the focal point of dated history and the calendar of the world was His. It was Christianized. Now we date time as B.C. or A.D. "Before Christ" or "In the year of our Lord."

3 ACKNOWLEDGED BY AN ENEMY

THE Roman emperor Julian had professed Christianity in his early years of power, and claimed to be a Christian. Then — without warning and without any known reason — turned viciously against the Christians and vowed to exterminate all Christian churches and Christians from the empire.

One day, as a particular Christian was being whipped by a Roman soldier, Julian was watching the event and then began to taunt the victim by saying, "Where is your carpenter of Nazareth now?"

This Christian replied, "He is driving nails into your coffin, O Emperor." This proved to be quite accurate. It's reported that when Julian next went into battle he was mortally wounded and that he then clutched some of his spilling blood in his hands and threw it into the sky with these words: "Thou hast conquered, O Galilean."

Four hundred years after His birth, the relevance of Jesus Christ was acknowledged by a powerful enemy!

4 WHAT DID HE LOOK LIKE?

NO one living today has ever seen the physical face of Jesus Christ! In fact, we don't even have a clue as to His appearance. Why? Because the Early Church strongly disapproved of idols or any kind of carved or "graven" image. Therefore, there is no contemporary record of Christ's physical looks.

However, the earliest representations show Him as a beardless youth and these date from the 3rd century. The traditional vision of a bearded Christ began only in the 4th century. There are many carvings, paintings, and castings dating from the 12th century which depict Him in facial hair.

Contrast this to His life and teachings which were recorded within about 70 years of His death. The earliest document was St. Paul's letter to the Romans, written about A.D. 58. Then in quick succession came Mark's Gospel; Matthew's, which was written for Jewish believers; and Luke's, which was written for Gentiles. The last written account was penned by the beloved apostle John about A.D. 100.

HOW MANY COMMANDMENTS?

5

DEVOUT Jews obey or attempt to obey 613 different commandments! And included are the "Ten Commandments." These commands are taken from the "Pentateuch," the first five books of the Old Testament, which for the Jew is the most important of all religious texts. Together these commandments provide a moral framework for life.

When Jesus was teaching about life here on earth, He boiled all of the 613 down to only two! The first is to love the Lord your God with all your heart, mind, soul, and strength and the second is to love your neighbor as yourself. Simplification . . . 613 down to 2! Simple, easy to understand . . . but a challenge to live out.

DID JESUS LAUGH?

6

DID the only Man who came from heaven to earth ever laugh? Do they laugh in heaven? The Bible puts this question to rest with the statement that in heaven there "no longer will be any curse" (Rev. 22:3). Yes, we all believe that heaven is one very happy place.

But did the Man who came from heaven laugh while He was here on this earth? Song creators, poets, writers, and artists have almost without fail portrayed Jesus as being the "man of sorrows . . . the man of griefs" but the Bible paints a very different picture.

Just consider one incident with me. The very first miracle Jesus performed was at a wedding! Have you ever attended a wedding that was sad? No! They are happy, joyous events. It happened in a small town, Cana. These Jewish weddings usually lasted for up to seven days and it was a matter of family pride that guests were to enjoy it to the fullest. Particularly with good food and wine that was to last all the way to the end.

On the third day of this joyous occasion there was a problem — they ran out of wine. Jesus turned six pots of water into wine! The master of ceremonies said, "Everyone brings out the choice wine first and then the cheaper wine after the guests have had too much to drink; but you have saved the best till now" (John 2:10).

Did Jesus laugh? Draw your own conclusions. At the very beginning of His ministry He makes use of His omnipotent power NOT to point out a solemn moral, NOT to relieve a sufferer's pain; NOT to preach — but to keep a happy wedding party from breaking up, to save a host and hostess from embarrassment!

Then, too, consider this: What kind of a self-portrait did Jesus paint of himself? He said He was a groom! A bridegroom who was celebrating with His followers! Yes . . . Jesus did laugh!

7 THE PEOPLE WHO COULD NOT WAIT

THE members of the "Order of the Star of the East," who were led by a Hindu mystic named Krishnamurti, held a strange belief about the return of Jesus Christ to this earth. In fact, they believed so strongly that they built a 2,000-seat amphitheater in 1925 which cost more than $100,000, in anticipation of this event which was to happen. Their strange belief was that Jesus would return to the earth, and in particular to this part of India. He would come walking across the Pacific Ocean to be welcomed by the waiting crowd in the seaside amphitheater. They gathered regularly for the next four years in preparation. When He did not arrive by 1929, this group finally gave up all hope and dissolved.

8 THE WORLD'S WORST CHURCH

THE "All Saints Church" of Sedlac, located in the former nation of Czechoslovakia, was completely looted of all its decorations and fine ornaments in the year A.D. 1600. However, this congregation was not deterred nor discouraged. These worshipers set about re-decorating their house of worship with human bones. They exhumed nearly 10,000 graves for what must be the most macabre interior in all of Christendom. The high-lights are a bony chandelier made up primarily of femurs and hundreds of skulls piled up in the shape of the "Schwarzenberk" family crest. It was all done in the name of Jesus Christ to honor some of His saints. In his well-known collection of books about travel, Fodor calls it a "ghastly fascination" and recommends that you stop in to take a look.

HE SERVED OTHERS

OFTEN, we underestimate the heart of God. We have a Creator who delights in giving . . . giving to us. Jesus said, "I always do what God asks me to do" (John 8:29). Then, later He also said that the father will do what you ask Him to (John 16:23). It's an interesting picture of the godhead . . . a picture of these two members serving each other.

In fact, Jesus even served food to other people. After the people who had followed Him returned, hungry, He fed them all (Mark 8:1–10). One of the first acts, after returning from the dead was to have prepared a lake-shore picnic complete with broiled fish for His disciples (John 21).

The bottom line is that Jesus is a servant.

10. A MOST UNUSUAL STEEPLE

IN the past, it was not unusual to see Billy Graham or young people who were followers of the "Jesus Movement," as well as others, flash the "one-way" sign. The right hand was raised with the index finger pointing heavenward. It may have seemed a new symbolism, but it was not new nor unique to the above.

This symbol has long been a favorite of any number of pulpiteers. An especially well-liked preacher of the First Presbyterian Church in Port Gibson, Mississippi, frequently used this gesture well over a hundred years ago. So in 1859, the worshippers of First Pres erected a steeple in his memory. On the very top, instead of the traditional cross, they placed a bronze cast of a hand with the index finger pointing upward toward heaven.

WHAT STAR?

THE Magi from the East came looking for the infant Jesus because of the appearance of a star! So, what star? What kind of star?

One hour and 20 minutes before sunrise on August 12, 3 B.C., the planet Jupiter rose in conjunction with Venus, the "morning star." This particular planetary alignment could have created a blazing light in the sky! Jupiter, which is considered, astrologically, the "Father of the gods" when co-joined with Venus could well have been interpreted as heralding the birth of a king . . . since Venus is the goddess of fertility.

Another consideration is noted by the American scholar E.L. Martin — that Jupiter was stationary in the heavens on December 25, 2 B.C. because it would have reached its orbital point and would have changed its direction of movement. It would have been in the direction of Bethlehem as seen from Jerusalem. This, he thinks was the date of the Epiphany.

WHEN WAS JESUS BORN?

THERE is no early tradition of the exact date given to the birth of Jesus! Further, there are no widely celebrated festivals which have been documented before the 4th century. Clement of Alexandria, quite early in the 3rd century, does write about the tradition that Jesus was born on the 20th of May.

The first use of December 25 as the birth date of Jesus begins in the year of A.D. 336 from Rome. To the pagan Romans this was the birthday of "Unconquered Sun." The emperor Constantine's family had been sun worshippers . . . then his vision of the Cross came to him from the sun. Therefore it was easy to transfer the festival to the "Sun of Righteousness."

In the East, Christmas was long celebrated on January 6, and to this day is still commemorated by the Armenian Church. More generally, this is "Epiphany," the appearance to the Magi, symbolically representing the Gentiles who were people of the world outside of Judaism. Whatever these events . . . it is certain that Jesus was born of a human mother, Mary, and that intellectuals and shepherds, Jews and Gentiles, angels and the heavenly host, were the first to celebrate the birth of a different kind of King!

YOU CAN SEE HIS NAME IN LIGHTS

ON Broadway, where all lights are bright, there have been two very popular musicals about Jesus. The first, called *Godspell,* was a long-running hit about the good news of the gospel of Jesus. An early sixties, feel-good fest, it gave new life to young people who followed His teachings.

But, then, nothing can top the impact of *Jesus Christ Superstar.* People everywhere sang and danced to the lively tunes and contemporary words superimposed on the gospel message. It was written by Andrew Lloyd Webber and his cohort Tim Rice.

THE UNDERGROUND CHURCH

THE world's largest active salt mine is located in Zipaquira, Colombia. Contained as part of the mine, more than 800 feet deep into the mountainside is the unique "Salt Cathedral." A remarkable place of worship . . . magnificent, yet so earth-bound. The three main corridors have ceilings arching 73 feet high supported by columns of solid salt. It took about six years to excavate and seats up to 5,000 people. It must give a whole new meaning to the statement of Jesus that "you are the salt of the earth" (Matt. 5:13).

HE WAS NOT A CAPRICORN

SCHOLARS are quite sure that Jesus was not born on December 25 of the first year A.D. Historically, we are also aware that before the 16th century, calendars were always inaccurate. Some were based on the 28-day lunar cycle, some on the solar. The Egyptians even had a "second lunar calendar" which featured a civil year upon which they determined various religious celebrations and duties. Throw in a few Roman superstitions about months with even numbers, the Jewish need for seven days in a week so the Sabbath could be celebrated, and we are still left wondering.

Since "Passover" falls ten days after the vernal equinox, it was decided that Christmas should be celebrated a few days after the winter solstice, which conveniently leaves nine months in between.

The traditional observation of Christ's birthday began somewhere about A.D. 336, which doesn't answer the question of what month in which He was born. To add another element to this puzzle, according to the Jewish calendar, which began with the creation at year 1, Jesus was born in the year 3761.

THE ULTIMATE ALLEGORY

16

WHEN speaking to the crowds Jesus often used parables, word pictures, and allegories . . . but none quite as imaginative as some of the religious writings to come out of England during the 17th century. How about trying some of the following on for allegorical essays?

"Eggs of Charity, Layed by the Chickens of the Covenant and Boiled with the Water of the Divine: Take Ye and Eat."

Or how about this one? "Spiritual Milk for Babes, Drawn Out of the Breasts of Both Testaments for Their Souls' Nourishment: A Catechism." And then, there was this one: "High-heeled Shoes for Dwarfs in Holiness."

Perhaps the most bizarre was *A Wordless Book,* which contained no words but still contained a message. In this book there are eight pages . . . the first two were black, the second two red, the next two were white, and the last two were gold. They symbolized, in order, the evil of mankind, the redemption of mankind, the new-found purity of the soul after it had been washed in the blood of the Lamb, and finally, the gold represented the eternal bliss awaiting the soul.

WHAT WAS JESUS' LAST NAME?

17

ACCORDING to Jewish tradition, your last name was always determined by your father's given name. Therefore, "Ben," which means "the son of," would precede your father's name. An example is shown to us in the movie *Ben Hur.* You would know that the protagonist, played by Charlton Heston, was the "son of Hur." It follows, then, that the Lord's complete name would have been "Jesus Ben Joseph."

18 COULD THIS BE THE WORST MIRACLE?

JESUS, during His earthly ministry, was noted for the performance of many miracles, which ranged from turning water into wine to raising people from the dead. And to this day many of His followers claim to be able to do the same.

In Bombay, India, in 1966, a Hindu yogi named "Rao" loudly announced his intention to perform the miracle of walking on water just like Jesus had done. Six hundred prominent members of Bombay society were invited to witness this miracle spectacle . . . with tickets being sold at $100 a piece!

At the appointed day and appointed time . . . now garbed in flowing white robes, the snowy-bearded mystic Rao stood majestically on the side of a five-foot deep pool. He bowed his head and prayed silently for a number of minutes, looked up, then stepped confidently and with boldness into the watery void. He sank immediately to the bottom! I wonder how many members of that Bombay society asked for a refund?

19 JESUS STANDS

THE Bible contains many references to Jesus "sitting at the right hand of God" but only once does it say He was standing (Acts 7:55–56). Stephen was a young Christian of great faith and power. Because he was so full of wisdom and the presence of Christ within and had a lifestyle that caused condemnation in others, many people became jealous of him and plotted to put him to death. He was then brought before the Council and questioned by the high priests. Stephen spoke with such truth and eloquence that those observing said his face became like that of an angel. In his closing statement, he turned on his accusers for betraying and murdering Jesus. The crowd became incensed and closed in on him and dragged him out of the city to be stoned.

Then, just before he was to be stoned, he looked up toward heaven and said, "Look! I see heaven open and the Son of Man standing at the right hand of God" (Acts 7:56). Following this they covered their ears, yelling at the top of their voices, and began the stoning of the first Christian martyr.

His last words as he fell to his knees under the stoning were these: "Lord, do not hold this sin against them" (Acts 7:60). Then he died. The young man holding the coats of those throwing the stones was named "Saul." His name was later changed to "Paul" and he became the great Apostle.

20. WHAT COIN?

JESUS called attention to a number of different coins as He made teaching points. Very likely the coin referred to by Him when He made the pronouncement about payment of tribute to Caesar would have been a "denarius," the small silver coin equivalent to a laborer's wage for a day's work.

The "two very small copper coins," perhaps better known as the "widow's mite," were the Greek "lepton," a coin of the very least value in circulation at that time.

The infamous "30 pieces of silver" paid to Judas Iscariot were most likely silver shekels, equivalent to approximately 120 "denarii." Incidently, this was the exact amount set by way of compensation or "blood money" which was to be payable for a slave who was accidently killed, according to the Old Testament.

THE JEFFERSONIAN BIBLE

THOMAS Jefferson created a special edition of the Bible based solely on selected moral teachings of Jesus. During the 18th century, the U.S. Congress did issue this Bible with all references to the supernatural in the life of Christ completely eliminated. The closing words of this special Bible edition are: "There laid they Jesus and rolled a great stone at the mouth of the sepulchre and departed." I for one am thankful that we have a complete Bible which includes the happy news that "HE IS NOT HERE, HE IS RISEN!"

THE REVERSAL
OF VALUES

22

THE Gospel according to John is the only recording we have of the account of Jesus washing the feet of His disciples at the "Last Supper." Peter protested this action, vehemently! Why? The dialogue which took place pointed symbolically to baptism and the cleansing from sin which Jesus' ultimate sacrifice would bring. However, this symbolically demonstrated the reversal of values, too. It was the traditional, customary duty of a wife or a slave to wash the master's feet when he entered the house because feet would become dirty and dusty after having walked about in open sandals with no paved streets or walks.

Jesus, in this incident, was showing all of us for all time that the way to glory is down and not up — not by the way of power but by the way of humility.

GARDEN TOMB'S SOIL
IS ANALYZED

23

HISTORICALLY, we know that Jesus was laid to rest in a tomb which had been prepared for somebody else. The location had been lost but was "discovered" in 1885. The British general Gordon was absolutely convinced that this was the place where the body of Jesus had lain. The Garden Tomb, which had been hidden for centuries, was covered with rubbish and overgrowth about 20 feet deep. When they first cleared the spot, they did it with great caution, gathering all the dust and debris within the tomb and carefully shipping it to the "Scientific Association of Great Britain." Every part of it was analyzed . . . but there was absolutely no trace of any kind of human remains. If this was the real tomb of Christ . . . then Jesus was the first to be laid there and He was also the last!

DESPERATION
IN ACTION

24

CONCERNED friends were so desperate that they tore off a roof to get their friend to Jesus! Was this as simple as it sounded? Judean houses were built of wood and plaster and had flat roofs. The account in Mark's Gospel tells of the friends of the paralyzed man "unroofing the roof" and "digging it out." This would have been fairly easy to do. In Luke's written version, he alludes to an adaptation of a roof constructed in Greece or Italy. His account has the men up on top of the roof to lower the paralytic in "through the tiles."

But whichever account is correct, both indicate the same kind of characteristics on the part of the helpers — determination and faith — two elements which are in such short supply today.

OLDER THAN HIS MOTHER THOUGHT?

25

JESUS was not born in A.D. 0 or even A.D. 1 as you might have been thinking. Many scholars place His birth at about 3 to 5 B.C. Creating calendars that really worked presented unsolvable problems for centuries. Julius Caesar developed a calendar to accommodate a year that lasted 365 days. Since a year is really 365.242199 days, 11 minutes and 14 seconds were unaccounted for every year. After 1,000 years, the Julian calendar was 7 days off . . . making it out of step with the seasons. Easter which was considered to be the highest Christian holiday, is determined according to the spring or vernal equinox. But by 1545, it was ten days later when compared to the lunar calendar. Of course, after much figuring, many retroactive adjustments were made. Hence, the pivotal person of the Christian calendar had His birth year moved back a few years.

WHAT ABOUT THOSE HIDDEN YEARS?

26

JESUS' fame came about in the last three years of His short life. His obscurity lasted ten times longer than His ministry . . . 30 years. We know almost nothing about those years because the Bible is strangely quiet about this time period. So we must speculate on what Jesus must have done in those silent years.

Nazareth was the village of His growing-up years — a nothing place off the main thoroughfares which had no historical roots in the Old Testament. Its reputation was so poor that the proud Jerusalemites laughed: "Can any good thing come out of Nazareth?" It was the place of life preparation for Him.

We know even less about the home life of Jesus. It seems very likely that Joseph died during Jesus' early teens because Joseph is not mentioned after the 12th birthday of Jesus. As the oldest son of Mary, He would have had to assume the heavy responsibilities at Joseph's death. He would have carried on the trade of His father, that of a carpenter. Can you imagine the craftsmanship of a dining table fashioned by the Son of God? This young carpenter must have had many delighted customers.

This Son of God would have honored manual labor as He built yokes, plows, and farm implements as well as houses and furnishings. We have a seriously distorted picture of Jesus if we think of Him as pale, timid, and frail. His arms would have bulged with well-exercised muscles. His mountain-tested legs would easily carry Him about the countryside. Jesus asked for and needed no help when He overturned the tables of the greedy moneychangers in the temple courtyard. Those hidden years would have made Jesus into a real man's man, preparing Him for the vigors of the life of ministry and for the culminating three years of His life!

HOW FAR-REACHING IS HIS INFLUENCE?

HIS active life work lasted a bit less than three years. He held no political position in public life. He had almost no money and very few material possessions. He never wrote a book, poem, or song. He never painted a picture. He is not known for any clever invention. He never used force, other than throwing the moneychangers out of the temple. He was hated by the religious and political authorities, arrested, condemned, tortured, and executed. And yet. . . .

His teachings are of enormous relevance for us today. If what He said was true, we have the answers, profound answers, to some of the greatest questions that have perplexed peoples down through the centuries of time. These are issues of life and death, God and humanity, humanity relating to each other, time and eternity . . . and a whole lot more. His life and character wrapped up in a single being what all of us would like to be in our best moments.

His death, beyond any question or dispute, was the most famous death in all of human history. No other death has aroused even a fraction of such intense feelings over these hundreds of years. This death is still the subject of study.

His resurrection was either the most outstanding event of all time or else a monstrous hoax perpetrated on a trusting humanity.

And today . . . about 2,000 years after these events took place in history . . . more than 1,400,000,000 people throughout this world profess to follow Him. (This is approximately one-third of the world's population.) Few have the luxury of being neutral about Jesus. No other human being has been so loved and so hated, so adored and so despised, so proclaimed and so opposed.

THE ANCIENT ROMAN EMPIRE AND TAXES

JESUS was born into a world at peace. However, it was a Roman peace, a peace watched over by the ever-vigilant Roman armed legions whose presence were enough to discourage any thought of a possible revolt even in the most remote corners of this vast empire. For the most part, this Roman peace triggered prosperity and luxuries for most provinces.

This was not true of Jesus' homeland, a region of some 8,000 square miles on the far eastern edge of Rome's domain. The million or so Jews living there had been placed under a heavy yoke when Pompey conquered Jerusalem in 63 B.C. This was considered not much more than another tax-paying unit in one of history's most extensive systems of taxation. This was a system built and dependent on the taxable contributions of all the conquered peoples from all over the empire.

The great public works of the Roman government . . . great roads, aqueducts which flowed with life-giving water, marble buildings, government projects, and public coliseums were all funded by taxes. Now these taxes, as in our day, would prove to be the most burdensome on the lowest members of the empire totem pole.

In this taxation, as in everything else Rome did, there was a strong-armed attitude. Rome was a harsh overlord. In order to pull this off, provincial governors were empowered to conduct a census to organize Rome's tax rolls. It was just such a Roman mandate that sent Joseph and the very pregnant Mary on a 90-mile journey to Bethlehem.

ANOINTING
WITH OIL

OILS were used to cleanse the skin and protect it from the dry, arid climate of the Middle East. Some of these oils were perfumed with plants, flowers, or barks from India and other faraway lands. Because these oils were rare and expensive, they were kept in "alabastrons," small alabaster or clay containers with narrow necks that restricted the flow.

Oils were also used for ceremonial purposes. Kings were to be anointed with holy oil at their coronation to show that they were consecrated to God. You can read about the anointing of King Saul or King David by the prophet Samuel. Interestingly, the term "Messiah" comes from the Hebrew "mashi'ah" meaning the "anointed one."

While Jesus was in Bethany in the home of a man known as Simon the Leper, a woman came to Jesus with an alabaster jar of very expensive perfume, which she poured on His head as He was reclining at the table. When the disciples watched this action they became indignant and demanded to know why this wasn't sold and given to the poor. Jesus replied that she had done a beautiful thing and this selfless action of hers would be told as a memorial. She knew or sensed something that none of those disciples had. To her, Jesus was the "anointed one," the MESSIAH!

CERTAIN POOR
SHEPHERDS

AFTER Jesus had been born and was asleep in the manger, shepherds were in the countryside about Bethlehem tending their flocks. These humble men would be the first to learn that a miracle had occurred that glorious night.

Shepherds played an important part in the story and life of Jesus. They remind us that Jesus descended from David, the Shepherd King. Jesus would later speak of himself as the "Good Shepherd" because everyone who lived in that part of the world would immediately grasp the significance. The relationship between the shepherd and the sheep was very special. And this relationship has forever been immortalized with this line: "The Lord is my shepherd, I shall not want . . ." (Ps. 23:1).

In those days shepherds led their flocks, while now, in the West, they are driven. Even today, you can still observe shepherds on the hillsides of Israel calling to their sheep in a distinctive voice so that every sheep recognizes that voice. Their lot wasn't easy . . . always outdoors in all kinds of weather. Usually this man ate only what he could carry, simple fare, bread, cheese, olives, figs, dates, and raisins. Finding water for the flock was always a problem.

Then, too, the hills around Bethlehem at that time were full of predators such as bears, leopards, jackals, and sometimes a stray hyena or more. To defend his sheep against such enemies the shepherd was armed with a slingshot and a rod, which was a wooden club likely embedded with sharp nails. It was not unusual for a shepherd to lose his life in warding off such attacks.

Jesus said for all people for all time: "I am the Good Shepherd, I lay my life down for the sheep" (John 10:14–15).

THE MOST UNUSUAL COMMUNION?

WHEN Lord Strothallan, a Jacobite hero, was mortally wounded in the Battle of Culloden Field on April 15, 1745, he requested communion before he died. A priest administered the last rites and offered him a Eucharist of whiskey and oatcake because there was nothing else immediately available.

However, you should be aware that there is also a controversy surrounding this story. A less romantic source agrees that the communion was observed, and there is also agreement on the fact that it was oatcake . . . but this source insists that Strothallan washed it down with water. All in observance of the Lord's Last Supper.

THE MOST PERSISTENT HERMIT

IN the book *Decline and Fall of the Roman Empire,* the author, Edward Gibbon, relates the life story of one Simeon Stylites, a humble Syrian shepherd who became an anchorite monk. After his novitiate, during which he repeatedly had to be rescued from committing "pious suicide," Simeon chained himself to the top of a column 60 feet high. And there he remained for the rest of his life . . . 30

long years, 30 hot summers, 30 cold winters, 30 changes of seasons! Imagine! To pass away the decades of time, Simeon prayed a lot and did sit-ups. His is a record which no contemporary or current flagpole sitter has even begun to approach.

Why? All in the name of serving Jesus Christ!

WHOSE IMAGE?

33

IN a "reliquary" in the chapel of the dukes of Savoy at Turin Cathedral lies a piece of cloth which measures 14 feet 5 inches by 3 feet 8 inches. This bears the faint image of the front and back of a man. Approximately four times in each century this cloth is put on display for thousands of pilgrims who flock to see it. It's believed that this cloth bears the image of Jesus Christ. Therefore, when viewing it, pilgrims believe they are looking at the very features of Jesus.

The "Holy Shroud of Turin" certainly is one of the most controversial pieces of cloth in the world. If it is the real thing, it has to be the most precious of all the relics from the time of Christ. It is believed to be the linen wrap in which Christ's body was placed in the tomb following His crucifixion. The image appears to have been imprinted on the cloth much like an old-fashioned photographic plate.

The shroud purportedly was to have been kept in hiding for the first three centuries while the Early Church was persecuted. Later it was taken by the Byzantine rulers of Constantinople and it remained in their possession until the city was captured in 1204. It was then taken by the Crusaders to Besancon Cathedral in the French province of Doubs, where it narrowly escaped being destroyed by fire in 1349. Finally . . . the shroud was presented to the dukes of Savoy in 1432. There it was slightly damaged in another fire at the palace. For safekeeping it was taken to the cathedral at Turin and has been kept there since 1578.

WHAT'S IN A PHRASE?

34

JESUS said: "It is easier for a camel to go through the eye of a needle than for a rich man to enter into the kingdom of God" (Matt. 19:24; Mark 10:25; Luke 18:25). Some scholars have claimed this memorable, even humorous, quotation is a translation that has been mistaken. Some Greek and Armenian versions of the Bible refer to a "rope" rather than to a camel. However . . . proverbs taken from the Talmud and the Koran do allude to a large animal, perhaps even one so large as an elephant, passing through a needle's eye. Jesus may have chosen the word "camel" for emphasis so that no one would forget the illustration.

Or another plausible explanation is that ancient cities which had walls built about them for safety also provided an "after hours" entrance — a very small gate or gateway which would allow a camel to go through it only if it were made to crawl through the gate after it had been unloaded. This was called the "eye of the needle." It was made very small for security reasons. Only one person or animal at a time could enter. If the people entering were bent on mischief or making trouble, they could be dealt with by the guards one at a time.

But in any translation, explanation, or interpretation . . . let's not lose the meaning. It is difficult for people who have learned to trust in their riches to humble themselves so that they, too, can enter the kingdom of God.

35 WHO ROBBED PETER TO PAY PAUL?

WHERE did this phrase come from? A common fable about this phrase that has been circulated is related to the fact that in 1550 many of the estates of St. Peter's, Westminster, England, were appropriated to pay for much-needed repairs on St. Paul's Cathedral.

But, supposedly, the origin goes back to common usage in the year 1380. The preacher John Wyclif was said to have declared, "How should God approve that you rob Peter, and give this robbery to Paul in the name of Christ?"

36 THE MESSIAH

THE name Jesus means "he will save" or "savior," and was given to the son of Mary to show that He would save His people from their sins. The naming of the Messiah was so important that an angel was dispatched from heaven to make sure He would be given the correct name. The Old Testament equivalent was "Joshua" or "jeshua." In the Hebrew language, Messiah, means "the Anointed One." At the time of the birth of Jesus, there was an intense hope among the Jews that an "Anointed One" would come in order to be the ideal king — one who would stand alongside an ideal high priest or perhaps a person who would embody both of these ideals into one person.

Later in His ministry when Christ asked His disciples, "Who do you say that I am?" Peter was ready with this simple phrase, "You are the Christ" (Mark 8:29). This phrase embodied all the hopes, yearnings, and promises of centuries for the Jewish people.

THE SEA OF GALILEE

THE Sea of Galilee is the world's lowest freshwater lake at 680 feet below sea level. This lake is about 13 miles long and as wide as 8 miles. In some spots it is as deep as 150 feet. It was also known as the "Lake of Chinnereth," the "Sea of Tiberias," or the "Lake of Gennesaret." This lake is in the center of some of the most fertile area of Israel. It is surrounded by bountiful fields and lush orchards.

It was the center of the fishing industry and a main source of income in Jesus' day. More than 40 different species of fish come from these waters. The fish that were caught were dried or salted and then exported through all of the region and beyond. It was here where Peter and Andrew were tending their nets when Jesus invited them to become "fishers of men."

It was from the seaside town of Capernaum that He launched His Galilean ministry. Mary Magdalene came from the tiny, nearby village of Magdala. It was on these beautiful shores that Jesus fed the crowd of 5,000 with the five loaves and two fishes of the boy's lunch. It was here that He drove the demons from the man possessed and into the herd of swine who drowned themselves in the lake. It was here that Jesus appeared to His fishing disciples after the resurrection with the invitation to come and eat the fish which He had prepared on the fire. And it was in this setting that Jesus restored Peter by commanding him to "feed" His sheep.

And would you believe it? To this day, it's still pure enough from which to drink!

THE BIG
FISHERMAN

38

SIMON Peter was a humble, brash Galilean fisherman when Jesus called him to become one of His disciples. Peter is often portrayed as being impetuous in his actions . . . but his faith in Christ was positive. He was the first to really recognize Jesus as the Messiah.

At the Last Supper, Peter boldly declared that he would never desert or turn away from Jesus. Despite the bravado, mere hours later he had denied that he had ever known Him. In spite of the denial, Jesus met with him and some of the other disciples and gave Peter an important role in the first church. It was this same Peter who preached on the Day of Pentecost when 3,000 joined the church in a day. Peter was also one of the first to realize that the gospel of Jesus Christ was for all people and not exclusively for the Jews. He was martyred for being a follower of Jesus Christ.

JESUS TELLS US
WHO HE IS

39

JOHN'S Gospel records some of the teachings of Christ which are not found in any of the other Gospel records. These are statements Christ made in regards to himself. These give us a composite picture painted by Jesus of who He considered himself to be:

I am the living bread that came down from heaven. If anyone eats of this bread, he will live forever (John 6:51).

I am the light of the world. Whoever follows me will never walk in darkness, but will have the light of life (John 8:12).

I am the gate for the sheep. All who ever came before me were thieves and robbers, but the sheep did not listen to them. I am the gate; whoever enters through me will be saved. He will come in and go out, and find pasture (John 10:7–9).

I am the good shepherd. The good shepherd lays down his life for the sheep (John 10:11).

I am the resurrection and the life. He who believes in

me will live, even though he dies; and whoever lives and believes in me will never die. Do you believe this? (John 11:25–26).

I am the way and the truth and the life. No one comes to the Father except through me (John 14:6).

I am the vine; you are the branches. If a man remains in me and I in him, he will bear much fruit; apart from me you can do nothing (John 15:5).

THE MESSAGE OF JESUS

MANY people today think only in terms of the "Sermon on the Mount" which can be summed up according to popular opinion in the "Golden Rule." Yes . . . it's in the Bible, too: "So in everything, do to others what you would have them do to you, for this sums up the Law and the Prophets" (Matt. 7:12). But the real essence of Jesus' message was that "the kingdom of God" had arrived in people's lives. The message that Jesus came to deliver can be summed up like this:

• The Kingdom of God . . . means that the rule of God is in the life of human beings. It also meant the realm or community where God's rule is obeyed. Jesus taught, particularly in His parables, that God is at work building the kingdom.

• Repent and believe . . . the kingdom of God is near but you must turn away from your sins and believe the Good News! People, in order to be a part of the kingdom, must repent and have a total change of heart. They are to accept the rule of God in their hearts.

• Jesus taught about himself . . . that the way to eternal life is through Him. That He and the Father were one and the same. He was the way to God.

• Joy . . . marked His life and teachings. There is a glorious note of joy in all that He did! The kingdom of God frees people so that they can live a full, happy, meaningful, complete, and joyful life.

• To be a disciple . . . was a great, wonderful privilege! He didn't lay great burdens on His followers . . . but told them that His yoke was easy and His burden was light (Matt. 11:30). His followers were to be like Him in life, actions, and ministry. They were to share His life, His joy, and His future glory!

41 SHILOH

THIS name comes to us from the prophecy of the aged patriarch Jacob who on his deathbed pronounced blessings on each of his sons. "The scepter shall not depart from Judah, nor a lawgiver from between his feet, until Shiloh comes" (Gen. 49:10). As you read the blessings you will also find scathing rebuke where there has been moral failure. Some instances of instability, lust, and cruelty forfeited the blessings of birthright. But you can also find special blessings reserved exclusively for the tribes of Judah and Joseph.

In the blessing pronounced on the descendants of Judah there is another piece of the mosiac of messianic prophecy. The specific tribe from which the Messiah would come is revealed. This blessing and prophecy gives us the name "Shiloh." Its root meaning is "to rest" or "to give rest." It is another Old Testament prophecy regarding the rest and peace which Jesus gives to all who follow Him.

There is a place in the state of Tennessee with this beautiful name, Shiloh. However, today it is known only as a place of bloodshed. Our history of the Civil War reveals to us that more than 25,000 men were killed on this battlefield. Those events are the opposite of the meaning of the word.

Jesus Christ is true to the meaning of all of the great titles given to Him. These are descriptions of His character and life mission. In this little-known title, He is the only One who can still bring rest to His people. Hear His promise once more, "Come to me, all you who are weary and burdened and I will give you rest" (Matt. 11:28).

42 JESUS WAS A JEW

CHRIST could have been born a Roman. The proudest claim of His day was "Civus Romanus sum!" (I am a Roman citizen.) At His birth, Rome ruled the world and to be citizen of Rome meant you could enjoy all the privileges of the empire.

Or Christ could have been born a Greek. This race has given to the world aesthetics and a beautiful language. Rome conquered Greece . . . but the Greek language would become the universal language.

But Christ did not choose to be identified with "The glory that was Greece or the grandeur that was Rome" according to Poe. Rather He became a member of the most downtrodden, despised race of people in His day. In fact, we are still dealing with anti-Semitism in our era. Just witness the horrors of the Holocaust. Jesus was a Jew!

Sholem Asch writes about being a Jew: "Jesus Christ is the outstanding personality of all time. . . Is still a Teacher whose teaching is such a guidepost for the world we live in. . . . He became the Light of the World. Why shouldn't I, a Jew, be proud of that?"

Why, then, do we today still attempt to portray Christ as having blond hair and blue eyes? Let's give respect to His heritage!

ALPHA AND OMEGA

43

WHAT a magnificent title! Three times in the very last book of the Bible is this title spoken and written. This is the same title in which God the Father refers to himself. This title, then, is another witness to the divinity and deity of Christ.

Alpha and *omega* are the words for the first and last letters of the Greek alphabet. Their meaning becomes very clear as Jesus gives it, "The beginning and the end, the first and the last."

He is alpha! The beginning, the first! First . . . before creation, before mankind, before the ancient world empires of Babylon, Egypt, Greece, Medo-Persia, and Rome! First . . . before time began, before geology, before the solar system! First . . . beyond the imagination of our finite minds! FIRST! ALPHA!

He is omega! The end, the last! After everything is finished, He is the exclamation point in all eternity!

Jesus has no beginning or ending. He is eternal! The alphabet, whether ours or the Greek — alpha to omega or a to z — are the same letters used to write the Bible or a play by Shakespeare or the Gettysburg Address by a president. These same letters make up lofty proclamations or guidelines given by a parent to a child.

As the alpha and the omega, He is the Lord of beginnings as well as being there in all our endings. There is comfort in this title. There is courage which can be derived from this title. He is God of all of our beginnings and endings. Jesus Christ is the alpha and the omega!

ALL
INCLUSIVE

IN the Greek monastery of Mount Athos, *nothing* female is ever allowed to enter through its gates. Men can enter but not women; boys can enter but not girls; roosters but no hens; stallions but not mares; bulls but not cows. The border is always patrolled by armed guards to absolutely ensure that nothing feminine passes through their gates. It has been this way since the 13th century.

What a contrast to the Church which Christ established. Paul wrote in his letter to the church at Galatia these words: "There is neither Jew nor Greek, slave nor free, male nor female, for you are all one in Christ Jesus" (Gal. 3:28).

SOME FASCINATING
RELIGIOUS TIDBITS

HAIRS from the tail of a mule ridden by the crusader Peter the Hermit brought huge prices as sacred relics throughout Europe during the 14th century.

There have been 263 popes.

On the stone temples of Madura in southern India, there are more than 30 million carved images of gods and goddesses.

Before the Chinese takeover of Tibet in 1952, 25 percent of the males in the country were Buddhist monks.

Hugnes was archbishop of Reims in the 10th century when he was only five years old.

In the 11th century, Benedict IX was pope at 11 years old.

The Puritans, in America, forbade the singing of any Christmas carols in their worship.

The toe of the bronze statue of St. Peter in St. Peter's Cathedral in Rome is worn down almost to a nub by the great number of pilgrims who have kissed it through the centuries.

There are approximately 370,000 churches of all kinds of denominations in America.

The American Bible Society, a group that has fewer than a million members, has distributed more than a billion Bibles since it was founded in 1816.

Forty-seven Bibles are sold or distributed throughout the world every minute of every day making it the number one seller of all time for non-fiction or any other kind of book.

THE DOME OF THE ROCK

46

THE "Dome of the Rock" in Jerusalem is one of the few shrines in the world simultaneously sacred to three religions: Christianity, Judaism, and Islam. According to the Jews, the rock beneath the dome marks the spot where Abraham prepared to sacrifice his son Isaac, and later it was the site where Solomon built his magnificent temple. For the Moslems, this is the holy ground where the prophet Muhammad made his famous "Night Flight" on the back of the winged barak.

Christians believe this to be the rock from which Jesus is once to have preached a sermon. Today . . . it is the very center of the unrest and conflicts which still plague the city of Jerusalem. We are still to "pray for the peace of Jerusalem" (Ps. 122:6).

THE CITY OF BETHLEHEM

47

THE name "Bethlehem" means the "house of bread." This is one of the most-remembered and known towns in Judea. It is near where Jacob buried his beloved wife Rachel, but at that time was named Ephrath. It is also called "Bethlehem-Ephratah" or "Bethlehem-judah." The old name lingered in usage long after the reign of King David.

This is a city which overlooks the main highway to Hebron and Egypt. The site of the city is on a commanding limestone ridge of the Judean highland. Then there was another conquest and the city fell into the hands of the tribe of Judah. Ibzan of Bethlehem judged Israel after the reign of Jephthah. This was the home of Elimelech, the husband of Naomi and father-in-law of Ruth. Boaz, who later married the Moabitess Ruth, was also a resident of this city.

David was born in Bethlehem and it was here that he was also anointed as the future king by the prophet Samuel. Here is the special well from which David's three heroes brought him water when he was running from the persecution of King Saul. This well is believed to be in existence to this very day on the north side of the village.

Here is where all the male children were slain by order of King Herod. Bethlehem is about five miles south of Jerusalem at an average elevation of 2,550 above sea level, which is about 100 feet higher than Jerusalem itself.

And of course, most importantly, Bethlehem is remembered because it was the birthplace, birth-city, of Jesus Christ.

WHAT IS A "PARABLE"?

48

ONE of the things for which Christ is best known is His telling of "parables." It's a word derived from the original Greek verb *paraballo* meaning to "lay by the side of, to compare such as a likeness or similitude." It's also the Hebrew *mashal*. As Jesus used parables they became instructive maxims, or proverbs.

It's really quite a broad term which covered more than the lengthened narratives. Many of the sayings of our Lord contained the germ of a parable . . . such as "Can the blind lead the blind?" or "Physician, heal thyself." The parable was used to set forth a spiritual truth, to make truth, doctrine, and theology more easily understood. These were not fables or myths. It is illustrative, an assist in making truth intelligible. It was a hook upon which to hang truth in the mind of the listener. The minds of the listeners were easily engaged by such vivid pictures — pictures which were not quickly forgotten. A fabulous teaching tool which Jesus used to perfection.

He told 38 parables . . . the numbers depend on who does the counting, but most scholars agree that it's somewhere in this number and is a bit subjected to argument. But of these 38, more than half of them dealt with money and the use of money. Did He know something about our day?

When we think of parables and Jesus, our minds center most on the parable of the "Good Samaritan" or the "Prodigal Son" and a whole host of others.

A most telling observation was penned by the Gospel writer Mark: "He did not say anything to them without using a parable!" (Mark 4:34). Jesus was the world's most fascinating story teller! No wonder people flocked to hear Him teach!

THE FINAL
WORD

49

CHRISTOPHER Wren was commissioned to rebuild St. Paul's Cathedral and much of London after the "great fire" of 1666. When he submitted his plans, a member of the city council insisted that the roof required better supports, more supports, and extra pillars to support the domed roof. In vain, Wren argued that his planned structure was perfectly safe. But the politician knew better. He also managed to spread alarm through the community and succeeded in pressuring Wren to add the supports.

Many years later, when both the artist and politician were dead, some repairs and cleaning were performed on the cathedral. The workmen were surprised to discover that, invisible from the floor below, the extra columns Wren put in were two inches short of touching and supporting the roof. Thus Wren, who claimed that he did his artistic/architectural designs because of spiritual inspiration he received from worship, had satisfied his critics and made his vindication as a designer. All in the name of Jesus Christ whom he claimed to be serving.

CHRIST'S LAST WILL
AND TESTAMENT

50

He left . . .
His purse to Judas.
His body to Joseph of Arimathea and Nicodemus.
His mother to John the Beloved disciple.
His seamless robe to the soldiers.
His peace to His disciples.
His last supper to His followers.
His baptism to new believers.
His love to the children.
His healing to the sick.
His teachings to the hungry in mind and spirit.
His church to society.
His Gospel to the world.
His hope for the hopeless.
His presence with all of God's children.

51   SWEET REVENGE

LORD Byron once presented his publisher, John Murray, with a beautiful, hand-bound copy of the Bible, which the latter proudly displayed in his house for all to see. One of Murray's many guests was leafing through the Bible when he noticed that there had been a slight alteration to the last word in the Gospel of John:

> I find no basis for a charge against him [Jesus]. But it is your custom for me to release to you one prisoner at the time of the Passover. Do you want me to release "the king of the Jews?" They shouted back, "No, not him! Give us Barabbas!" Now Barabbas was a *PUBLISHER* (John 18:39–40).

52   CALVARY

WHEN Henry Huntington, the railroad tycoon and avid art collector, was in the hospital and about to undergo surgery, he solemnly summoned his agent for buying rare books, Dr. A.S.W. Rosenbach, and his art dealer, Sir Joseph Duveen. When they arrived he asked them to sit on either side of his bed, where he lay with his arms outstretched. After some small talk, during which the dealers muttered encouraging hopes for the health of their largest and most prolific customer, Huntington turned to the art dealer and asked: "Sir Joseph, do I remind you of anyone?" Duveen looked startled but could not think of an answer. Then the patient turned to his book dealer, and asked the same question: "Dr. Rosenbach, do I remind you of anyone?" The good doctor could not think of what his patron meant. Henry Huntington stretched his arms out a little wider and said with a wicked smile: "Well . . . I remind myself of Jesus Christ on the cross between two thieves."

53   THE INTERCESSION OF CHRIST

THIS activity belongs to the office of Christ as priest and refers generally to the aid which He extends as mediator between

God and mankind. In a very particular sense, Christ is represented as drawing near to God and pleading on the behalf of mankind. This is in agreement with the idea of intercession and therefore He is also called our "Advocate." Thusly, the prayers and praises of believers are acceptable to God through the intercession of Christ.

The objects of Christ's intercession are in part the whole of humanity, the world. It's on no other legal grounds that we can understand how a guilty people could be permitted to extend their existence upon the earth under the moral government of a holy and just God. In the broadest meaning of the term, the prophet Isaiah says, "He made intercession for the transgressors" (Isa. 53:12).

Also, the other object of this intercession is the great body of His people, believers, followers, who from time stand united with Him. For these He prays especially. The Bible says "If any person sins we have an ADVOCATE with the Father" (1 John 2:1).

JOSEPH, THE FOSTER-FATHER

54

WHAT kind of man was this Joseph, the husband of Mary and foster-father of our Lord? Very little is written about him in the Bible. However, Matthew traces his line of descent — in fact, a royal line of descent. He is said to have been the son of Jacob, whose lineage is traced through David all the way to Abraham.

The writer Luke, however, gives the line of natural descent and represents him as the son of Heli and then traces his origin to Adam. Just a very few statements about Joseph appear in Holy Writ. While living at Nazareth he was espoused to Mary, and discovering that she was pregnant was apparently quite grieved at the news. He must have been some kind of a wonderful, compassionate man. And if culture and custom tell us anything . . . he must have been much older than Mary who was believed to have been still a teenager.

Following the birth of Jesus, he took his little family down into Egypt and remained until the "all clear" was sounded by an angel. He intended to reside in Bethlehem but apparently changed this because of a fear of Archaelaus and lived instead in Nazareth, which was a fulfillment of prophecy. There he took up his trade as a carpenter and apprenticed the son, Jesus. Don't you wish you could have seen a video of this relationship? The last we are told of Joseph is when he and his wife took Christ up to Jerusalem. What a man he must have been, mentoring the Son of God through early life. What did his presence put into Jesus? What life lessons did he teach this miracle child? What a special man this forgotten man of the Bible must have been!

55   THE MONEYCHANGERS

THESE were the "money brokers" or "bankers" who sat in the "Court of the Gentiles" or on its porch. For a fixed discount they changed all foreign coins or currencies into those which were acceptable in the temple.

Every Israelite, rich or poor, who had reached the age of 20 was obliged to pay into the sacred treasury, whenever a census was taken, a half shekel as an offering to Jehovah. This tribute must in every case, without exception, be paid only as prescribed . . . a Hebrew half shekel.

These "moneychangers" exacted a fixed charge which must have brought in a very large windfall . . . since not only the native Judeans might come without the statutory coin, but all the foreign Jews who presented themselves on special occasions at the temple for a feast or to worship. It's impossible to estimate the profits of these changers.

But that was not all . . . money was needed in the temple area for other things — the purchase of whatever was needed for the feast in the way of sacrifices and their adjuncts and for purification. It was always better to get the right money from the authorized changers than to have to deal with other "dealers." And through their hands would have passed the immense votive offerings of proselytes as well as other foreigners.

The very strong language and vigorous action of Jesus is to be accounted for by the fact that avarice and greed had taken up its abode in the temple to carry on its huckstering and money-changing. Jesus entered the temple area and drove out all who were buying and selling there. He overturned the tables of the moneychangers and the benches of those selling doves. "It is written," He said to them, "My house will be called a house of prayer, but you are making it a den of robbers" (Matt. 21:12–13).

NATHANAEL

THIS is one man who was a follower of Christ about whom we have just a few lines written, in the Gospel of John. His name means "God has given." His story is interesting. It seems that after Jesus was proclaimed to be the "Lamb of God" by John the Baptist that He made His way to Galilee. He had already called Philip to follow Him who in turn hurried to Nathanael to inform him that the Messiah had now appeared.

Nathanael immediately expressed his strong opinion and mistrust that any good thing could come out of Nazareth. However, he did follow Philip and as they approached Jesus, Jesus greeted him: "Here is a true Israelite, in whom there is nothing false." Nathanael was stunned and asked: "How do you know me?" The answer is equally stunning: "I saw you while you were still under the fig tree before Philip called you."

This more than convinced Nathanael that Jesus was more than a mere man. Listen to his declaration: "Rabbi, you are the Son of God; you are the King of Israel!" (John 1:47–49). This purportedly took place about A.D. 25. From there we meet with this man only once more in the Bible as being part of the small contingent of disciples at the Sea of Tiberias to whom Jesus showed himself following His resurrection. Have you ever wondered how it was that Jesus "saw" Nathanael while he was still under the fig tree?

A SHYSTER'S CONSCIENCE

IN 1720, the year celebrated for the bursting of the scheme called the "South Sea Bubble," a gentleman came calling quite late one evening, just before closing, at the banking house of Hankey and Company. He was in his carriage and refused to get out but requested that one of the partners come outside to him. Then, into the hands of this surprised banker, he placed a parcel, very carefully sealed up. His directions were that the banker would take care of it until he would return for it at a later time.

Days passed, a few weeks, then a few months . . . but the stranger never returned. At the end of the third year, the partners agreed that it was time to open this sealed mysterious package. They found the huge sum of 115,000 English pounds with a letter stating that it had been obtained by false pretense in the "South Sea" speculation. This letter directed that it should be placed in the care of three trustees, whose names were mentioned, and the interest be given to the relief of the poor, because Jesus had brought a conviction to his conscience, that this thievery should be made right.

58 VILLAGE LIFE

IN the first century A.D. the vast majority of people in the Holy Land lived in rural villages where farming determined just about every aspect of the daily lives — traditions and habits, holy days and beliefs. Such a place was Nazareth, the boyhood home of Jesus. It was situated high in a sheltered valley some 1,300 feet above sea level. The lush, fertile countryside around this village, even today, is beautiful.

The Jewish historian Josephus, wrote: "The land is everywhere so rich in soil and pasturage and produces such variety of trees, that even the most indolent are tempted . . . to devote themselves to agriculture. In fact, every inch of the soil has been cultivated by the inhabitants."

The hub of the village of Nazareth, like other typical villages, would be centered around the marketplace as well as the street of shops where craftsmen made and sold their wares. The smithy and the carpenter were in high demand to make and repair farm implements. These two tradesmen were usually located close together to facilitate their crafts. Almost everything was handmade. Other necessary craftsmen would be the mat makers, potters, and basket weavers.

When Mary and Joseph returned from Egypt they went home to Nazareth, where the boy Jesus "grew and became strong." It's easy to imagine that many of His teachings, stories, word pictures, life applications, and parables would have been drawn from this idyllic setting.

59 PHYLACTERIES

IT was customary for male Jews to strap "phylacteries" to their foreheads and left arms for morning prayer, except on the Sabbath and other festivals. What is a "phylactery"? They were strips of parchment with four passages of the Scripture written upon them, including the Ten Commandments. Each strip of parchment was tightly rolled up, tied with the white hairs of a calf's or cow's tail and placed in one of the compartments of a small box. During prayer these phylacteries were firmly attached to the forehead between the eyebrows and on the left arm by leather strips, so as to be near the heart.

This practice originated with a very literal interpretation of the Old Testament command: "This observation will be for you like a sign on your hand and a reminder on your forehead that the law of the Lord is to be on your lips" (Exod. 13:9). The boxes for the phylactery were ordinarily one and one-half inches square with the three-pronged Hebrew letter "shin" on the outside which was designated as an abbreviation of the divine name "Shaddai" (Almighty). Then on the other side or left side it had a four-pronged "shin" with the two constituting the sacred number seven.

These are still in use today in Jerusalem, especially when celebrating a bar mitzvah and the passage into religious maturity.

Jesus said, "The teachers of the law and the Pharisees . . . make their phylacteries wide and the tassels on their garments long" (Matt. 23:2–5). This practice was to make the leather straps wider, requiring a larger box, thus making themselves more conspicuous and more pious-appearing in front of others. Jesus castigated them for their pride when He said, "For whoever exalts himself will be humbled and whoever humbles himself will be exalted" (Matt. 23:12).

60   ATONEMENT

THE writers of the Bible, both Old and New Testament, were concerned with one problem above all the others: How can people come into a meaningful relationship with God? They were equally concerned with the problem that stands in the way of that enjoyment . . . sin! Because of sin, people are separated from God and therefore the basic need is to be made "at one" with Him. This is the simple meaning of atonement . . . being "at one" with God!

In order to make this happen, in the Old Testament people offered animal sacrifices to atone for their sins. But this could not be the final answer as these writers looked forward to a better way.

The New Testament describes how God sent His only Son to do just that — become the better way, become the living way, become the sacrifice for their sins. Jesus has "atoned" for the sin of the world!

61 ACCOUNTABLE STEWARDSHIP

RICHARD Reynolds was an English merchant in Bristol, England, who had amassed a huge fortune in the early part of the 19th century. He was a deeply religious Quaker who often referred to himself "merely as a steward of the Almighty." One of his contemporaries wrote the following about Reynolds:

He devoted his entire income, after deducting the moderate expenses of his family, to charitable purposes, and he thought his round of duty still incomplete, unless he devoted his time likewise. He often deprived himself of slumber to watch beside the bed of sickness and pain to administer consolation to those in trouble. On one occasion he wrote a friend in London, requesting to know what object of charity presented itself . . . . His friend informed him of a number of persons confined in prison for small debts. Reynolds paid the whole sum, and swept that miserable abode of its distressed tenants. Most of his donations were enclosed in blank covers, bearing a modest signature of "A Friend." A lady once applied to him on behalf of an orphan, saying: "When he is old enough, I will teach him to name and thank his benefactor."

"Nay," replied the Quaker, "thou are wrong. We do not thank the clouds for rain. Teach him to look higher, and thank Him who giveth both the clouds and the rain. My talent is the meanest of all talents . . . a little sordid dust; but as the man in the parable was accountable for his talent, so I am accountable to the great Lord of all."

62 THE FLEET-FOOTED SAINT

SAINT Gregory, the fleet-footed one, died on November 16, A.D. 270. He had once been a student of the "super" saint, Origen.

However, when troubles forced Origen to go into hiding in order to save his hide, Gregory ran away . . . in fact he ran so successfully that he was gone for three years.

Later, when Gregory was chosen to be a bishop, he ran away again! But the members of his church pursued him, caught him, brought him back, and made him bishop anyway. Perhaps there was a shortage of eligible bishops. Then, near the end of his life, Saint Gregory warned his church members to flee from the wrath of the emperor Decius and he was the first one out the door. Old habits die hard.

It follows then that if Saint Martin is remembered as a soldier with half a uniform, and Saint Catherine is remembered for jumping over fire, and Saint Anthony for having wet boots, and Joan of Arc for her martyrdom — then Saint Gregory's trademark for all of posterity could be . . . running shoes?! Quite contemporary, huh?

JESUS CHRIST

63

THE double title "Jesus Christ" has a deeper meaning which is over and above the titles when used separately. "Jesus" means "savior" and is the New Testament equivalent of the Old Testament name of Joshua. This is the human name given to Him. "Christ," which means the "Anointed One," is His divine name. These two names link His humanity and divinity. And when used together in combination it is an acknowledgment of our Lord as both man and God!

THE 40 DAYS OF LENT

64

LENT is the season in which the "Church" as a whole enters into an extended retreat. Jesus went into the desert wilderness for 40 days and 40 nights according to the account. The practice of Lent is to be a participation in the solitude, silence, and privation of Jesus.

The 40 days of Lent bring into focus the 40-day concept found in many places in the Bible. Back in the Genesis account, the rain fell for 40 days and nights during the great flood in which Noah and his family survived. Elijah walked 40 days and nights to the mountain of God, which is Mt. Horeb. The Israelites wandered in the wilderness for 40 years before they were allowed to enter the Promised Land.

The biblical desert wilderness was a place of purification, a place of passage. It's not so much a place of wind, sand, stones, and sagebrush . . . but a process, today, of inner purification which is to lead to liberation from the false which will not work in the human life.

Jesus deliberately took upon himself the human condition — fragile, broken, away from God, proud, rebellious, and sinful. Jesus went into the wilderness to prepare for His sacrificial ministry. He went into the wilderness to begin to heal these human conditions. This was ultimately completed in the culmination of His life with death on a sacrificial cross. Jesus redeemed us from the consequences of our human condition. In this desert experience, Jesus was tempted by the primitive desires of the human race . . . and came out victorious! That's what Lent is all about! Each Lent we are reminded of His invitation to join Him in the desert and share in the purification.

THE UNIQUE CHRIST

65

HIS birth was contrary to all the laws of nature and conceptions of life.

His death was contrary to the laws of justice, the laws of humanity, and the laws of death.

He had no wheat fields nor fisheries but He could spread a table for 5,000 with bread and fish to spare.

He walked on no beautiful carpets nor silk rugs but on the dusty roads of Israel and on the Sea of Galilee.

He preached for only three years but after two milleniums of time He is the central character of human history.

He wrote no books, built no temples, founded no schools, and had no monetary funds but built an organization that is alive today!

His parents were not famous, His home was humble, but He is the pivotal personality of human history!

SCOURGING

66

SCOURGING was a common punishment in the East. This instrument of punishment in ancient Egypt was usually the stick applied to the soles of the feet . . . the "bastinado." Under the Roman method, the culprit was stripped, stretched with cords or thongs on a frame, and then beaten, primarily on the back. This punishment was prescribed by law in the case of a betrothed bondwoman who was found guilty of unchastity. This was from the law as written in the Book of Leviticus. Also, it was prescribed in the case of both the guilty persons who might be caught in the same sinful act. The guidelines were such that if a judge was to use scourging as a sentence, he could not prescribe more than 40 . . . thus, 39 stripes to make sure that one wasn't missed or counted twice or the number was exceeded.

The instrument used was called a "scorpion," a whip with barbed points of sharp bone or bits of metal. The points were likened to the sting of a scorpion. Scourging was frequently mentioned in the New Testament and the most memorable scourging of all was when Jesus was scourged preceding His crucifixion.

67 PUBLICANS

THE Roman senate had found it most convenient at an earlier period, probably about the time of the second Punic war, to farm out the "vectigalia" (direct taxes) to capitalists. These capitalists were to pay a given sum annually to the treasury and had the rights to a protected territory. Usually these lucrative contracts fell into the hands of the "equites," the richest class of Romans, and most were written for a five-year period. Sometimes they formed a "joint-stock" company and took in other investors, and appointed an agent or managing director ("magister"). This chief officer, who usually resided in Rome, transacted the business, sharing the profits with the shareholders. Under their direction were the "portitores," the actual custom house officers who collected the tax.

It was this last group of people, "portitores," who were the hated "publicans" of the New Testament times. These publicans were encouraged by their overseers to charge as much as the traffic would bear and if they resorted to illegal means or threat, so much the better. There was no court of last appeal in this system. And often the publicans were residents of the province in which they collected taxes. They overcharged, brought false charges, accused the people of smuggling and thus collected hush money, and all other means of extortion. No wonder they were hated by the Jews.

To the Jew of Jesus' day, the publicans were regarded as traitors, apostates, dupes for their oppressors, and defiled by their contact with the Gentiles. They were for the most part excommunicated from society. These were some of the earliest disciples of John the Baptist and Jesus. Zacchaeus was considered a "chief among the publicans." One of the worst!

68 PALM TREES

THE palm is a beautiful and useful "branchless" tree crowned with a tuft of fan-shaped leaves. Israel came upon 70 palm trees at Elim. To the weary, hungry, thirsty traveler the palm was a most welcome sight because it signified a place of shade, rest, food, and refreshing. Where palms grow, their long tap roots strike water. If properly cared for and watered, palms will grow in Jerusalem. The date palm can live more than 200 years and furnishes juicy edible dates. Some of the other uses for palm trees were wax, sugar, oil, tannin, dyes, resin, and an alcoholic drink called "arrak." Jericho was called the "city of palm trees."

The palm tree was used as a decorative motive in Solomon's temple as well as in Ezekiel's temple. Palms were among the "goodly" trees to be used in celebrating the "Feast of the Tabernacles."

The palm became the symbol of the righteous enjoying their well deserved prosperity. They were used by the Early Church to express the triumph of the Christian over death through the resurrection. Also, these symbols appeared on tombs along with the monogram of Christ, signifying that every victory of the Christian is due to this divine name and symbol. Then, finally, the palm became the sign of martyr-dom in the primitive church. Thus, it was fitting that the worshipers would wave palms as Jesus made His triumphal entry into Jerusalem on that most fateful of all weeks.

69 CHRISTMAS CARDS

NO one can fail to notice that most Christmas cards of today have nothing to do with Christ or Christianity. But did you know that "Christmas" greeting cards were secular from their inception? The fact is that many of the customs we use to celebrate Christmas have nothing at all to do with religious commemorations. And some of these customs pre-date Christianity itself!

For starters, the date of Christ's birth is nothing more than conjecture. There is no historical evidence that He was born on December 25. It wasn't until A.D. 440 that the Church proclaimed this day as the official date of His birth. Conveniently, December 25 already marked a holiday among many European peoples. It was the beginning of the winter solstice.

When did the first Christmas card appear? The idea dates back to the Middle Ages. An engraving by "Master E. S." depicting the infant Christ stepping from a flower has been dated to about 1466 but is thought to be a copy of an earlier design. Calendars in the 17th and 18th centuries often carried yuletide greetings with domestic winter scenes.

As to the first legitimate "Christmas card" there is controversy. According to some accounts, the idea of a Christmas card came from Sir Henry Cole, the first director of the Victoria and Albert Museum in London. In 1843, Cole commissioned John Collcott Horsley, an artist of the time, to design his first card. Cole had a thousand copies printed and issued by Summerby's Home Treasury Office. Only a dozen of these exist today and two are found in the Hallmark Collection.

70   SALT

AS we eat and drink we consume hundreds of chemicals combined in lots of appetizing forms. Then our bodies do the work of separating and using them. But there are two chemicals that we still consume in their pure form and these are two of the most important: H20 and NaCl . . . water and salt.

But fortunately these are two of the most abundant of all the chemicals on our planet. Two-thirds of the world is covered with water and the oceans are about 3 percent sodium chloride . . . ordinary table salt. It seems odd to us today that in ancient times salt was even used as money.

Salt was used to seal covenants among the ancients because its preservative quality made it a fitting symbol for a long-lasting agreement. The Arab expression "there is salt between us" means a binding agreement has been reached. The Persian term "untrue to salt" refers to broken covenants.

The most saline of all water is the Dead Sea located in Israel. It covers about 350 square miles and contains some 11.6 billion tons of salt. The highly saline River Jordan pours six million tons of water into the Dead Sea daily, which after evaporation leaves behind about 850,000 tons of salt each year, most of it in the form of sodium chloride.

When Jesus told us to be the "salt of the earth" He implied that there was an "eliteness," a specialness, a responsibility to preserve relationships with others.

EPILEPSY AND VISION

CHRISTIANITY and Islam are two of the world's major religions today . . . but at least one of these owes much of the success to an attack of epilepsy.

Paul the Apostle was previously "Saul the Pharisee" who was determined to persecute and eliminate all the Christians he could lay his hands on until . . . there was that special "vision" of Jesus Christ on the road to Damascus. The biblical account says, "Suddenly a light from heaven flashed around him. He fell to the ground. . . ." And the men traveling with Saul "heard the sound but did not see anyone" (Acts 9:3–7). There are some who believe it was some kind of an epileptic seizure that he experienced but that doesn't explain the light and sound. Saul, as a result of his vision had his name changed and became the chief ambassador of Christ for Christianity. He traveled around the Mediterranean spreading the gospel and founding churches.

On the other hand, Muhammed, who was a recluse, was subject to ongoing epileptic seizures, when he had a vision of the angel Gabriel in A.D. 610. In this vision, which occurred during one of his seizures, he saw the angel who told him the Word of God. He then took the message to the Arab communities of Mecca and Medina. By the time of his death this faith was well established in the Near East.

Interestingly, Muhammed had no sons. A major split occurred over the status of successors. The minority Shiite sect believes Muhammed's son-in-law Ali to be the true successor. The majority Sunni sect holds that Ali's three predecessors were legitimate caliphs.

DID A VISION SAVE CHRISTIANITY?

72

HISTORIANS tell us that a vision in the heat of a battle possibly saved Christianity from extinction.

In the middle of a crucial battle in which the Romans were fighting the barbarians in A.D. 312, the emperor Constantine had a vision of a cross in the sky. This sign or vision or what have you in the sky was accompanied by the words which only he had heard: "By this sign you will conquer." He won the battle! Not only that, but he embraced this new faith of Jesus Christ, which was in a struggle with the Roman Empire. Constantine pronounced that Christianity would become the official religion of the Roman world and therefore its future was assured . . . but at what price?

HOW CHRISTIANITY CAME TO FRANCE

73

KING Clovis, who was married to Clotilde, a committed Christian lady, was about to be defeated at the Battle of Tolbiac in A.D. 496. Desperate for victory, he promised in prayer, "God of Clotilde, if you grant me to win this battle, I'll become a Christian like her."

He won! Give him credit . . . he kept his promise! He became a Christian with her help and France was turned to Christianity following his leading. Thus, a promise, a vow, a prayer prayed in the heat of battle was the turning point. And so this victory and vow was responsible for France becoming a Christian nation!

THE TEMPTER

74

MANY people today laugh at the idea of a real devil. They say that such a being doesn't exist other than being some sort of depraved influence in this world. Such people have never met the devil in person like Jesus did in the wilderness.

The biblical account reads like this: "Then Jesus was led by the Spirit into the desert to be tempted by the devil" (Matt. 4:1). This is a dangerous adversary. The Bible, in both the Old and New

Testaments, expose the deeds of this evil being. Jesus called him *Satan,* which is a Greek word meaning "adversary" because the devil is in opposition to God and all the good in this world. This opponent attacked Jesus at His weakest, after 40 days of fasting and prayer. The spirit of Christ was acutely tuned to the Heavenly Father but His body would have been weakened by hunger. But Jesus had a wonderful strategy for victory!

NOBLE THINGS

75

LET'S think about some of the leaders found in the Bible. Then take a look at the things they prayed for. Many were given opportunities to express these directly to God the Father who said in essence: "I will give you whatever you ask." Here's my list and I also discovered that they all asked for the more noble things of life . . . not for personal needs or desires.

Abraham requested: "Help me follow you."

Moses requested: "Help me set your people free."

David requested: "Help me kill the giant of oppression to free your people from bondage."

Esther requested: "Help me save my people from annihilation."

Solomon requested: "Give me wisdom."

Isaiah requested: "Give me lips that are clean so I can speak your words."

Peter requested: "Help me to care for and feed your sheep."

Jesus requested: "Help me to show them your love and be their perfect sacrifice."

Isaiah, the prophet, who requested clean lips also wrote, "But the noble man makes noble plans, and by noble deeds he stands."

Jesus . . . the noblest of all, asked for noble things!

LIGHTNING STRIKES

76

THE leader of the "Protestant Reformation" in Germany became a Christian because of a thunderstorm and a lightning strike.

Martin Luther (1483-1546), as a young man, was walking on the road near Erfurt, Germany, during a thunderstorm when a lightning strike knocked him off his feet into the mud. He was immediately filled with such a fear of death, consciousness of sin, and dread of the future that he renounced the world. He confessed his sins and entered the monastery of the Augustinian Eremites. The apostle Paul wasn't the only one arrested by the Lord through a special intervention!

77 DANIEL WEBSTER AND JESUS

THIS story is supposedly true and it's about Webster when he was in the prime of his life and livelihood. He was dining with a prominent businessman of Boston. During the dinner the conversation turned to the subject of Christianity. Mr. Webster frankly expressed his belief in the divinity of Christ and his utter dependence on the atonement of the Savior. The listener then replied: "Mr. Webster, can you comprehend how Christ could be both God and man?"

Mr. Webster promptly replied, "No, sir, I cannot comprehend it. If I could comprehend him, He would be no greater than myself. I feel that I need a super-human Savior."

78 THE WORLD'S SMALLEST CHURCH

THE church of Monte Cassino built near the city of Covington, Kentucky, is considered the smallest church in the world. The church, which is built of brick and stone, can accommodate only three people at a time. There are three rough-hewn wooden pews or benches. These face a tiny altar. The walls are eight feet high with a vaulted ceiling. The midget belfry is so tiny that it cannot hold a bell.

This miniature church was built in 1850 to honor Jesus Christ by Benedictine monks. They named it after the very first Benedictine monastery, Monte Cassino, in Italy. The original was reduced to rubble by bombs in 1944 during World War II.

79 FIRST U.S. FEMALE MISSIONARY

HARRIET Newell, along with Ann Judson, are believed to have been the very first overseas female missionaries from the

United States. They both began their ministries in 1812, however, Harriet is the first woman missionary from the U.S. to have died on foreign soil.

She was born in Haverhill, Massachusetts, in 1793 and married Samuel Newell in February of 1812, a student at Andover Theological Seminary. Together they planned to serve as missionaries to India, a country previously unvisited by American missionaries. They reached India in June of that year and spent some time with British missionaries . . . but the British East India Company was opposed to any attempt to convert Indians to Christianity and forced them to leave the country on August 4. After a long and difficult ocean voyage, they landed on the Isle of France (later to become Mauritius) in October.

While the Newells were sailing, an infant daughter was born prematurely, to them. The baby died five days later and was buried at sea. Harriet, weakened by an onset of tuberculosis and the rigors of the premature childbirth, died a month after they arrived at the Isle of France.

She was the first U.S. female missionary to the gospel of Jesus Christ to have died and been buried on foreign soil.

SEVEN SAYINGS ON THE CROSS

THE seven sayings by Jesus on the cross are commemorated each Good Friday in many churches around the world. These are treated as the last sayings which have eternal significance. Three of these are recorded by Luke only, three in John only, and one in Mark and Matthew.

• The first calls for forgiveness of those who are executing Him: "Father, forgive them, for they do not know what they are doing" (Luke 23:34).

• The second is a promise to one of the bandits crucified with Him: "I tell you the truth, today you will be with me in paradise" (Luke 23:43).

• The third commends John to Mary and Mary to John: "Dear woman, here is your son," and to the disciple, "Here is your mother" (John 19:26–27).

• The fourth is a cry of despair which is a partial quote from Psalm 22: "Eloi, Eloi, lama sabachthani?" which means, "My God, my God, why have you forsaken me?" (Matt. 27:46; Mark 15:34).

• The fifth is a statement of His physical thirst. "Later, knowing that all was now completed, and so that the Scripture would be fulfilled, Jesus said, 'I am thirsty' " (John 19:28).

• The sixth is the cry of triumph, the final note to the life He had lived. It's the culmination of His life work: "It is finished" (John 19:30).

• The seventh is the indication that He died in faith and had fulfilled the Father's plan: "Jesus called out with a loud voice, 'Father, into your hands I commit my spirit' " (Luke 23:46).

OLD TESTAMENT PROPHECIES

81

APPROXIMATELY 25 percent of the Bible is composed of prophecies. What if the prophet gave a wrong prophecy, a prophecy that was proven false, a prophecy that didn't come to pass? If you were a Jewish prophet and if you lived in Old Testament times and you were wrong . . . you were stoned until dead.

Contained in the Old Testament are more than 300 specific prophecies alone that concerned Jesus, the promised coming Messiah. These were written from 450 to more than 2,000 years before His birth. They were so vivid that the argument among many was that ordinary people could not have written them. The Dead Sea Scrolls established that these were indeed written hundreds of years before the birth of Christ and covered such aspects as to where and how He was to be born, where He was to be raised, how He was to die, etc. It's been calculated that the probability of just 8 of the more than 300 prophecies being fulfilled by chance is 1 in 10^{17}. It is beyond calculation to figure the probability of all 300-plus coming to pass in one life.

JESUS WAS FOR THE LITTLE PEOPLE

82

ZACCHAEUS, come down [from that tree] immediately. I must stay at your house today" (Luke 19:5). What do you think this must have done to this little man in the eyes of the public? How do we know he was a little man? The biblical account tells us that "being a short man he could not see Jesus because of the crowd, so he ran ahead and climbed a sycamore-fig tree to see him" (Luke 19:3–4).

Jesus was always encouraging people who were considered the little people, the downtrodden, the wallflowers, the ones nobody else wanted to be around. "Simon," He said, "from now on I am calling you the Rock." "Mary Magdalene" He said at another time, "they want you dead but you are worthy of eternal life." Then to the little children, parents, and disciples for all time, He said, "Bring them to me, don't push them back. They need to be in the center of things." Jesus was always looking out for and offering protection to the little ones.

To the woman caught in adultery He said, "Woman, neither do I condemn you . . . but go and sin no more." When He looked up at Zacchaeus He essentially said, "Come on down and let's be equals. It will be an honor for me to have supper with you tonight."

The rich provided a burial plot for Jesus . . . but He spent the largest majority of His time with the common folks, the little people, the unimportant of this world. Jesus cared for the common folk.

HUMOR ABOUNDS

83

IT'S really too bad that while we humans can frequently enjoy humor, we are hesitant to connect humor to the Scriptures and especially the teachings of Jesus. Humor and the comic spirit are part of the human nature — and who put it there? It's one of the most valuable gifts bestowed upon all of us, because we have been created in the image of God.

It's too bad that any humor found in the Bible has been lost in the many translations by grim, unsmiling people. Today we are being exposed to new studies which are revealing an original sense of humor.

Jesus often used hyperbole, comic exaggeration, and comic reversal to make His point. When Jesus talked about the rich man going through the eye of a needle . . . don't you suppose that was a knee-slapper to His crowd? He often used humor to reveal more facets of truth. Also, if you look, there is a clear link between the use of His humor and His compassion!

Some of Jesus' harshest words were reserved for the self-righteous who took themselves too seriously. Such people robbed themselves and others, as well as life and worship of all joy. Jesus, today, would be a favorite dinner guest. Why? Because He was full of joy. The Bible describes Him as a man who was anointed with the oil of gladness above all others. In other words . . . He was the happiest man to have ever lived because He was filled with more gladness than anyone else.

THE WRITER
IRENEAUS

84

IRENEAUS (A.D. 130–200), was likely born at Smyrna, which is a few miles from Ephesus. He also may have accompanied the Early Church father Polycarp on his journey to Rome in A.D. 154. Ireneaus was elected a bishop of Lyons in A.D. 178. He is remembered and known for his literary and religious writings that were part of early Christian literature.

Recent discoveries of some of his works in 1904 (I guess that's not so recent) give credence to his life. The major discovery was *In Proof of the Apostolic Preaching* in which he lists many of the events of early Christianity and records many incidents from the life of Christ. His is a non-biblical perspective of biblical events, most particularly the life of Christ. He said this of Jesus: "For he has made known to us in all wisdom and insight the mystery of his will, according to his purpose which he set for in Christ as a plan for the fullness of time, to unite all things in him, things in heaven and things on earth."

HEROD
THE GREAT

85

HEROD the Great ruled Israel for 30 years preceding the birth of Jesus from 37 B.C. to 4 B.C. His reign was noted for being opulent and oppressive. During his 33-year reign, not a single day passed without someone being put to death. In 37 B.C., as he was establishing his rule, he killed 45 of the brightest and best in Jerusalem who belonged to the Maccabaen family and took all their property. In 29 B.C. he strangled his own wife, Mariamme; his mother-in-law, Alexandria; and the 300 men who were their supporters. He killed all of the Sanhedrin except one member. Thousands of Pharisees were put to death for refusing to swear an oath of allegiance to the emperor of Rome and to Herod.

Josephus records that a riot ensued and 20,000 were killed in retaliation. Not only were times tough because of Herod, there were natural calamities. In 31 B.C. an earthquake struck Judea killing 30,000 people. Six years later there was a famine, which further devastated the area.

Herod was a man of his times. — an era which produced men of intellect without morals, ability without scruples, and courage without honor. Herod beautified Jerusalem with lots of buildings in his honor.

Two of the most respected rabbis, Judas and Matthias, believing at one point that Herod was dead, led a gallant band of men who were determined to wipe out all vestiges of Herodian idolatry. This band of 40 was captured and Herod, on his deathbed on March 12, 4 B.C., was carried on a couch to preside as judge. The little band of rebels was all burned alive.

One historian said this of Herod the Great: "He stole along to his throne like a fox, he ruled like a tiger, and died like a dog."

It was into this distraught world that Jesus was born!

86 ONLY A COMMA

THERE is only a comma in the "Apostles' Creed" that fills the gap between Jesus' birth and His death: ". . . born of the Virgin Mary, suffered under Pontius Pilate. . . ." Strange, isn't it, that His life is taken care of by a simple comma!

Most people are identified by what they do or have done. But in the life of Jesus . . . what did He do other than lead a life which took Him directly to the cross? Is the Apostles' Creed correct in placing the stress on the birth, death, and resurrection of Jesus as being most significant for our faith? Everything about Jesus has to do with His birth, death, and resurrection. Could He have avoided going to the cross? Yes, I believe it was possible that He willingly and purpose-fully directed His life toward that cross. It's almost as though Jesus understood that His life was to be a "comma" — the pause between — when God came down to mankind in the form of the Savior.

87 I'LL TAKE YOUR PLACE

DURING World War II there was a wonderful Russian nun, Mother Maria. At that time she lived under the Nazi rule in

Paris and did her best to relieve the suffering of all people, especially the persecuted Jews. However, on one particular day, when the Nazi SS were lining up the Jewish girls in her convent school to take them off to the execution chambers . . . one high-school girl became so frightened that she collapsed in fear. Mother Maria took off her nun's habit and quickly put over her head the yellow scarf which marked the Jew and gently said to the girl: "I'll go for you; I'll take your place." And Mother Maria died as a Jew.

Now, what would cause this nun to become a substitute for another whom was condemned to die? The teachings and example of Jesus Christ is the only meaningful answer. This was the meaning of the cross . . . Jesus went in our place.

JESUS: THE MAN OF JOY

WHAT do you think was the real secret of the life of Jesus? I believe it was a whole lot of inner joy! If you read the account of His life in the New Testament you can only come to the conclusion that this life was very special. Another thing has become clear to me — Jesus was a cheerful and joyful person with a merry heart.

Gilbert Chesterton wrote: "He [Jesus] concealed something . . . He restrained something. . . . There was something that He hid from all men . . . some one thing that was too great for God to show us when He walked upon our earth; and I have sometimes fancied that it was His mirth."

The joy of the Lord was present at the tomb of the resurrected Lazarus. Joy was there when the one out of ten lepers returned to express his thanks to Jesus. Joy was very much present when the woman caught in adultery was forgiven. Joy surely was there when the deaf heard, the blind saw, and the lame walked! Joy was also there on the mountainside as the throng of people listened to the profound teachings of Jesus! Joy was there when little children flocked to Jesus! Joy was surely present when the boy gave Jesus his lunch so another miracle could be worked! Joy had to be there as Jesus stood up and quieted the storm on the Galilee! Joy was there on that special resurrection morning when the stone had been rolled away!

Joy preceded and followed Jesus everywhere He went! The Bible points out to us that the message of salvation wrapped up in Christ is a message of love dipped in joy! The word "gospel" literally means "good news" or "happy tidings." The bottom line is that joy is an attribute of God expressed in the life of Jesus!

 89 BREVITY — THE SOUL OF WIT

"BREVITY is the soul of wit," Shakespeare said and much of Jesus' wit was brief and to the point.

The most important documents of all time are all remembered because of their brevity among other things. Consider:

The "Declaration of Independence" has only 300 words.

Lincoln's "Gettysburg Address" contains 266 poignant words.

The creation story in Genesis is told with but 400 words.

The "Ten Commandments" in Exodus has 297 words.

The "Lord's Prayer," as given by Jesus, has only 67 words in it!

Yet . . . when the Federal government decided to place price restrictions on the price of cabbage during World War II, it took 26,911 words!

90 THE PHARISEES

THE Pharisees were separatists. Their name comes from the Greek "farisez" meaning "separate." This was a lay political/religious party which came into being about 200 years before Christ came on the scene. Their original purpose was to resist the encroachments of "Hellenism." This expression, "Hellenist" was used of Jews who adopted the Greek language and to some extent the Greek customs or culture. The aim of the Pharisees was to defend Judaism and turn Israel into a nation of priests. They were political opponents of the Sadducees who cooperated with the Roman officials.

The Pharisees were experts in the Old Testament law. They were the master interpreters of oral traditions of the rabbis. Most of these came from the middle class. The historian Josephus tells us that when important decisions had to be made the people relied on the opinions of the Pharisees rather than the king or high priest. Often these individuals were chosen for government offices because they were trusted by the people. More than

6,000 Pharisees lived in Israel during the lifetime of Jesus.

However . . . the Pharisees did not like Jesus because He didn't fulfill their expectations. They criticized Jesus because of many of His actions . . . actions that were contrary to many of their religious rules. Their interpretations of Old Testament law took them into every area of living . . . they always had an answer. They ensnared the people in all kinds of specifics about living. It was a bondage from which Jesus came to set people free! But the Pharisees were doing everything in their power to destroy their Messiah!

THE SHEEPFOLD DOOR

91

VISITORS to the land of Israel seem to always be interested in the illustrations used in the Bible to portray truth. The land and customs shed light on the Book and it enables the western reader to understand it better. Prominent among the pictures painted in words are the life and customs of the shepherd. Some visitors noticed the usual sheepfold on the side of a hill . . . nothing but a low wall built of mud and stones. But on closer examination they were puzzled because there was a single opening but no gate or door across it to make the fold secure at night. The shepherd was asked about it and he answered, "I am the door." It is the custom for the shepherd to lie down at night in the opening so no sheep can escape without his knowledge . . . nor can any intruder — man or beast — get inside without going through the shepherd. When Jesus said, "I am the door for the sheep" (John 10:7), everyone knew exactly what He was saying.

FAME AND IMMORTALITY

92

EVERY person in the Bible whose name became linked with the name of Jesus Christ has also become immortal. Think of some of them . . . Mary of Magdala, Stephen, Lazarus, Zacchaeus, Peter, Paul, John, and many more were unknown personalities and nobodies until they met Jesus. But on that day, when the link was forged, they became listed among the immortals of history.

Then there is the name of Fredric Handel. He had become so discouraged in his attempts to give London an opera that he left and moved to Dublin. Just before his departure a friend gave him a section of Scripture from the Book of Isaiah and asked him to write an oratorio on it. It was from that suggestion, which kept turning over and over in his mind, that he wrote *The Sacred Oratorio*. We know it today as *The Messiah*. With the linking of his name to that of the Messiah, he, too, has become famous.

93 THE DOORKEEPER

IN the ancient world of the Bible, the job of protecting the entrances to important places was held by people known as "doorkeepers" or "gatekeepers" or "keepers of the threshold." Eunuchs were chosen by kings to guard the gates of their harems. Special gatekeepers were chosen from among the Levites to watch over the ark of the covenant. The doorkeepers at the temple also had the important job of collecting money from the people who came to worship. Women could also serve as doorkeepers.

After Jesus had been arrested and led away . . . Peter was questioned by a woman who was obviously guarding the gate to the high priest's courtyard where they were holding Jesus.

94 THE GENERAL'S EXPERIMENT

ON a train, two friends from Civil War days sat talking. Both men . . . a general and a colonel, were professed infidels. Soon their conversation moved to the place of Jesus Christ in religion.

"I think it's a shame that the historical Jesus has become so encrusted with supernatural superstition," one said. They continued debunking various Gospel miracles as nothing more than legends or myths. Finally the general suggested, "Someone ought to write a novel about the real Jesus."

"That's a good idea," retorted the colonel. "General, you should do it. You could portray Jesus as He really was — a wonderful man, but nothing more."

"I'll do it," the general said.

He began careful research on the life of Christ, intending to prove that Jesus was only a man and not divine. The book was finally written and published. Its subtitle was *A Tale of Christ*. It became a best seller and sold more than two million copies. A movie of the book has proven to be one of the most popular motion pictures of all time. The name of the book and movie: *Ben Hur*. The author: General Lew Wallace. The colonel who challenged him to write the book: Colonel Robert Ingersoll, America's "Great Agnostic."

Oh yes . . . while researching and writing the book, General Lew Wallace became a devout believer in the divinity of Jesus Christ!

95 THE NEGRITOS TRANSLATION

ROY and Georgialee Mayfield, who were missionaries with the Wycliffe Bible Translators, were the first white Americans to live in the vicinity of the small settlement of Negritos in Cagayan Province in the Philippines. They often wondered how the Negritos would speak of them as well as other Americans. This opportunity came when fellow missionaries serving another tribe came to visit the Mayfields. Their Negrito neighbors saw the visitors and called out, "Itta ya kagittamuy," which literally means, "There is your same kind." "Kagittamuy" is the Negritos word for describing anything that is of the same appearance and/or essence as another.

This provided an answer. When the Mayfields came to translate "and the Word was God" from the opening verse in the Gospel of John, into the Negritos language, they were no longer stumped on how to do it. The phrase means that Christ, the Incarnate Word, was of the same nature and essence as God. Therefore they translated it like this, "a kagitta na Namahatu ya uhohugen." When we translate it into English it means "and the Word was the sameness or equalness of God."

96 LOOSED INTO THE WORLD

IN John Masefield's powerful drama *The Trial of Jesus,* Procula, who is the wife of Pilate, overhears the report that Jesus is no longer in the tomb but has risen from the dead. She asks Lonoginus, a Roman soldier, in great excitement, "Do you think He is dead?"

Longinus replied, "No, I don't."

Procula asks, "Then, where is He?"

And Longinus declares, "Loose in the world, lady, where neither Jew nor Roman nor anyone else can stop Him!"

97 HOLY LAUGHTER

AN Early Church tradition holds that following the thrill of the resurrection on Sunday, these Christians gathered together on Monday to feast, sing, and dance. One author writes in commenting on this practice, "With Eastertide began the laughing of the redeemed and the dancing of the liberated." Now . . . we do not know if this tradition is true. However, we do know what was to have inspired this practice. It was the famous Easter midnight sermon of John Chrysostom, of the fourth century. In that message he described a vision of Christ's confronting the devil and laughing at him.

However, this theme has been echoed down through the ages in the Christian experience. St. Francis of Assisi advised, "Leave sadness to the devil. The devil has reason to be sad."

Martin Luther wrote: "God is not a God of sadness, but the devil is. Christ is a God of joy."

John Wesley wrote: "Sour godliness is the devil's religion."

The bottom line truth is simply that the devil can't stand the sound of holy laughter which comes from a relationship with Jesus Christ!

98 JOYOUS MARTYRS

IN the book *Lives of the Saints,* by Alban Butler, there are many accounts of victorious martyrs for the cause of Christ. Here are three of the many that exhibited joy in their martyrdom:

In A.D. 203, five young people who lived in the city-state of Carthage were arrested as Christians and imprisoned. An account written by one of them, a young woman named Perpetua, survives. Perpetua, who was carrying a small baby, wrote that after the judge "condemned us to the wild beasts, we returned joyfully to our prison."

Another victim of third century persecution was a brother named Laurence. He was a deacon in the Roman Church who, when he heard he was to be arrested, "was full of joy . . . and gave everything to the poor." He refused to deny the faith or sacrifice to idols. He was, therefore, stripped, bound, and placed on a large gridiron above burning coals. After suffering a long time he said with a cheerful smile, "Let my body be turned; one side is broiled enough." After he was turned, he said, "It is cooked enough. You may eat." And then he died.

Lastly, the bishop of Tarragon, Spain, was roused from bed and arrested, along with two companions, under orders of the Roman emperor. Condemned to be burned alive, "the martyrs exulted to behold themselves on the verge of a glorious eternity."

History confirms that the blood of martyrs is the seed of the Church!

ENRICHING OTHERS

99

CONSIDER . . . Socrates taught philosophy for 40 years, Plato for 50, Aristotle for 40, and Jesus Christ for only 3. Yet the influence of Christ transcends the impact left by the years of teachings from these men who were among the greatest philosophers of all antiquity.

Consider . . . Jesus painted no pictures, yet some of the world's best-known paintings of Raphael, Michelangelo, and Leonardo da Vinci were inspired by the desire to capture Him in vivid color.

Consider also . . . that Jesus wrote no poetry, yet Dante, Milton, and scores of others were inspired to write by Him.

Consider, too . . . that Jesus composed no music, and still, Haydn, Handel, Beethoven, Bach, and Mendelssohn reached their pinnacle of highest perfection when composing hymns, symphonies, and oratories about Him.

Think . . . name a single sphere of human greatness which has not been enriched by this humble Carpenter of Nazareth!

THE ANCIENT PRACTICE OF MEDICINE

100

ACCORDING to anicent sources, Jesus is not the only person who healed people. Many held to the belief that the king could heal the sick and many cases of healing were attributed to the Roman emperor Vespasian. Other miracle cures were also associated with Apollonius of Tyana, who was an itinerant philosopher during the first century A.D.

There were also miracles of healings inside the religious world through the Samaritan, Simon Magus. Then there were the Jewish "holy men," such as Rabbi Hanian ben Dosa. Interestingly, all of the "healers" were accused of being magicians just like they had accused Jesus. And yes . . . the disciples and other followers of Jesus were able to heal the sick through prayer and faith.

Int those days there were no public health institutions and few communities had a public doctor. Sickness could bring financial and social ruin. Often the physically sick, the mentally ill, the demon-possessed, and always the lepers were driven from their homes to eke out an existence as beggars. It's no wonder that Jesus was such a popular figure in His day . . . the crowds thronged Him. Jesus' power to heal was the power of God at work through Him.

THE
101 CORNERSTONE

THE Jews tell this story based on a statement made in the Psalms. According to them, when the Temple of Solomon was being built, the masons sent up a stone from the quarry that was different in shape and size from all the others. Looking at it, the builders decided that there was no place for this stone. It must have been a mistake, so they rolled it down the edge of the cliff into the valley of Kidron below the temple area.

Time passed — remember that it took seven years to build this temple. Also recall that there was to be no sound of pounding or chiseling . . . it was to be erected in silence.

They were ready for the cornerstone to be set in place and the builders asked the quarry masons to send up the stone. But they were told that it had been already cut and had been sent up to them a long time ago. They searched all around the building site but no such stone could be found . . . until one workman recalled the incident. It had been rejected and rolled into the valley below. Men were sent into the valley to find it and when they brought it up . . . it fit perfectly into place . . . the headstone of the corner.

Paul the Apostle wrote of God's household like this: ". . . built on the foundation of the apostles and prophets, with Christ Jesus himself as the chief cornerstone. In him the whole building is joined together and rises to become a holy temple in the Lord" (Eph. 2:20–21).

SOME TRIBUTES TO CHRIST . . .

"CHRIST is the great central fact of the world's history. All lines of history converge upon Him. All the great purposes of God culminate in Him." — Charles Spurgeon

"The life of Christ, the holiest among the mighty and the mightiest among the holy, has lifted with its pierced hands empires off their hinges and turned the stream of centuries out of its channel, and still governs the ages." — Jean Paul Richter

"I find the name of Jesus Christ written on the top of every page of human history." — George Bancroft

"If Christ be not divine, every impulse of the Christian world falls to a lower octave, and light and love and hope decline." — Henry Ward Beecher

"The three short years of the public ministry of Jesus have done more to soften and regenerate mankind than all the moralizing of all the moralists, and all the philosophizing of all the philosophers since the world began!" — Leckey

PONTIUS PILATE

LOTS of people are remembered because of their contact with Jesus. Of these it is likely that Pilate is the best known to us from history. Pilate was the 5th prefect of Judea who had been appointed by the emperor Tiberius. He held his office from A.D. 26 to 36. As the governor — the direct representative of the emperor — he had unlimited power. He also was charged with the judicial jurisdiction over Judea.

When he was appointed governor, the first thing he did was to show his contempt for the Jewish people by making a "graven image" and displaying it in Judea. He also decided that Jerusalem needed an extra water supply, so he robbed the temple treasury to build an aqueduct which brought water from the Pool of Siloam to other parts of the city. The fact that he was allowed by the emperor to remain in this office for ten years probably attests to the fact that he thought a good job was being done. Pilate was a loyal servant of the empire.

Pilate married Claudia Proculla, the daughter of Julia, who was the third wife of Tiberius and granddaughter of Augustus Caesar. After marrying into this family, Pilate received the emperor's commission as procurator of Judea.

The Bible, however, presents Pilate as being weak. He knew the charges against Jesus were fraudulent and sought to release Him but his judgment was swayed by the angry mob. He was coerced into giving Jesus up to the crowd.

It is believed that when Jesus talked about the 18 worshipers who were killed when the tower of Siloam fell . . . that He was referring directly to an accident while building the aqueduct. So Pilate is remembered because of his time with Jesus.

JESUS EMPOWERED WOMEN

104

GOD sent an angel to a young woman named Mary and told her about a wonderful plan of which she was to be a part. In the very beginning of the Gospel accounts, God elevated the status of women and gave them a significant part in the plan. The first appearance of Christ following the resurrection was to a woman who was asked to go and convince the more doubtful males among His followers.

Mary Magdalene and Martha were the first to recognize the miracle of the resurrection when it happened. Jesus spent hours walking on the road to Emmaus with some of His male disciples after His resurrection and they didn't recognize Him! Mary, however, recognized Him almost instantly! Wealthy women had financially supported Jesus and His traveling troop while they were carrying out their mission. Women were the last to remain at the crucifixion while most of the male followers had disappeared.

Jesus didn't make the mistake that lots of men and society as a whole make . . . He enlisted female help and energy. What would have happened if Pilate had listened to his wife? He ignored her and her advice and ultimately signed Jesus' death warrant and forever secured his infamous place in history.

Jesus said to both men and women, "The kingdom is within you." And He delegated equal power, position, and authority to both female and male. He also told us that in heaven there is neither male nor female . . . under His leading we have equal status. He was way ahead of His time — but Jesus elevated and empowered women.

THE BREAD
OF LIFE

THE multitude had just been a part of the miraculous feeding of the 5,000 with the five loaves and two small fishes from a little boy's lunch. To attempt to escape the pressure of the crowd, Jesus went up the mountain and then crossed the lake to the other side. But the people followed Him. As we listen again to their inquiries we see that they were still looking for more fish sandwiches. Jesus must have stunned them when He said, "I am the bread of life" (John 6:48).

What did He mean with this statement? What bread is to the physical life, He was to be to the soul. This "I am" takes on more meaning when we consider that Jesus was born in Bethlehem, which was known as the "house of bread." Bread is called the staff of life. It is one of the basic of all staples for existence. Jesus Christ is absolutely necessary to life and sustenance!

THE
AMEN

"AMEN" is one of those wonderful, great biblical words! Literally it means, "so be it" and it affirms something to be trusted and positive. In the Old Testament Book of Deuteronomy there is a section in which "all the people shall say, 'AMEN' " 12 different times. In the Book of the Psalms, this word is introduced as the word to be used in conclusion of praise.

In the New Testament it's frequently used with expressions of prayer or praise. For example, the doxology of Paul ends like this: "To Him be the glory forever! AMEN!" It's the very last word that concludes many of Paul's epistles.

This word was frequently used by Jesus . . . at least 51 times in the Synoptics and 50 times in the Gospel of John. It's translated "verily" and is always doubled in John, for example: "Verily, verily I say unto you…" When Jesus used this expression He was giving special emphasis to some truth He was stating. The popular NIV translates this word as "I tell you the truth." Therefore it's not very surprising that in the final book of the Bible it literally becomes a title for Jesus Christ himself! "These are the words of the *Amen*, the faithful and true witness, the ruler of God's creation" (Rev. 3:14).

THE FIRST SUNRISE
107   SERVICE

THE year was 1909 . . . the place was Mount Roubidoux in California . . . it happened at the Mission Inn . . . the guest was Jacob Riis. Riis was the well-known social crusader and the "father" of slum clearance in New York City. As Riis was looking at the crest of Mount Roubidoux, he caught a vision. Later, at the evening service of the inn, he shared his thoughts with Frank Miller, the owner of the inn and the assembled guests. Essentially he said: "I see in the days to come an annual pilgrimage . . . call it what you will . . . winding up the steeps of Mount Roubidoux, climbing ever higher toward the cross that crowns the summit, where the dell peels out its message of peace on earth and good will to men, and gathering there to sing the old songs that go straight to the hearts of men and women."

Riis was a prophet . . . but even he had no idea how his prophecy would come true. The following Sunday was Easter and Miller decided to make the observance special and memorable. He invited 100 of his guests and friends . . . Riis had left by then . . . to climb with him to the summit of Mount Roubidoux and there to welcome and hail the breaking of Easter Sunday with a simple but impressive service of praise and worship.

In the light of that 1909 Easter dawn . . . the first "sunrise" service on record took place with these 100 pilgrims.

AN OLD
108   PRAYER

THERE is a prayer, more than 1,500 years old, which still has a powerful message and stirs the heart. Who first prayed it or who wrote it has been lost in antiquity. It is called "St. Patrick's Breastplate" and here it is in part:

Christ be with me. Christ in the front. Christ in the rear. Christ within me, Christ below me, Christ above me. Christ at my right hand, Christ at my left. Christ in the fort, Christ in the chariot seat, Christ at the helm. Christ in the heart of every man who thinks of me. Christ in the mouth of every man who speaks to me. Christ in every eye that sees me. Christ in every ear that hears me.

LEONARDO
DA VINCI'S CUP

WHEN the great artist Leonardo da Vinci was 43 years of age, Duke Ludovinco of Milan commissioned him to paint the dramatic scene of Jesus' "last supper" with His disciples. He worked slowly and meticulously, spending more than three years in completing it. He carefully selected his models and grouped them on either side of the central figure of Christ. You can recall that the arms of Christ are outstretched and His right hand holds the communion cup.

When this masterpiece was completed, da Vinci invited a friend to view it. He said, "Observe it and give me your opinion."

"It's wonderful!" exclaimed the friend. "The cup is so real I cannot divert me eyes from it!"

Immediately . . . Leonardo took a brush and painted across the sparkling cup! He exclaimed as he did it: "Nothing shall detract from the figure of Christ!"

SET FREE BECAUSE
OF A HYMN

A German youth was taken prisoner by the Turks in a conflict and no one was able to effect his release. He was only released from his prison cell but compelled to live as a slave among the fanatical followers of Mohammed. He grew up . . . but never lost his Lutheran faith. Jesus was his Lord and Savior.

One Easter morning he was forced to plow his Mohammed master's field. But as he worked, he kept thinking in his mind and heart about the celebration of Easter. As he walked the furrows behind the plow he sang in his native tongue one of Luther's hymns: "Jesus Christ today is risen, and o'er death triumphant reign."

At that moment the consulate of the German government who was stationed in Constantinople happened to be riding by. Amazed at hearing a German hymn in that land, he got out of the carriage and went to the man. The man told his story of capture and still being held as a slave with all hope of release gone. But he was determined to keep his faith alive in this land. The consulate succeeded in obtaining the man's freedom and he was sent back to the fatherland where he continued to live and celebrate Easter.

THE CARPENTER

THE question was asked by people who were amazed at His teachings, "Isn't this the carpenter?" The original Greek word for "carpenter" is "tekton" which means an artisan, a craftsman, or a person who is a builder. These few words in the form of a question speak volumes about the silent, long years of His young manhood. The term indicates long hours of honest, sweaty, grubby, hard work. And the absence of the mention of Joseph in the Gospels also suggests that he had died during that time and traditionally Jesus, as the oldest son, would have been responsible for the support of the family by the trade which He had mastered in His father's shop.

At some point, likely after He had mentored and trained younger brothers in the trade, He would have made His last yoke, His last table, His last door . . . shook off the wood shavings and went out to build an eternal kingdom.

THE POWER OF CONVICTION

IT'S quite easy to imagine the setting and the story. . . . It was just after dawn. A crowd had gathered about Jesus in the temple court. Just as He was about to begin teaching, the Pharisees dragged in a woman. It was a trap, a set-up, for the woman and Jesus. There is no doubt that she was guilty as charged.

Give them credit . . . the Pharisees were clever. They kept saying, "She was caught in the act!" Whichever way Jesus answered, He could be in trouble. If He said, "Let her go," then He would not be upholding the law which demanded death for adultery. If He said, "Put her to death," He would be in trouble with Roman authorities, who, when they began ruling the Jews, had withdrawn their power to use capital punishment.

Jesus was particularly calm in this confrontation. Having stood up to meet the accusers and the woman . . . He bent back down, kneeled down on one knee and began to write in the dust. The Greek word used to describe this action literally means "to write down," so we know He wasn't doodling in the dust. There is still a lot of speculation on what He must have written . . . names of some of the crowd who were also guilty? The name of the other party who might have been one of them? The sins of the accusers? A Scripture text from the Old Testament? They kept pushing until Jesus stood up and said, "If any one of you is without sin, let him be the first to throw a stone at her" (John 8:7). Talk about the power of conviction! This can be a disturbing story. No lecture. No condemnation . . . only forgiveness — and to the woman He said, "Leave your life of sin" (John 8:11).

THE TRIUMPHAL ENTRY

113

THE rabbis had a saying: "When the Messiah comes, if Israel is ready, He will come riding a white horse. But if Israel is not ready, He will ride a foal." When Jesus Christ of Nazareth came riding into Jerusalem, He was riding a foal!

Today, this procession is called the "Triumphal Entry." But that doesn't really capture what this was about. It was hardly a triumph in our sense of the word. His followers were throwing down their garments and waving palm branches they had apparently cut near or in Jericho, the "city of palms." In that area Jesus had restored sight to blind Bartimaeus and such a miracle would have stirred this crowd of followers. The crowd was also still talking about the resurrection of Lazarus who also might have been in the crowd.

It was customary for pilgrims, when coming up over a rise to see Jerusalem for the first time, to burst into joyful praise. Yet the writer Luke tells us that Jesus was weeping. The word he used, "klaio," refers to weeping out loud, sobbing. When Jesus saw this city He literally sobbed over it. The disciples had been talking about thrones and Jesus had been talking about crosses. The disciples thought Israel was ready for the Messiah but Jesus came riding a foal!

THE SPEAR OF LONGINUS

114

IN 1909 at the Hofburg Museum in Vienna, a thin, pale, shabby young man was transfixed by one small item: the remains of a spear which was now dull and black with age. The visitor was Adolph Hitler and the object was the "Spear of Longinus."

This spear is reputed to have been the one used to pierce the side of Jesus as He hung on the cross. There were at least three other "holy" spears in Europe at this time. One was in the Vatican, the second had been taken to Paris during the Crusades, and the third was in a church in Cracow, Poland. BUT it was the Spear of Longinus which was considered the most authentic one. It was named after the Roman centurion who had used it. In addition, it also had attached to the handle a nail which purportedly had been used in the Crucifixion.

The spear was said to have acted as a powerful charm for Constantine the Great; Charles Martel, who drove the Arabs out of 8th century France; Charlemagne; and the Holy Roman Emperor, Frederick Barbarossa. According to the legend, whoever possessed the spear would be victorious in battle. That's what fascinated Hitler.

The Austrian scholar Dr. Walter Stein revealed this secret about Hitler and the spear. When Hitler added Austria to the Third Reich in 1938, one of the first things he did was to visit the Hofburg Museum and claim his "Spear of Destiny." He took it to Nuremberg where it was placed in a church that, on his order, was turned into a Nazi shrine. When the Allies bombed the city, the spear was hidden in a special vault in the foundation of the Nuremberg Castle. In 1945, U.S. troops fought their way into Nuremberg and entered the vault and came upon the spear. Today it's back in the Hofburg Museum.

WHAT HAPPENED
115 TO THE CUP?

AT the Last Supper of Jesus with His 12 apostles, He broke the bread, the unleavened bread of the Passover, and concluded with, "This cup is the new covenant in my blood" (Luke 22:20). But what happened to the "cup?"

There's a controversy with the cup at the center. There are a number of legends based on early Christian writings. One of the accounts is that it came into the possession of Joseph of Arimathea, the wealthy Jew who may also have been the uncle of Jesus, who took the body of Jesus for burial in his own tomb.

When the body of Jesus disappeared, the outraged Jewish elders accused Joseph of stealing it. They threw Joseph into prison and left him to starve. Then, Jesus is said to have appeared to Joseph in a vision and made him the official guardian of the "Holy Grail." It is then said that for the remainder of his stay in prison that Joseph was miraculously kept alive by the appearance each day of a wafer in the cup . . . brought to his cell by a dove.

Finally, when he was released in A.D. 70, Joseph went into exile and eventually arrived in Britain where the legend says he had once taken Jesus as a child. He founded the first Christian church in Glastonbury in Somerset and . . . somewhere . . . there in the church . . . many believe the "Holy Grail" is still hidden.

Could there be some truth to the Indiana Jones movie about the search for the Holy Grail?

A MIRACULOUS JAILBREAK

116

SADHU Sundar Singh was positive he was going to die. He had been stripped naked, left in the bottom of a dry well, and the cover on top was locked. He found himself lying on a mass of corpses, some putrefying, some nothing but bones of previous victims. All he had done in Tibet was preach the gospel of Jesus Christ. In despair he prayed the words of Christ: "Father, why have you forsaken me?"

On the third night of his imprisonment he heard a noise from above . . . the cover was being opened. He heard a key turn in the lock and the cover was pulled back. A voice told him to catch the rope. He put his foot in the loop at the end and was pulled to freedom.

Lying on the ground, his pain gone, Sundar heard the cover being replaced and locked. He turned to thank his rescuer . . . but no one was there! Sundar offered praise and thanksgiving to God for his escape. He had yet to understand how miraculous it was.

When he had recovered from his ordeal in that appalling prison he began to preach the Gospel again. Word spread that the dead man was alive, and he was arrested again. He was dragged before the head lama who totally rejected Sundar's story and flatly stated that the key had been stolen. But the key was exactly where it had always been . . . chained to the lama's own belt! The lama was speechless with amazement and then fear. He ordered Sundar to leave Rasar, fearing that such a powerful god as Sundar served would bring some kind of a disaster upon this city.

So . . . it happened again much like the jailbreak of Peter in the Book of Acts! Another miraculous jailbreak!

HE SANK WITH THE TITANIC

117

W.C. Stead was a notable journalistic figure in his era. He also went down with the *Titanic* on that fateful April night in 1912. One of the survivors reported later that he saw him standing alone at the edge of the sloping deck as if he was in prayer or profound meditation.

Stead was a courageous reformer who campaigned to protect young girls and raise the age of consent. He was arrested on some technicality, convicted, and sentenced to some prison time. One day he was writing a letter to a girl he was encouraging to become a Christian and stand fast. He was in the organ loft of the prison chapel, looking down on the more than 600 prisoners when he heard a voice say to him, "Why are you telling that girl to be a Christian? Never again tell any one to be a Christian. Always tell them to be a Christ."

CHRIST REFLECTS DEITY

118

THE next time you travel to Rome, make it a priority to visit the "Rospigliosi Palace" where Guido Reni's most famous fresco, "The Aurora" has been painted on a ceiling. This painting is a work unequalled in that period for line, texture, color, and poetry. As you stand on the floor and look up, your neck begins to stiffen, your head grows dizzy, and the figures become hazy. And so, eventually, the owner of the palace placed a mirror on the floor. Now, you can sit and study the wonderful work of art in comfort.

Jesus Christ does the same thing for us when we try to get some notion of what God is like. He is the mirror of Deity. He is the express image of God. He interprets God to our searching hearts. He makes God visible to us. He is God coming down to our level.

WHERE THE REFORMATION BEGAN

119

MANY pilgrims who make their way to Rome will pay a visit to the "Scala Santa" or the "Sacred Stairs" of the judgment seat of Pilate. Whether or not these are the same stairs is open to discussion

. . . experts tell us it is possible that the actual marble steps of Pilate's judgment seat are genuine. However, that's not the point of this fact.

Roman Catholic superstition says a special type of merit will be upon every pilgrim who ascends these stairs on their knees. It was when he was in this very act of devotion that Martin Luther, a pilgrim to Rome from Germany, heard the words ringing in his ears which later would become the battle cry of the Reformation: "The just shall live by faith!"

JESUS AND WOMEN

ISRAEL was most definitely a patriarchal society. Men were almost always the leaders of families and government. While God has given women equal status, they were not given equal importance by men. There was a noted Jewish prayer of men in the first century which thanked God for not making them women. Here were some of the laws created to restrict women in their legal functions:

• Normally only men were allowed to own property . . . a daughter could, but only if there were no sons.
• A wife could keep a pledge only if her husband agreed to allow her to fulfill it.
• If a woman failed to have a child . . . it was assumed to be her problem and a sign of God's disapproval.
• A woman, before marriage, was expected to give proof of her virginity. Such a sign for males was impossible.
• A woman's life was considered to have half the monetary value as that of a man.

With this background, you can easily see how Jesus' attitude toward women left the doors open for criticism. Jesus crossed all kinds of social barriers to elevate women to a place of equal status. Some of the taboo things which He did in relationship to women were: He included women in His inner group of followers; He taught spiritual truth to women; He entered their homes; He met with women in public, which shocked His followers; He allowed women to touch Him; He attracted prostitutes who followed Him; and He even championed the rights of women when it came to divorce.

No wonder women gladly heard Him and followed Him!

OUR ERRONEOUS CALENDAR

121

SINCE all of history is tied into the dating of events . . . we should be aware of how one man's error has affected the dating of history for the past 1,500 or so years. Our calendar may be off by 4 to 20 years . . . give or take a few. Since the sixth century, the West, and much of the world, has numbered the years by citing "Year One" as the year in which Jesus Christ was said to have been born. This was based on the calculations of a monk, Dionysius Exiguus, who presented his research on Jesus' birth in A.D. 525. Dionysius, who was said to have been one of the most learned men of his century, made a serious error which went unnoticed and since has not been corrected.

Prior to Dionysius, the world followed the Roman calendar which began the year in which Rome is said to have been founded . . . 753 B.C. But at that time the year was called 1 A.U.C., which is the abbreviation for the Latin "anno urbis conditae" which means "the year of the establishment of the city."

When Dionysius advocated renumbering the years based on the birth of Jesus Christ he made a mistake trying to determine the year. According to the *New Catholic Encyclopedia* he "wrongly dated the birth of Jesus to 754 A.U.C., some 4 years, at least, too late."

Today, scholars place the birth of Christ as far back as 20 B.C. to as far forward as A.D. 6. The point of reference is that Jesus was born during a census taken by King Herod who died in 4 B.C. The census could have taken place up to three years previously. Jesus was not born A.D. 1, thus all our dating systems are incorrect all because of a error by a monk in 521 or 519 or. . . .

BIBLICAL PRINTING ERRORS

122

IN London in 1631 an authorized edition of the Bible was printed without the negative in the listing of the 7th of the 10 Commandments. It read, "Thou shalt commit adultery." And as a result of this error the Bible came to be known as *The Wicked Bible*. The printers, Robert Barker and Martin Lucas, were fined 3,000 pounds.

Then, during the 17th century many Bibles were printed in cheap editions in Holland. So it was inevitable that errors would creep in.

Therefore, a large printing of "Dutch English Bibles" were burned by order of the Assembly of Divines. One typo which really incensed them was a mix-up of a Scripture in Ruth in which the Lord, instead of giving her "conception" gave her "corruption."

Then there was Carlo Guidi (1650–1712) who was an Italian poet who worked diligently translating a religious work into Latin. He was about to present his work to Pope Clement XI when he discovered the typographical errors. The Latin word "sine" which means "without" had been misprinted as "sin" throughout the entire book. Guidi took the mistake so seriously that he dropped dead upon discovering the error.

123 THE AFFIRMATION

ABOUT 1930 the infamous Russian Communist leader Bukharin traveled from Moscow to Kiev. His purpose was to be the speaker at a huge gathering of people — who were forced to attend, we might add. His subject was "atheism." For more than a solid hour he aimed his heavy artillery at Christianity . . . hurling argument, scorn, and ridicule. Finally he finished and looked over his audience, gloating in the smoldering ashes of Christianity. Bukharin demanded at his conclusion: "Are there any questions?"

A solitary man stood to his feet and asked permission to speak. He made his way up the platform . . . moved close to Bukharin. The audience waited in breathless silence as the man looked over the crowd . . . first to the right, then to the left. At last he shouted the ancient Orthodox greeting, "CHRIST IS RISEN!"

This huge crowd jumped to its feet as one person and shouted back their response which came crashing against the arguments of atheism like a mountain avalanche, echoing, reverberating through that auditorium: "HE IS RISEN INDEED!"

124 THE GREAT SACRIFICE

THIS story was shared at the International Youth Triennium in Bloomington, Indiana, in July of 1980 when Professor Bruce Riggins of McCormick Theological Seminary spoke to the 3,800 attendees.

He had met an unusually dedicated Christian working in the slums of London, England. He wanted to know what had inspired her faith and life action. She shared her story of seeing another person's faith in action which converted her to Christianity: She was a Jew attempting to run away from the German Gestapo in France during WW II. She knew she was close to being caught and was ready to give up. She made her way to the home of a French Huguenot. A widow lady came to that home to say that it was now time for her to run to a new hiding place. This Jewish lady said: "It's no use, they will find me anyway. They are so close behind."

The Christian widow said, "Yes, they will find someone here, but you must leave. Go with these people to safety. I will take your identification and wait here." The Jewish lady understood the plan.

As the professor listened to this story, the Christian lady of Jewish descent looked him in the eye and said, "I asked her why she was doing that and the widow responded, 'It's the least I can do; Christ has already done that and more for me.' " The widow was caught and imprisoned in the Jewish lady's place giving the other time to make an escape. In less than six months, the widow was dead in the Nazi concentration camp . . . and the Jewish lady never forgot. She, too, became that follower of Jesus Christ.

125 LUTHER AND MYCONIUS

WE believe it was his sense of being in the center of the will of God which gave Luther his boldness in prayer. In 1540, Luther's close friend and associate, Frederick Myconius, became very sick and was expected to die in a short time. On his deathbed he wrote a loving note to Luther expressing his farewell.

Luther took one look at the letter and fired this letter in reply: I command thee in the name of Jesus Christ to live because I still have need of thee in the work of reforming the church. . . . The Lord will never let me hear that thou art dead, but will permit thee to survive me. For this I am praying, this is my will, and may my will be done, because I seek only to glorify the name of God."

These words are bold and almost shocking to us. Why? Because we live in a cautious day. When Myconius received this letter in reply, he had already lost the ability to speak. However, shortly he

recovered. He recovered completely and lived six more years to out-
live Martin Luther himself by two months!

THE BASIC
WARDROBE

THE well-dressed first-century Israelite usually wore a
money bag and an extra shawl or shoes in addition to the essential
basics. The most important was a "cloak," an outer garment like a
sport coat or jacket. It was little more than a square of cloth with a
hole in the middle for the head. They could be very colorful or plain,
depending on the owner. It could be used as collateral when in financial difficulty but had to be returned to the owner at night because it
doubled for a blanket. When Jesus made His entry into Jerusalem,
those who lined the streets spread their "cloaks" as a gesture of honor.
Most owned only one cloak.

Then . . . there was the inner garment, which was the most basic
of Jewish clothing. It functioned much like a long shirt, open at the
bottom, and like the cloak was made of wool or linen, but lighter in
weight. The clothing which Jesus had worn and which was taken by
the soldiers must have been the inner garment because the purple
robe had been put on and then taken off.

The belt or girdle or loincloth was important. It was to hold the
loose-fitting inner garments close to the body. Belts, in Christ's day, also
held other things such as daggers, knives, swords, money, or inkhorns.

Headgear or headdress is rarely mentioned in the Bible, but prac-
tically everyone wore some kind of covering. Most likely it was a
head-square. On hot days it was protection from the sun.

Ancient footwear was of two types . . . sandals and shoes. Both
of these play important roles in the Bible.

What was the wardrobe that Jesus used? Likely a cloak, inner garment, belt, headdress, and sandals. Simple, yet effective for that climate.

PRUNING

ANNUALLY, drastic pruning of the grapevines guaran-
teed maximum yields. The branches that did not yield fruit were cut
off, usually with a pruning hook or sharp knife. A pruning hook was

a metal blade shaped sort of like a modified fishhook with a wooden handle. Usually the pruning was done immediately after the vine had blossomed and before the blossom became a grape. In Israel, a vineyard that was not pruned was considered to be abandoned. But there was one exception to the annual pruning — according to Levitical law, a farmer was to not prune the vineyard every 7th year.

Notice this beautifully symbolic word picture Jesus paints: "I am the true vine, and my Father is the gardener. He cuts off every branch in me that bears no fruit, while every branch that does bear fruit he prunes so that it will be even more fruitful" (John 15:1–2).

The ultimate promise about ending wars says that people will beat their swords into plowshares and reshape spears into pruning hooks.

ROMAN EMPERORS OF CHRIST'S DAY

TO help understand the political scene of the time of Christ let's take a look at the five men who reigned in succession as emperor:

Augustus Caesar (29 B.C. to A.D. 14) — He and his army defeated Egypt along with Antony and Cleopatra in 31 B.C. It was his decree which brought Mary and Joseph to Bethlehem to be taxed. Augustus really treated the Jews quite well.

Tiberius (A.D. 14–37) — He was emperor during the ministry of Jesus. It was his face on the coin when Jesus asked about the inscription. He was an insecure man and may have suffered mental illness later in life . . . he was a libertine.

Gaius (A.D. 37–41) — Also known as Caligula. He was most likely insane and imagined himself to be a divine. He ordered a statue of himself to be placed in the Holy of Holies in Jerusalem. He died before this decree could be fulfilled.

Claudius (A.D. 41–54) — Early in his rule he showed some benevolence toward the Jews . . . however, later he became suspicious and restricted their movements. He prohibited the Jews in Rome from gathering and so forced them to leave.

Nero (A.D. 54–68) — He began his rule on a decent note . . . however, there is little positive to say about this madman who had his own mother murdered. He is known for his persecution of Christians . . . tortured, burned, and more gruesome kinds of death for his amusement and to divert attention from his political problems. It was to Nero's justice that the apostle Paul appealed and it was Nero who executed Paul as well as Peter.

A Roman emperor was generally considered a god and was worshiped as such. His power was absolute.

129 PIGS

THE Jews had very strict dietary laws as well as strong feelings about eating pork. These were written in the Old Testament law. The pig was considered an unclean animal. However, there were farmers who raised and sold swine because it was profitable. Just because there was a law against doing something didn't mean that it wasn't done anyway. In Israel there were wild pigs and there were domestic pigs. It was at Gadara that a herd of these domesticated pigs ran to their death in the Sea of Galilee following the deliverance of the demoniac by Jesus.

And you remember the story of the prodigal son which Jesus told, of how he finally found a job tending pigs in a faraway country before he came to his senses and returned home.

130 WAS JESUS POOR?

VERY interesting question . . . because poverty is a relative term. Here is some of the evidence that must be weighed.

Joseph was a carpenter and would have had the advantage of a skilled trade . . . but he was the father of six or more kids. The offering which they brought to the temple was that of a poor couple . . . but it could have been that they were just getting started or were away from their home. On the other hand, consider that the Magi came visiting bearing expensive gifts . . . likely after the family had returned to Bethlehem after the ceremony in Jerusalem.

Jesus lived in a house which is described as being His in one place in the Gospel of Matthew . . . while, later, He did say that He had no place to lay His head. He might not have been the owner but had reference to the family home. There is nothing written to imply that Jesus had totally denied himself any of the possessions of life. He was not an ascetic such as John the Baptist. And He did not identify himself with any of the groups which practiced voluntary poverty.

It's strongly hinted that during the years of His ministry, Jesus depended on others for support. The demands of ministry would have affected His ability to have time to continue with His carpentry. So you call it . . . was Jesus poor or not? He had some things worth much more than worldly possessions.

HOW OLD IS OLD?

BIBLICAL longevity is an interesting study. The Bible records tremendous changes in length of life over its duration. Before the flood these patriarchs lived amazing lives. Adam lived to 930 years of age; Mahalaleh was 895; Methuselah, the oldest of all, lived to 969; and Noah died at 950 years of age!

The Bible did not keep statistics or averages, but we do know that longevity changed following the flood in that Arphaxad lived to be 403, Peleg made it to 209, Reu died at 207, and Nahor lived to be 119.

By the time of the kings or the monarchy, ages were much more like our modern times. King David lived to age 70 and this seemed to be the acceptable three score and ten. But in the Psalms if a person reached 80 they were presumed to have unusual strength. Ninety was considered extremely unusual.

By the New Testament time 70 seemed to be the expected life span. The apostle John may have reached the age of 90 before he died.

Jesus Christ died prematurely at age 33!

THE BETROTHAL

A great deal of significance was placed on the betrothal or engagement period which normally lasted for at least one year. Quite often there was a feast, a ceremony, and an exchange of gifts to make it official. Interestingly, in Old Testament times a betrothed or engaged man was exempted from any kind of military service so he could not be killed before he was able to marry.

The major part of these arranged marriages was the transaction or negotiations of finances — how much the father of the bride was to receive and in what form. Then there was a discussion of the dowry and what goods and how much were to go with the bride. Usually there was a "refund" type of clause that was agreed on in case the husband were to die or if the marriage was to be dissolved. It centered on what was to be returned.

After the betrothal the couple was referred to as husband and wife. However, they did not consummate the union until the wedding ceremony a year later.

Mary and Joseph at the time of her pregnancy with Jesus were legally betrothed and had already completed whatever negotiations had been necessary. In keeping with Jewish custom they had no sexual relations until after the wedding ceremony. Breaking the betrothal would have caused major embarrassment for the couple and for the families involved. The Bible indicates that the loving and kind Joseph was seeking a way to dissolve their betrothal which would not reveal that Mary was pregnant . . . until the angel appeared to him and told him the truth of the matter.

DID JESUS WEAR A BEARD?

THIS is not one of those earthshaking theological questions. However, it's interesting. I do not know if Jesus wore a beard or not and nobody else alive today does either. Most artists have taken artistic liberties to portray Him almost exclusively with a beard.

There are, however, some circumstantial facts which may support the fact that He probably did. Beards have been common among the Jews for centuries. Jeremiah, the weeping prophet, said that clipped beards were the sign of a defeated people. Those Levites who served in the temple were not to enter with sideburns shaved. But many men in Jesus' day may have been influenced by the Greco-Roman culture in which men did not wear beards.

PROPERLY WASHING THE HANDS

IN the Jewish society where everybody ate with their hands it was very important that people washed before eating. It was a practice to wash before and after the meal . . . cleansing those sticky, oily hands.

One of the major debates that raged about Jesus and His disciples centered on the practice of the washing of hands. The Pharisees had an elaborate little ceremony when washing the hands before a meal. The water had to be poured on the hands and allowed to run down from the fingers to the wrists. If not done properly, it had to be done all over again until the washer got it right. They also regulated the size and shape of the container from which the water was to be poured . . . no smaller than one and one-half eggshells in size.

The Pharisees were indignant, even angry, that Jesus did not wash His hands according to their regulations, and vociferously complained about it. Jesus attached very little significance to their myriad rules because He taught the higher love of God for humankind.

135 FUNERAL BIERS

FUNERAL processions were quite common among the Jews in Jesus' day. The body was carefully carried on a wooden "bier" which consisted of little more than flat boards. Custom also dictated that the bier would carry some kind of symbol which indicated the occupation or social status of the deceased. Also, if a young lady had been betrothed and died before the marriage ceremony, a canopy would be used to cover her bier. This practice can be traced back to the time of King David.

It was one of these funeral processions with a bier carrying a dead boy that Jesus stopped. He touched the "bier," or in some translations it says "coffin," but the original word indicates it was a bier. Miraculously, the young man, as Jesus addressed him, "sat up and began to talk, and Jesus gave him back to his mother" (Luke 7:15). What an awesome incident that must have been!

136 JESUS IN THE FOUR GOSPELS

IF you can really master and retain this simple outline you can be familiar with what the Gospels are all about. It will be a guide for you for life.

KING . . . Matthew presents Jesus primarily as King! This book was written mostly for the Jew. Jesus is seen as the son of David and

His royal genealogy is given to us in the 1st chapter. In the "Sermon on the Mount" the laws of His kingdom are presented.

SERVANT . . . Mark pictures Jesus as the Servant! This was written primarily to the Romans, therefore there is no genealogy. Why? Romans weren't interested in the genealogy of a servant. There are more miracles from Jesus' ministry recorded here than in the others because, again, Romans didn't care for words, they were interested in actions and deeds.

MAN . . . Luke presents Jesus as the perfect Man! This gospel was written for the Greeks. The genealogy here goes back to Adam, the first man, instead of Abraham. As the perfect Man, Luke portrays Him as being in prayer and that angels ministered to Him.

GOD . . . John paints the word picture of Jesus as the Son of God! This book was written for believers as well as unbelievers with the purpose of bringing all people to Christ. Everything here is recorded to illustrate and demonstrate His divine relationship. Even the opening verse takes us back to "the beginning."

Why then, these four Gospels? Each of these writers is absorbed with a facet of Christ's life . . . the four give us a more complete, composite picture. Each of these writers develops a different theme with power. It's this perspective that gives us the true scope of Christ — His life, His person, and His ministry.

SOME INTERESTING BIBLE FACTS

THE Bible can be expressed in six words: God, man, sin, redemption, justification, and sanctification. In two words: grace and glory. In one word: JESUS!

Christ, in His teachings, quoted from 22 different Old Testament books: In Matthew He made 19 O.T. quotations; Mark, 15; Luke, 25; and John, 11. In Hebrews there are 85 quotations and allusions and in Revelation, 245.

D. L. Moody said: "Christ quotes the very passages most avoided by the Bible's critics . . . the flood, Lot, manna, brazen serpent, and Jonah."

Here are some other miscellaneous or trivial facts about the Bible you might be interested in knowing:

Number of verses . . . 31,102

Number of words . . . 775,693 (King James Version)
Longest chapter . . . Psalm 119
Shortest chapter . . . Psalm 117
Longest verse . . . Esther 8:9
Longest book in the Old Testament . . . Psalms
Longest book in the New Testament . . . Luke

And . . . it's also a fact that Ezra 7:21 (KJV) contains all the letters of the alphabet except the letter "j."

138 COURAGE AND TAKING A STAND

WHEN Honorius was emperor of Rome, about A.D. 400, the great Colosseum was often filled with spectators who viewed the games. Gladiators battled, sometimes prisoners were pitted against wild hungry beasts in combat . . . killing and blood sport held the attention and the highest thrill was watching the death of a human being. The crowds turned such contests into a holiday atmosphere.

On one such game day, when the crowd was watching a contest, a Syrian monk named Telemachus, who had dedicated himself to serving Jesus Christ, was also present. He had come with purpose. He was torn up by the utter disregard for the value of human life.

He leaped into the arena in the middle of the gladiatorial show and shouted: "This thing is not right! In the name of Jesus Christ this thing must stop!" Because he was interfering with their pleasure, the authorities gave the command for Telemachus to be run through with a sword, which was done. And so he died . . . a martyr . . . but in his death he lit a flame in the conscience of the thinking people of the Roman Empire. History tells us that because of this single act, within a few months gladiatorial combats began to decline and disappeared. Why? Because one lone man, following the leading of Christ, dared to speak out for what was right! He changed the course of history.

139 NAMES OF THE LORD'S LAND

THE physical land where Jesus was born, matured, ministered, died , and was resurrected has been called by several names:

CANAAN . . . The grandson of Noah, the son of Ham, whose

name was Canaan, originally settled in this territory and gave his name to the land. Ancient Abraham, father of the Jews, was called by God to leave Ur of the Chaldees and travel to Canaan. And Moses was directed to bring the children of Israel back to the land of Canaan, a land which flowed with milk and honey.

ISRAEL . . . When Jacob had his named changed by God to "Israel" he was also promised the land of Canaan. Later, after Joshua had led his people into the land and it had been conquered, the land was divided up among the tribes of Israel and was referred to as the "land of Israel." When the Romans conquered Israel, they connected this land with the province of Syria and called it "Coele Syria." However, the name Israel stuck until the times of the emperor Hadrian.

PALESTINE . . . The emperor Hadrian was despised by the Jews because he renamed Jerusalem and dedicated it to pagan gods. This was the reason for the revolt under Bar Kochba (who renamed it again). Hadrian decided to name it after one of the enemies of Israel . . . the hated Philistines. He called it "Palestine" which means "the land of the Philistines." This all occurred in A.D. 135, and this name stuck until modern times. In 1948 the state of Israel was recognized and it became known as "Israel" once again.

THE WAILING WALL

140

"HEROD'S Temple" and all that it entails covered an area of about 26 acres and was known as the "Haram esh-Sharif" or the "Noble Enclosure." The walls which surrounded this area were separate from the walls surrounding the city. Part of the temple walls which were built by Herod were constructed of huge stones which were a characteristic of his work and can be seen today. The most famous and well-known part is the "Western Wall," formerly known as the "Wailing Wall."

THE ETERNAL CHRIST

141

JESUS Christ has no beginning or ending! He is the *eternal* Son of God as well as being the Son of Man. He is from everlasting to everlasting! However, He lived on this earth in the form of mankind for 33 years.

To consider His life it might be well to think of a *"pre-incarnate"* state — this is the life He lived before His coming to earth in the flesh. Then the *"incarnate"* state is His earthly journey in human flesh. This is His birth, childhood, public ministry, death, resurrection, and post-resurrection ministry before He again left this earth. Thirdly, there is His *"post-incarnate"* state and ministry. These are the things He is doing right now — the intercession for His people, being seated at the right hand of God in the heavenlies.

Therefore we must conclude that Christ is eternal . . . He always was and always will be!

WHERE DID THE WISE MEN COME FROM?

THE word for the "wise men" who came is "Magi." It's the root for our word "magician." Likely, according to historians, these would have been astrologers who attempted to interpret religious meanings from the stars. Also, they may have been into special magical illusions, much like a stage magician of today.

The Bible gives one more clue: "from the east." "East" could mean anyplace east of Jerusalem. More likely it was an area in Mesopotamia — possibly Babylon or some Persian city such as Shushan.

Remember that the children of Israel, at least some of them, had spent more than 70 years in captivity in some of these eastern cities and might have left a witness as to the true God. I remind you that Darius of Media had acknowledged that the God of Daniel was the true God. Nebuchadnezzar had also declared that there was a real God in the heavens who could be involved in the affairs of men. During the reign of Ahasuerus of Persia the Jews had been honored and were granted the right to protect themselves from the wicked Haman who wanted to destroy all of them.

We can speculate that these mystics out of the East may well have been looking towards Jerusalem for the great king to come. It could well have been Ezekiel, Daniel, Mordecai, Esther, or some other Jew who was knowledgeable about prophecies concerning the coming Messiah that planted the seeds of curiosity as well as awe over the promised event.

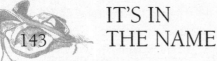

IT'S IN
THE NAME

143

OFTEN, truth is stranger than fiction. Some of this stuff you just can't make up. Such is the following. . . .

A burglar who specialized in plying his trade during the day had a technique that worked for him. He would case out a neighborhood to discover the homes where people were gone and would come back later to let himself in. One day he noticed the family loading up the SUV with luggage in the back as well as on the top carrier. Obviously they were leaving on vacation. After making sure they had left, he returned after dark to do his thing. Just to make sure, he rang the doorbell, pounded on the door . . . then picked the lock. As he entered, in the darkness he heard a voice: "I see you and Jesus sees you!"

He was stunned! He was positive no one was at home. The voice came again, "I see you and Jesus sees you!" He didn't know what to do . . . caught in the act. He snapped on his flashlight and focused on a cage at the end of the front room with a parrot in it who once more said, "I see you and Jesus sees you." The burglar let out a sigh of relief and laughed a nervous laugh. But as he flicked around his flashlight . . . it focused on a Doberman on the floor beneath the cage, with teeth bared. THEN, the parrot said, "Sic 'em, Jesus! Sic 'em, Jesus!"

How do we know this might be a true story? Purportedly the burglar showed up in a hospital emergency room to be treated for dog bites!

THE QUESTION OF
TRIBUTE MONEY

144

THE Pharisees were legalists and did all in their power to trip up Jesus. They felt they were the keepers of Jewish separation from the all things Gentile. In contrast, the "Herodians" were willing compromisers with the then-developing western culture which was called "Hellenization," brought upon them by the Herodian family. While the Herodians embraced the theater, Greek drama, track and field events of the hippodrome . . . the Pharisees hated these events. The Pharisees saw it as brutality, nakedness, and evil. The two were natural enemies, but they joined efforts in a common cause to oppose Christ.

They wanted to lay a trap for Jesus . . . anything they could get Him to say that was contrary to the law or Word of God was their aim. The Greek word used here, "pagideusosin" means to "lay a trap." Here's their question: "Tell us then, what is your opinion? Is it right to pay taxes to Caesar or not?" If He said yes, they would accuse Him of denying Moses and Jewish law. If He denied that they should, He could be accused of treason against Rome. He could anger the Jews or the Romans.

Jesus turned the tables on them when He said, "Show me the coin used for paying the tax." They then gave Him a "denarius" which would have been the Roman penny. This coin would have been minted in Rome and had on it the image of Caesar. Christ's answer was a classic for all times: "Give to Caesar what is Caesar's and to God what is God's" (Matt. 22:17–21; Mark 12:14–17; Luke 20:21–25). In other words . . . let Caesar have his coins . . . but let God have your lives because you belong to Him! Caesar's image was on the coins . . . but God's image was upon all of mankind! Therefore, Jesus said that they were responsible to do both . . . taxes to Caesar, obedience to God. Once more they "marveled" and left without their prey!

HOW MANY ANOINTINGS?

145

MATTHEW, Luke, and John each describe an instance in which a woman anointed Jesus. Two happened in Bethany and one in the Galilee region. Two instances were in the home of one named "Simon." But one of these was "Simon in Galilee" and the other a "Simon in Bethany." Two instances indicate the ointment was in an alabaster container and the response of Jesus was the same.

On these three separate happenings, Jesus was anointed by grateful women who sacrificed one of their most valued possessions — costly perfume — for the anointing. One took place two days prior to the Passover, another happened six days prior to the same Passover, and the third took place during the second preaching tour in the second year of Christ's public ministry. Two of them merely refer to some "woman," while John specifically refers to "Mary."

Interestingly enough, in one of these anointings a Pharisee complains, in the second it is Judas who complains, and in the third it is the disciples who register the complaint.

WHAT CALENDAR IS CORRECT?

146

WHEN midnight January 1, A.D. 2000 happened, Christian countries and others who have adopted the Christian calendar celebrated the beginning of a new century and a new millennium. But in much of the world that day had no significance.

In Jerusalem, the Jewish calendar marked Tebet 23 in the year 5760. In Buddhist Colombo, in Sri Lanka, the year is 2544. In Delhi the Hindu calendar showed a date of 11 Pausa in the year 1921. In Mecca the date of the Muslim calendar is Ramadan 24 in the year 1420. And to the world's astronomers who are into using very large numbers so they can escape the confusion of all the dating systems of this world, January 1, A.D. 2000 is the Julian date 2,451,545!

It is an interesting study in how such diverse points came about . . . but that is another book or at least a chapter or two. Back to the Christian calendar, which is dated to the birth of Christ — we have a problem there, too. It seems that the 6th century theologian Dionysius calculated that Christ was born in the 28th year of the reign of the Roman emperor Augustus. It's still considered to be quite accurate with the exception that our good monk was off a bit — A.D. 1 should have been the year he called 4 B.C. Therefore, when Christians celebrated the beginning of a new millennium, they all were four years too late. It should have been marked in 1996! Oh . . . well.

WHAT'S IN A CLICHÉ?

147

MOST people tend to speak in cliches. How about you? Do you use them? They are convenient in that they describe in a graphic kind of way, a shorthand kind of way, what we wish to say or mean. Let's just consider one.

"Hold the fort!" This was the message General William Tecumseh Sherman sent from Kennesaw Mountain to General John Murray Corse at nearby Allatoma, Georgia, during a Civil War battle in October of 1864: "Hold the fort! I am coming!"

This quote became a cliché . . . in fact it was so popular that an old Christian camp meeting song with the name "Hold the Fort" was compiled and written in 1874 by P.P. Bliss. Here are a few lines from it:

Ho, my comrades! See the signal waving in the sky!
Reinforcements now appearing, Victory is nigh.
CHORUS:
"Hold the fort, for I am coming," Jesus signals still;
Wave the answer back to heaven, "By Thy grace we will."

Well . . . not too biblical but it sure inspired lots of camp meeting crowds of years past. Everybody was encouraged to get out a handkerchief and when you sang the chorus, "Wave the answer back to heaven," wave the handkerchief as the answer back to heaven. I wonder how clean and germ-free those hankies were?!

THE VERY FIRST VALENTINE

THE story of "Valentine's Day" begins in the 3rd century with an oppressive Roman emperor, Claudius II and the Christian, Valentinus. Claudius had ordered all Romans to worship 12 gods and made it a crime punishable by death to associate with Christians or worship their Lord. Valentinus was dedicated to the ideals of Christ and nothing could keep him from practicing his beliefs. He was arrested and imprisoned.

During the last weeks of Valentinus' life a remarkable thing happened. The jailer, knowing that Valentinus was a man of learning asked if it would be possible for him to teach his daughter Julia, who had been blind since birth. Valentinus read to her, described the world of nature to her, taught her mathematics, and told her about God and Jesus. She, for the first time, began to see the world through his eyes. She trusted in his wisdom and found a special comfort in his quiet strength.

"Valentinus, does God hear our prayers?" Julia asked.

"Yes, my child, He hears each one," he replied.

"Do you know what I pray for every morning and every night? I pray that I might be able to see. I want so much to see everything you've told me about!"

"God does what is best for us if we will only believe in Him," Valentinus said.

"Oh, Valentinus, I do believe," Julia said intensely. "I do!" She then knelt and grasped his hand. They sat quietly, she kneeling, he sitting, each praying. Suddenly there was a brilliant light in the prison cell! Radiant, she screamed, "Valentinus, I can see! I can see!"

His death was carried out, February 14, 270. He wrote a farewell note to Julia and signed it, "From Your Valentine!"

RICHARD THE LIONHEARTED

KING Richard, "the Lionhearted," was king in England for ten years . . . but spent only about six months at home? Why? Because he was so busy crusading to rescue the Holy Land in the name of Christ and for the honor of England.

Returning from the Holy Land, Richard was captured and imprisoned by King Modred of Almain (Germany). Modred's daughter Margery fell in love with him and bribed the jailer to allow him to spend his nights in her chamber. On the seventh night they were discovered. King Modred wanted to have Richard killed then and there but his counselors were alarmed by the idea of executing a king and preferred to arrange an "accident." The lion in the royal menagerie was to be starved for a few days and then allowed to "escape" into the captive's cell. Margery learned of the plan and begged Richard to attempt an escape but he would not hear of it.

Instead he asked her for 40 silk handkerchiefs which he then bound around his right arm. When the lion burst into his cell and leapt hungrily upon him, Richard simply thrust his hand down the lion's throat and tore his heart out!

Then, pausing to give thanks to God . . . he strode up to the great hall, still bearing the warm heart in his hand. Before the astonished gaze of Modred and his court, Richard thumped the heart down on the banquet table, sprinkled salt over it, and proceeded to eat it with relish. Well . . . at least, so goes the legend.

FOOTPRINTS IN THE SAND

JESUS Christ . . . His life, ministry, and teachings have inspired countless artists, poets, writers, musicians, and others in their work. One of these works is entitled: "Footprints in the Sand."

The author is unknown. You may have read it or listened to it as Wayne Watson has put music to these wonderful words. In case you haven't heard or read it, here are the words:

One night I had a dream. I dreamed I was walking along the beach with the Lord and across the sky flashed scenes from my life. For each scene I noticed two sets of footprints in the sand. One belonged to me and the other to the Lord. When the last scene of my life flashed before us I looked back at the footprints in the sand. I noticed that many times along the path of my life there was only one set of footprints. I also noticed that it happened at the very lowest and saddest times of my life.

This really bothered me and I questioned the Lord about it. "Lord, you said that once I decided to follow You, You would walk with me all the way. But I noticed that during the most troublesome times in my life there was only one set of footprints. I don't understand why, in times when I needed You most, You should leave me."

The Lord replied, "My precious, precious child. I love you and I would never, never leave you during your times of trial and suffering. When you saw only one set of footprints . . . it was then that I carried you!"

151 HOW TO ESCAPE THE HANGMAN'S NOOSE

IT seems hard to believe in our day . . . but, simply by memorizing and reciting the first verse of Psalm 51 from the Bible, a convicted murderer could escape the hangman's noose in medieval England! In those days, the court showed no mercy, sentences were harsh, and the death sentence was applied to anything from treason to stealing a horse.

BUT in the church courts there was no death sentence. Anybody who had a connection with the church would have their trial held instead in an ecclesiastical court, which saved many a life. To prove this connection with the church was quite easy. If a person could read, that obviously meant they were a Christian cleric and entitled to claim "benefit of the clergy." This was a church law that exempted the lawbreaker from hanging or other harsh sentences.

But the majority of the population could not read. So they got around this by memorizing what would popularly become known as the "neck verse." "Have mercy on me, O God, according to your unfailing love; according to your great compassion blot out my transgressions." As you can imagine, this exemption led to all kinds of corruption and chicanery but it saved the neck of many a criminal.

This law in England was finally abolished in 1841. However, it was brought to the United States by the early Colonial settlers and was later abolished in 1790 for federal crimes. And then, by the mid-19th century was finally abolished for all crimes and disappeared from United States courts.

152 UNIQUE COMMUNICATION METHODS

JESUS was the most exciting communicator to ever exist . . . His methods were many and varied; in fact, He invented new ways never before used. For example . . . recall or read the encounter with the Samaritan woman at the well from John's Gospel and you will find that:

HE BROKE THE RULES! In His day, no self-respecting male was to be seen in public communicating with a woman. And further, no self-respecting Jew was ever to speak to or speak well of a Samaritan. He did! He met her at the well outside of Sychar.

HE BROKE THE ICE! How? By asking her for a drink. She was very surprised and taken back. Just remember her reply: "You are a Jew and I am a Samaritan woman. How can you ask me for a drink?" (John 4:9). Then…

HE BROKE THE NEWS! The dialogue is quite interesting but it comes down to this bottom line: "God is spirit, and his worshipers must worship in spirit and in truth" (John 4:23). She was so motivated that she went back into her town and invited them all to also come and meet this special man.

What a plan — break the rules . . . break the ice . . . break the news! Jesus' method of communication!

153 JESUS AND WORRY

CLYDE S. Kilby said: "I shall open my eyes and ears. Once every day I shall simply stare at a tree, a flower, a cloud, or a person. I shall not then be concerned at all to ask what they are but simply be glad that they are. I shall joyfully allow them the mystery of what (C.S.) Lewis calls their 'divine, magical, and ecstatic' existence."

When creation was completed, God pronounced it as being "very good." Therefore, all that we see of nature around us . . . all are part of that good creation. And Jesus said that the Heavenly Father takes into account a falling, wounded sparrow, that He numbers the very hairs of each head, and that He clothes the lilies of the field.

Therefore, Jesus says to get our living into a right relationship with God and we do not have to worry about anything!

THE MOTH

154

THE Holy Land seems to have a great number of moths who along with the butterfly belong to the order "lepidoptera" and could really be any of a number of winged insects. The Bible, however, only refers to the kind of moth that eats clothing. This insect has been associated with the weakness of humanity, the destructiveness of sin, and the quickly passing nature of the material world.

Jesus talked about spiritual deeds which could not be eaten by moths: "But store up for yourselves treasures in heaven, where moth and rust do not destroy" (Matt. 6:20). The letter James wrote warned the wealthy that their clothes had become moth eaten (James 5:2).

WHAT'S IN A SONG?

155

THE Reverend Samuel West was the pastor of a tranquil congregation in jolly old England. Things went along quite smoothly until there was a controversy with the choir about choices in musical selections. It began to take on a life of it's own until there came one particular Sunday when the choir refused to sing or even to lead the congregation in their singing. More weird things happen in the name of the Lord and His church!

So on this infamous Sunday, the shrewd clergyman introduced the service with the hymn "Come, We That Love the Lord." But he asked that the congregation begin their singing in worship with the second verse: "Let those refuse to sing who never knew our God. . . ."

HE CHALLENGED
THEM

JESUS constantly challenged people to do it! Take up your bed and walk. . . . Lazarus, come forth. . . . Come on, Peter, walk on the water. . . . Go show yourself to the priests who shall pronounce you clean. . . . Fill the empty pots with water . . . and many more! One of the Bible's saddest stories has to be of the tribes who chose to remain on the desert side of the River Jordan rather than going on into the Promised Land. They really got all they asked for, believed for, and exercised faith for . . . the bottom line is that all they asked for was sand and they got it.

How frustrated Jesus must have been to see people with great potential settle for less and act like nobodies. Perhaps we have asked for too little. Jesus kept challenging people to do it!

THE VIA
DOLOROSA

THE "Via Dolorosa" winds along the streets of the old city of Jerusalem and is considered to be the traditional route Jesus followed when bearing His cross from Pilate's Judgment Hall to Golgotha. These words are Latin, *via dolorosa*, which means "the sorrowful way" or "the way of sorrow." This was first used by the Franciscan boniface of Ragusa in the late 16th century. This way, or walk, was divided into 14 "stations" or segments, stops where pilgrims were to pray. However, there are no references in the Gospels to stations 3, 4, 6, 7, and 9.

This historical "Way of the Cross" begins in the area of the modern citadel just inside of the Jaffa Gate. The present-day Via Dolorosa was developed out of a series of stops on the circuit of holy places that the Franciscans developed for pilgrims sometime in the 14th century. It was customary for 14th-century pilgrims to the Holy Land to spend somewhere between 10 and 14 days in Jerusalem in order that they could see everything systematically while on their pilgrimmage.

The Via Dolorosa is not laid out by history but by tradition and the generations of Christians who deeply desired to have some sort of contact with all that had to do with the life of Christ. We do know that the distance from the scene of the trial to the place of crucifixion was approximately a mile. Jesus may have traveled this way or another.

THE 13TH DISCIPLE

158

MATTHIAS, meaning "gift of Jehovah," was the man chosen to replace the traitor, Judas. We know nothing of this man, except the single mention of him in the first chapter of the Book of the Acts. Here there were 120 gathered in the Upper Room waiting for the advent of the Holy Spirit. It was suggested that someone should be selected to replace Judas, the betrayor of Jesus Christ. The qualifications were outlined by Peter and two men were put forward . . . Joseph, called "Barsabas," surnamed "the Just," and Matthias.

The final decision was decided upon by drawing "lots." There is some speculation as to how this was done. According to Grotius, this was accomplished by the means of two urns. In one they placed two rolls of paper with the names of Joseph and Matthias on them, and in the other two rolls, one with the word "apostle" and the other blank. Then one roll was to be drawn simultaneously from each urn and the selection was read aloud and made.

Matthias was chosen . . . but we have never heard of him in the Bible since the selection. According to Eusebius and Epiphanius he was believed to have been one of the 70 disciples. He was to have preached the gospel in Judea and then been stoned to death by the Jews. Others make him a martyr by crucifixion in Ethiopia.

HEBREW NAMES

159

TO the Hebrew, names are designed to distinguish objects, and originally expressed special relationships or objects. Wouldn't it have been interesting to have observed Adam giving animals their names as God brought the beasts to him?

Some names were given prophetically as in the name of Jesus "the Savior." Quite often parents gave names to a child which meant a natural object as in Jonah (meaning dove), Tamar (palm tree), or Tabitha (gazelle). Sometimes a name kept alive the memory of some national event as in Ichabod (the glory of God has departed).

Also, you should know that the Israelites were fond of playing on names. Names, to them, were signs of something very special. Therefore names rarely were hereditary in Hebrew. But this tendency to play on names can be seen throughout the Bible as in Dan (judge) who was to judge his people.

THE MOUNT OF TRANSFIGURATION

160

WHERE is this "high mountain apart" on which Jesus was "transfigured" with Moses and Elijah? None of the Gospel writers identify which mountain this happened on . . . so we are left to speculation once more.

We do know that pilgrims to the Holy Land, as early as the 6th century, honored Mount Tabor, southeast of the Sea of Galilee as being the sacred spot. It seems, however, that the triple-peaked Mount Hermon in northern Israel, known today as the "Chief of the Mountains," could have been the more likely spot. Mount Tabor is 1,843 feet high while Hermon reaches to 9,166 feet. It's a huge mountain mass covering an area about 5 miles wide and almost 20 miles long. Furthermore, Tabor isn't near to Caesarea Philippi where Jesus and His disciples had gone for a retreat away from the crowds. There is one peak on Hermon which directly overlooks this city at an elevation of 8,500 feet.

Mount Hermon can be seen from almost anywhere in Israel. Its melting snows feed the River Jordan and it has a huge shadow which falls 30 to 40 miles westward at sunrise and eastward all the way to Damascus at sunset. Also of interest is that the "dew of Hermon" is heavier than anywhere else on the face of the earth.

NICODEMUS

161

HIS family history is unknown . . . but some say he was known as "Nicodemus Ben Gorion," the brother of Josephus, the well-known early Jewish historian. Some things we do know . . . this man was a member of the Sanhedrin and considered to have been one of the three most wealthy men of Jerusalem. It is also said that after all the recorded events he became poor because of rejection and persecutions for having embraced Jesus and Christianity.

He was also a Pharisee and was convinced by the miracles that Jesus was a "teacher" who was sent from God. He wanted a personal interview but the fear of the Jews caused him to come under cover of darkness to Jesus. Later, when officers were sent to apprehend Christ and returned empty, he defended Christ and for this received taunts from other members of the Sanhedrin.

However, at the burial of Christ, perhaps emboldened by the example of Joseph of Arimathea, Nicodemus assisted in the burial of Jesus. He came with a mixture of myrrh and aloes, about a hundred pounds or so, with which to anoint and embalm the body.

Nothing further is recorded about this man so we rely on tradition to tell us that after he had publicly declared himself to be a follower of Jesus and had been baptized by Peter he was removed from his office with the Sanhedrin and expelled from Jerusalem.

SOMEONE WITH SKIN

162

IT was a small high-pitched voice that penetrated the stillness of the night. It came from the bedroom across the hall, "Daddy, mommy, I'm scared!"

Out of your groggy, fuzzy, quick, sharp state of mind, you reply with, "Honey, Don't be afraid. Daddy and mommy are right here across the hall."

After a brief pause . . . the little voice can be heard to say again, "I'm still scared."

By this time, your quick insight helps with the reply: "Honey, you don't need to be afraid because Jesus is with you. He loves you. He promised to never leave you."

This time the pause is longer . . . you think the problem is solved. But the voice comes back once more, "I don't care about Jesus, Daddy! I want someone with skin on!"

Great logic used by a little child is almost exactly the reason for the "Incarnation." So after thousands of years of being unsuccessful in convincing His people that He really loved them, our Creator decided the best way to demonstrate His great love for us was to send "someone with skin on" — and His name is Jesus! Not too scholarly but it works for me! How about you?

SOMETHING DONE RIGHT

163

CHARLES Malik, the Lebanese ambassador to the United Nations, asked in a speech: "What has been the greatest American contribution to the rest of the world? Has it been money? Has it been food? Has it been medical skill? Has it been military might? Has it been industrial know-how?" He paused . . . then answered his own question: "The greatest thing to come out of America has been the American missionary effort: the quiet, selfless men and women who have left the comfort and security of their homeland to bring the gospel of Jesus Christ to less-favored nations."

FINDING THE CAUSE

164

MARIAN Preminger was born in Hungary in 1913, raised in a castle with her aristocratic family, surrounded with maids, tutors, governesses, butlers, and chauffeurs. While attending school in Vienna, Marian met a handsome young Viennese doctor. They fell in love, eloped, and married when she was only 18. The marriage lasted a year and she returned to Vienna to begin her life as an actress.

While auditioning for a play, she met the brilliant German director Otto Preminger. They fell in love and soon married. They went to America where he began his career as a movie director. Marian was soon caught up in the glamour and lights, and lived a sordid life. When Preminger discovered it, he divorced her.

Marian returned to Europe to live the life of a socialite in Paris. In 1948 she learned that Albert Schweitzer, the man she had read about as a little girl, was making one of his periodic visits to Europe and would be staying at Gunsbach. She phoned his secretary and was given an appointment to see Dr. Schweitzer the next day. When she arrived in Gunsbach she discovered he was in the village church playing the organ. She listened and turned pages of music for him. After a visit he invited her to have dinner at his house. By the end of the day she knew she had discovered what she had been looking for all of her life. She was with him every day and was invited to return to Africa to Lambarene to work in the hospital.

She did . . . and found herself. There in Lambarene, the girl who was born in a castle became a servant of Jesus Christ. She changed bandages, bathed babies, fed lepers . . . and became free!

165 JESUS AND MONEY

AMAZINGLY, Jesus talked and taught and preached a great deal about money! In fact, He talked about money more than He did about heaven or hell! He told 38 parables (earthly stories with heavenly or spiritual meanings) . . . and of these 38 . . . 16 are concerned with how to handle money, possessions, and how to establish the proper priorities in regard to these material things.

In the four Gospels, an amazing 1 out of 10 verses (288 in all) deal directly with the subject of money. The Bible offers 500 verses on prayer, less than 500 verses on faith, but more than 2,000 verses on money and possessions!

166 A ONE-TIME OPPORTUNITY

ONE of the great disasters of history took place in 1271. In this year, Niccolo and Matteo Polo (the father and uncle of Marco) were visiting the Kubla Khan. At this point in history, the Kubla Khan was a world ruler who ruled all of China, India, and the Far East. It was a huge empire.

He was attracted to the story of Jesus Christ and Christianity as Niccolo and Matteo told it to him. He said to them, "You shall go to your high priest and tell him on my behalf to send me a hundred men skilled in your religion and I shall be baptized, and when I am baptized all my barons and great men will be baptized and their subjects will receive baptism, too, and so there will be more Christians here than there are in your parts."

Niccolo and Matteo returned home with this message. Nothing was done for about 30 years and then two or three missionaries were sent. Too few and too late!

It boggles the mind to think what a different world this would be if in the 13th century China, India, and the Far East had become Christian nations! It's just another tragic example of mankind frustrating the purposes of God.

CHRISTIANITY
AND PATRIOTISM

THE followers of Jesus Christ and patriotism have much in common. It's significant to note that:

Our patriotic hymn, "My Country, 'Tis of Thee," was written by a Baptist clergyman, Samuel Francis Smith.

The "Pledge of Allegiance" to the flag was written in 1892 by another Baptist minister, Francis Bellamy.

The words "In God We Trust," which are carried on all of our coins, can be traced to the efforts of Rev. W.R. Watkinson of Ridleyville, Pennsylvania. His letter of concern, addressed to the Honorable S.P. Chase, was dated November 13, 1861. Seven days later Mr. Chase wrote to James Pollock, director of the U.S. Mint as follows:

> No nation can be strong except in the strength of God, or safe except in His defense. The trust of our people in God should be declared on our national coins. Will you cause a device to be prepared without delay with a motto expressing in the finest and tersest words possible, this national recognition?

The president of the College of New Jersey, the Reverend John Witherspoon, was the only clergyman to sign the Declaration of Independence. Tragically, he is a much-too-forgotten man in our history books. Perhaps it was he who had the most far-reaching influence on democracy. Why? He had personally taught several of the signers of the document and nine of them were graduates of the little college over which he presided at Princeton!

A LITTLE FABLE
ABOUT PEACE

WHEN Christ was born "The Prince of Peace," the angels declared to the frightened shepherds: "Glory to God in the highest, and on earth peace to men on whom his favor rests" (Luke 2:14). But, unfortunately, this weary world has seen very few years of peace since our Prince of Peace came. I came across this wonderful little fable on peace which I hope will also challenge you.

"Tell me the weight of a snowflake," a sparrow asked a dove.

"Nothing more than nothing," was the answer.

"In that case, I must tell you a marvelous story," the sparrow said. "I sat on the branch of a fir when it began to snow — not heavily, not in a raging blizzard — no, just like a dream, without a sound, and without any violence. Since I did not have anything better to do, I counted the snowflakes settling on the twigs and needles of my branch. Their number was exactly 3,741,952. When the 3,741,953rd dropped onto the branch, nothing more than nothing, as you say, the branch broke off." Having said that, the sparrow flew away.

The dove, since Noah's time an authority on the matter, thought about the story for awhile, and finally said to herself, "Perhaps only one person's voice is lacking for peace to come to the world."

169   THE CHANGED LIFE

WHEN Leonardo da Vinci was painting his masterpiece *The Last Supper,* he selected as the person to sit for the character of Christ a young man, Pietri Bandinelli by name, who was connected with the Milan Cathedral as chorister. Years passed before the great picture was completed, and when one character only remained . . . that of Judas Iscariot, the painter noticed a man in the streets of Rome who he selected as his model. With shoulders far bent toward the ground, having an expression of cold, hardened, evil, saturnine, the man seemed to portray a model true to the artist's conception of Judas.

When in the studio . . . Pietri, the profligate began to look around, as if recalling incidents of years long gone. Finally, he turned and with a look half-sad, yet one which told how hard it was to realize the change which had taken place, he said: "Maestro, I was in this studio 25 years ago. I, then, sat for Christ."

170   THE FOUR EVANGELISTS

THERE is a rich, symbolic tradition for the four "evangelists" or Gospel writers — Matthew, Mark, Luke, and John — which developed quite early in the Christian era. Christian artists borrowed from the Greek and Roman styles, and showed writers seated at their desks or standing holding a copy of the Gospel which they had written.

Much of their artwork also depicts them with or as the four-winged creatures of the Revelation . . . a man, a lion, an ox, and an eagle. Matthew is linked with the man because his Gospel begins with the genealogy and birth of Jesus. Mark is pictured with the lion as his symbol because he begins with the account of John the Baptist as the voice crying in the wilderness. The writer Luke is depicted with the ox or calf because of his telling of Zechariah's sacrifice in the temple. And John is linked with the soaring eagle because of the image of the "Word" which he paints.

The clergy of the Middle Ages also associated these four with the greatest prophets of the Old Testament — Isaiah, Jeremiah, Ezekiel, and Daniel.

JOHN THE BAPTIST IN THE WILDERNESS

TODAY, we tend to view John the Baptist's life and mission in a whole new light. We're discovering how the Hebrew attitude toward the wilderness was linked in tradition with the Sinai wasteland of the Exodus. The general thinking was that the wilderness was to be associated with wild animals, robbers, hunger, and thirst. But God changed that when He made a covenant with the Israelites during their 40 years of wanderings. Then the desert was seen as a place of cleansing and purity.

John, who was six months older than his cousin Jesus, went into the wilderness while he was in his youth. There is a possibility that he became a part of the sect of the Essenes. These were idealists who lived communally in preparation for the coming war between good and evil. They engaged in ritual bathing and believed themselves to be the real true Israel. They prayed for the day in which they would gain control of the temple from the worldly priesthood.

John began to attract a following with his fiery preaching, using language much like an Old Testament prophet. Such inflammatory language eventually cost him his life. He wore a distinctive garb and ate an interesting diet. However . . . the message of John was to all people. He specifically dealt with the coming of the One who was to be mightier than himself. It was he who introduced the rite of baptism, which was the symbol of the passing from a sinful life to being a follower of God.

FIRST WOMAN ORDAINED

EVEN though Jesus elevated the status of women in His day, the churches built in His name have been a bit slower to recognize them in leadership positions. For example . . .

Rachel Henderlite was the first woman to be ordained as a U.S. Presbyterian minister. She was approved unanimously by 125 commissioners in the Richmond, Virginia, presbytery to become pastor of the "All Souls Presbyterian Church" in Richmond in 1965. She was also the first woman professor of Christian education at the Austin Theological Seminary in Texas in 1966 and the first woman president of the "Presbyterian Council of Church Union" in 1976.

In 1980 she became president of the "Consultation on Church Union" in which ten other leading Protestant denominations participated. This group took significant steps toward ecumenical unity by approving a proposed form of ministry that would include bishops as well as recognized lay ministers.

SIN AND SICKNESS

WHAT is the connection between the sins we commit and the sicknesses we have? We're not really sure. However, in the time of Jesus, it was widely believed that people became sick because of some wrong or sin they or their parents had committed. The writer Luke tells us the story of how Jesus healed a man who was paralyzed. And in it, we have some insight into this ancient belief.

As Luke tells the story, "the power of the Lord was present" to heal on this day as Jesus was teaching. The first words to the man were not: "Get up and walk" but rather "Your sins are forgiven" (Luke 5:17–20). The man had two needs . . . health as well as to be forgiven. Jesus gave priority to forgiveness.

But this doesn't mean that every time you get sick, you must have your sins forgiven. At another time, as Jesus healed a man, the question was asked, "Who has sinned this man or his parents?" To which Jesus answered, "Neither this man nor his parents sinned," said Jesus, "but this happened so that the work of God might be displayed in his life" (John 9:2–3).

On the other hand . . . we also must know that the sins we commit can have a serious effect on our health. For example, if we harbor bitterness, anger, or resentment . . . eventually it can express itself in many ways that affect the body as well as the soul.

The bottom line is that Jesus has the answer for the healing of both soul and body!

HOW IMPORTANT WAS PRAYER TO JESUS?

174

JESUS was raised in a pietistic Jewish home and so it would have been most natural for Him to pray. Likely He was taught to pray as a young child and to pray frequently. Also, He would have been taught to pray at specific times during the day.

All the Gospels portray Jesus as a man of prayer, but it is Luke who puts the most emphasis on this aspect of His life. Luke tells us that Jesus prayed on a number of specific occasions such as when He was being baptized by John in the River Jordan; He prayed on the Mount of Transfiguration; He prayed for Peter that his faith would not fail him in the trial which was ahead; and as He was being crucified He prayed for the people who were crucifying Him.

There is also another passage written by Luke which shows Jesus praying by himself and His disciples came to Him asking Him to teach them how to pray. In answer to this request He gave them what we today call "The Lord's Prayer." Following this prayer, Jesus spent some time in teaching further about prayer and the attitude of prayer. He tells of two men who came to the temple to pray. One told God how good he was and the other came in humility. Jesus pointed out to all of us that it was the second man who was heard by God and not the first. If we are to be effective in our praying, we must do it in humility of mind, body, and spirit.

THE HIGH COST OF FOLLOWING JESUS

175

MARGARET Dehqani-Tafti is the wife of the Anglican Bishop of Tehran. Altogether they had spent more than 30 years working for the Lord in Iran before the revolution broke out in February of 1979. Early in 1980 an attempt was made on the life of the bishop but he managed to miraculously escape. But in May of that same year, their son Bahram was murdered on the outskirts of Tehran. After his murder, Mrs. Dehqani-Tafti wrote the following:

> We had prayed for our children for 24 years, and I had, in my mind, in my heart, in my prayers, given my children to God to use as He felt best. And we had prayed that God would use our family for His service in Iran. But, of course, how could I imagine that it might cost me the life of my son? When I came to it and I had felt the pain and the suffering and the human side of it, which any parent will feel, I then realized . . . well, if God needed him who was I to keep him? God's generosity to me became far greater. Everything I have is from God. It made it much clearer in my mind that really our children are God's too, and we must use them and love them as God's. So the cost was great, but God's love for me is greater than that.

THE OLDEST MANUSCRIPT

176

ONE of the oldest, if not *the* oldest, *complete* New Testaments in existence today is displayed in the British Museum. It was copied in the fourth-century A.D. and is known as the "Codex Sinaiticus." But there are individual books and other fragments that can be dated earlier than the Codex Sinaiticus.

For example, a fragment of John's Gospel exists that was copied around the year A.D. 130. It was found in southern Egypt and means that a copy of the Gospel must have been in circulation about only 40 years after the Gospel was originally written.

WHY WAS JESUS ARRESTED?

177

THE religious authorities were angry, frustrated, and had been looking for the right moment to arrest Jesus and subsequently silence Him forever. It happened around the biggest of the Jewish celebrations . . . the Passover. As He arrived in Jerusalem for this feast they began to actively plan ways in which they could manage to have Him put to death. This would not be as easy as it seemed. He was popular with the people, constantly surrounded by crowds.

Luke writes of their dilemma: "Every day Jesus taught in the Temple. The chief priests, the teachers of the Law, and the leaders of the people wanted to kill him, but they could not find a way to do it, because all the people kept listening to him, not wanting to miss a single word" (Luke 19:47–48).

To have attempted to arrest Him in broad daylight, while He was teaching, preaching, or healing the sick, no doubt would have provoked a riot. But to their delight, the ideal moment was to be provided by one of His own disciples, Judas. He offered to inform these authorities as to the whereabouts of Jesus at night, when no crowds would be present. Why were they so determined to kill Him?

LOVE FOR THOSE WHO PERSECUTE

ONE of the major principles which Jesus taught is about loving our enemies and praying for those who do us wrong. Festo Kivengere, an Anglican bishop in Uganda, faced this very problem under Idi Amin's rule. On February 16, 1977, Archbishop Janani Luwum was murdered by the security forces of Amin. Bishop Festo, who wrote the book, *I Love Idi Amin* described some of his feelings upon hearing of the death of the Archbishop:

> Early in the morning the paper came with the headline that the archbishop and the two cabinet ministers had died in a car accident between the place of arrest and another place for questioning. And then the whole country was paralyzed by that terrible news. And yet, on Sunday, four days after his death, St. Paul's Cathedral in Kampala was crowded out with nearly 5,000 worshipers: students and young people who walked to church singing. That singing was of course very difficult because it was singing with tears and with joy. And those who were present tell me that it was just like being in heaven.
>
> The title of my book, *I Love Idi Amin,* of course can give the wrong impression, as if it were just one of those little Christian clichés. But it in fact came out of a press conference when I arrived in the Unites States as an exiled bishop. The Amin thing was still very hard, and I faced

some tough questions. One black man said to me, "Why is it that you hesitate to condemn Amin . . . a terrible man? Don't confuse us, condemn him!" Then I said, by the help of the Holy Spirit, "My ministry is not the ministry of condemnation. My ministry is the ministry of reconciliation."

The above is merely one more example of how following Jesus is to work out in real life in the real world!

179 CHRIST IN COMMON PEOPLE

ONE of the great biblical themes is almost comic in the fact that Christ was found among humble people in humble places. Can anything be more common and humble than places such as Nazareth? Bethlehem? On Lake Galilee? Human wisdom tends to look for God in the palaces and temples of worldly ambition and imagination. Christ, however, was as likely to be found in the mangers and carpenter shops of our lives.

Joan of Arc, the 15th century French heroine, combines both of these themes. George Bernard Shaw wrote the play *Saint Joan,* and in it he captures both of these themes. Joan is a peasant maiden from a small French village who claims to have visions from God asking her to help the French in their fight against the invading armies of England. She has undertaken to lead and inspire the French troops despite the fact that she is a woman of only 18 years. She did this quite apart from the authority of the king, the military, or the church.

In this play, Joan has been summoned before King Charles VII. The king has commanded her to explain how she, who was nothing more than a peasant maiden, had the audacity to involve herself in this war. By whose authority had she been marshaling the troops and taken them into battle? Innocently, but boldly, Joan stands before the king, alone, surrounded by courtiers, soldiers, nobles, and church officials.

Without hesitation and bravely, she tells the king how she felt the presence of God speaking to her and compelling her to help her country in this time of need. The weakling King Charles interrupts: "O your voices, your voices! Why don't the voices come to me? I am the King of France, not you!"

And I think there is a great bit of comic relief in heaven, too.

NOW YOU SEE IT — NOW YOU DON'T

IN Matthew 24, Jesus' disciples ask Him to reveal the time of the end, the consummation of history. Jesus begins by telling them to look at the magnificent temple, then claims that one day, not one stone would be left upon another. Clearly, this would have astonished His followers, since the temple, in all its sparkling splendor, was the geographical and spiritual focal point for the entire region. That it had once before been destroyed (by the Babylonians) seemed of little consequence.

However, as with all the Bible's predictive prophecy, the event happened, and barely a few decades later.

To squelch yet another Jewish revolt, Rome sents its legions against Jerusalem in A.D. 68, under the leadership of Titus. Laying seige to the city, the Romans finally broke through two years later and torched the temple complex, then pushed even the foundation stones over the Temple Mount. Today, but for two Moslem mosques, the entire plaza is flat as can be!

THE PURITANS AND CHRISTMAS

DID you know that less than a century and a half ago, Christmas was not celebrated in many Protestant churches?! Not only were the secular celebrations frowned upon . . . there were NO religious observances, either! In fact, the two most controversial issues being debated in many of our churches before the Civil War were slavery and the celebration of Christmas. We presume that the more liberal clergy were for Christmas and against slavery while the more conservative were against Christmas and for slavery. Oh, well . . . there we were, at it again.

The major arguments against celebrating Christmas were that most of the customs were pagan and that too much drinking and merrymaking took place during this season. The further argument was that the Catholics, Episcopalians, and Lutherans did it so therefore the other Protestants shouldn't.

Interestingly enough, earlier in American history the Puritans, who observed Thanksgiving, had passed a law against making merry during the Yuletide season. The year was 1659 and the law was: "Whosoever shall be found observing any such day as Christmas and the like, either by feasting, forbearing labor, or any other way . . . every such person so offending shall pay for each offense five shillings as a fine to the country."

REDEEMING CHILDREN AND PURIFICATION

182

IT was required that following a 40-day period, the firstborn male was to be taken to the temple in Jerusalem to be consecrated before God. Part of this observation goes back to Egypt where the firstborn had been saved by the application of the blood of the sacrificial lamb of the Passover and thus belonged to God. Each mother was also expected to become purified after the birth of the first child.

This firstborn male was presented to the priest and the parents paid five shekels to buy him back or redeem him. The mother was then expected to pay a yearling lamb and a pigeon or a dove for her own purification. If, however, she could not afford a lamb . . . two doves or pigeons would be acceptable.

When Mary presented her firstborn, Jesus, at the temple, she must not have had very much money since she offered "a pair of doves or two young pigeons" (Luke 2:24).

HOW WERE THE HANDICAPPED TREATED?

183

WHEN children were born handicapped or with deformities, there was only one restriction and this barred them from the priesthood. Otherwise, it seems as though they were kept at home and helped as much as possible. For example . . . there is the story of the lame man who was brought daily to the Gate Beautiful who was unable to walk since birth. But it's obvious that someone cared for him . . . until Peter and John encountered him and he was healed by the power of God.

On another occasion, Jesus healed a man who was born blind whose parents had not rejected him but had cared for him since his birth.

FOUR MARYS
AND JESUS

NOT only did Jesus minister to many women while He was on this earth, but a large number of women were part of His inner circle. These women came from a wide spectrum of society and economic strata. The four Marys are the most familiar to us.

Mary, His mother, was a woman of great faith who must have had a remarkable influence over Him in His growing-up days. She was apparently a frequent companion in His ministry, but in a spiritual sense, Jesus also considered many women His mother.

Mary Magdalene, who was formerly possessed with demons, was probably a woman of some financial means. Tradition tells us that she was a former prostitute but there is no solid biblical reason to believe this. She was one of several women who traveled with Jesus and His troop as they evangelized from town to town.

Mary of Bethany, the sister of the resurrected Lazarus, was another dedicated follower of Christ. She is pictured in the Bible as a contemplative, sensitive person. This is the Mary who sat at the feet of Jesus to learn and washed his head with expensive perfume, which caused some consternation among some of the practical-minded male disciples.

Mary, the mother of James and John, attended most of the major events in the latter part of the life and death of Christ as did Mary Magdalene. She was also part of His group on evangelistic trips to other places.

One fact is most noteworthy about these ladies — during the most trying hours of His arrest, death, and burial, these women were daring enough to remain close to Jesus. In turn, they were among the first to share in the enormous joy at the news of His resurrection!

FIGS

PHILIP, "the Evangelist," found Nathanael sitting under a sprawling fig tree, according to John's account, and told him that Jesus was the Messiah. This was a typical Palestinian picture because of the many fig trees in Israel and because their foliage is thick and shady. Incidently, these are the same leaves from which clothing was fashioned for Adam and Eve as they left the Garden of Eden.

Often, if conditions are right, the typical fig tree in Israel will yield two annual crops; the first in May or June and the second in September. Closely related to the ordinary fig tree is the "sycamore-fig" which doesn't produce a good fig and is considered to be an inferior tree. And it was this sycamore-fig which Zacchaeus climbed up into to get a better view of Jesus.

Jesus also told the story about a man who had a fig tree that gave no fruit for three years. He decided to give it one more year by digging around the roots and fertilizing it. If that didn't work it was to be cut down. And . . . it was to a place of many fig trees that Jesus sent His disciples to find a colt for Him to ride on into Jerusalem — Bethphage, which means "house of figs."

HOW FAR DID 186 JESUS TRAVEL?

TIME and distances are an interesting study. The time duration of a journey usually depended upon the method of travel, weather, safety, and the physical condition of the traveler. One of the good things Roman rule did for Israel in the time of Christ was to make traveling on roads pretty safe for the traveler.

The people who traveled by foot likely averaged 15 to 20 miles per day. The actual distance between Jericho and Jerusalem is only 15 miles but this road is narrow, winding, and steep. From Jerusalem to the Sea of Galilee is almost 80 miles and from Bethlehem to Galilee is just a bit more than 80 miles.

Except for His trip to Egypt as a child . . . Jesus may have never traveled more than 85 miles from home. Contrast that with Paul the Apostle who traveled extensively around the Mediterranean Sea . . . hundreds of miles.

ANIMAL 187 TRANSPORTATION

THE world that Jesus lived in was likely more sophisticated than what we normally are led to believe. When it came to travel and transport . . . much of the travel was by wagons, carts, chariots, and the use of animals as beasts of burden.

Camels . . . Sometimes people rode these "tall ships of the desert" but the greatest value lay in their ability to haul heavy loads. Camels could be compared to our trucks today. They could carry half a ton of merchandise about 25 miles per day.

Donkeys . . . These sturdy, lightweight animals functioned much like a modern day pickup truck would. There are many biblical references to donkeys and they were the animals of choice for the common people. It was one of these on which Christ rode into Jerusalem.

Horses . . . The Romans used horses, especially to equip and move their mobile armies. These were too expensive for the common folk . . . but used often by government officials.

Elephants . . . Seeing these beasts in Israel would have been quite rare. Transportation was their best function. Their more practical role was like that of a bulldozer, or crane. Once, Lyoias used 32 elephants as he fought the Jews in a battle which took place in 163 B.C.

SOCIAL CONFLICTS
AND PREJUDICES

188

WHEN Jesus lived in Israel He was surrounded by bigotry, prejudices, and social conflicts. He himself was slandered by others. Often when a Jew in this biblical setting heard the word "Gentile," an ugly feeling bubbled up within. The word "Samaritan" could make the blood boil of a self-respecting Judean. It's very likely that when Caiaphas, the High Priest, heard the name of Jesus used, his heart probably raced from the adrenaline of hatred.

It is important for us to understand a bit of the prejudices that controlled people's emotions in Jesus' day. A person's prejudices often indicated how they would feel and act if completely free to do so. Naturally, we'll never know the emotions and feelings stirring in the souls of the Jews in Jesus' day but we can attempt to understand some of those thoughts. It also gives us a bit more of an insight as to many of the happenings recorded in the Bible.

The Old Testament prophet Jonah is a prime example of a man who acted upon his bigotry and prejudice. When he was called of God to preach to the city of Nineveh, he refused because he didn't want to see God's grace given to his bitter enemies.

So what has changed from Christ's day to ours in regards to this subject? We hope lots. But the world is still trapped by social conflicts, prejudices, and bigotry . . . from which Jesus came to free us.

WHY A "SYNAGOGUE"?

IN the time of Christ . . . the "synagogue" was extremely important. It was the center of Jewish religious education as well as being the center of Jewish community life. We do not know when the first synagogue was begun but we can be fairly certain as to why the concept. Just think back on the long history of the Jews . . . they have faced all kinds of serious threats to their continued existence; they have been murdered, captured, deported, and infiltrated by people who hate them. Consequently, if they were to survive, some form of educational and religious center had to be developed to facilitate survival.

It is likely that some of the Jews in exile decided to organize so they could more effectively teach their children about God so they wouldn't forget and be overrun by the pagan religions all about them. Over a period of years these facilities became more sophisticated and eventually became known as "synagogues." Ten Jewish males were necessary to form a synagogue and these had great diversity of physical design as well as teaching standards. These were much like denominations are today. The only standard adhered to were the ten males . . . other than that there was much choice. The Pharisees led in this development and were the strong forces behind this movement.

When Christ came ministering, the synagogue was a force to be reckoned with. Next to the temple in Jerusalem, the synagogue held the highest place of importance and authority. The major advantage to the synagogue is that it brought religion into close proximity to the common people.

SHEEP

190

IT would be difficult to exaggerate the number of sheep in the land of Israel. For example, when Moses defeated the Midianites he received over 600,000 sheep; when Solomon dedicated his temple, he sacrificed 120,000 sheep and goats; during the reformation of Asa, 7,000 sheep were sacrificed. This might give us just a bit of an inkling as to their numbers. Also, it helps us to appreciate that the word "sheep" appears more than 500 times in the Bible.

It's a specific breed distinguished by a broad tail which can weigh

10 to 15 pounds and was considered prime eating. If a particular sheep wandered away too often, the shepherd might tie one leg to its tail. In Israel, most sheep are white but can be brown, black, red, or spotted.

The disposition of sheep is between meek and dumb. They lack aggression and make easy targets for predators. Their very vulnerability makes them totally dependent upon a shepherd. Because of their disposition, sheep are quite affectionate and this accounts for some of the close relationship between sheep and shepherd. The dependency on a shepherd is one of the major themes in the Bible, particularly in the New Testament. Jesus pictured people as sheep who are tired and wandering aimlessly without a shepherd. When Jesus spoke of believers as sheep, He particularly emphasized their need for help. But He also insisted that we are worth much more than sheep.

191 INNS AND INNKEEPERS

INNKEEPERS have come in for a bad rap simply because of the one we are so familiar with who turned away the pregnant Mary and her humble husband, Joseph. Originally, when traveling, people took their chances by camping out or staying in private homes. Soon, however, life became more sophisticated and as travel increased there was a need for commercial inns. Rahab "the harlot" may well have been an innkeeper in Jericho. Later these became known as "caravanserais" which cared for people as well as their animals. And by the time of Christ's birth, most populated areas would have had inns.

According to one of the stories Jesus told (we know it as the story of the "Good Samaritan"), some innkeepers, at least this one, were caring and dependable. They would have provided only the barest of necessities — no hot showers there!

192 WHAT ABOUT LOCAL DOCTORS?

COULD you have made an appointment with your local family physician in Jesus' day? Yes! However . . . you must know this was a mixed bag. Some respected them and others considered them the worst of all crooks. Because of the doctors' poor reputations the Hebrew rabbis invented proverbs to describe them such as, "The best among doctors deserved Gehenna," or hell. Another warned, "Live not in a city whose chief is a medical man."

Jesus also alluded in His teachings to another of those well-known proverbs about doctors: "Physician, heal yourself." This saying was also to be found among the Greeks and Chinese. It was a skeptical way of telling the doctor that if his medicine is so good he should use it on himself first . . . then if he survived, others might also try it.

Another negative statement is found in Mark's account. This lady had been sick for 12 years and this Scripture tells us that she had suffered much at the hands of her doctors who had exhausted her funds. Interestingly, Luke, himself a doctor, writes about the same story but leaves out the harsh criticism of the medical profession!

193 GOLD

GOLD . . . from its color, malleability, durability, and occurrence, was without a doubt the first metal to really attract the attention of mankind. The ancients knew the value of gold as a use of exchange but also for use in all kinds of art forms. Go to any respectable museum on ancient history and you will observe objects made of gold, plated with gold, covered with hammered gold, and overlaid with gold. Gold was the choice for making idols, no doubt going back to the golden calf of Moses' time.

Therefore, gold, as the most precious of all metals, should be a most fitting gift to be given to the newborn King by the visiting Magi!

194 FRANKINCENSE

IN a hot land which was short on water, such as Israel, perfumes often took the place of a good bath or shower. After a day of heavy, sweaty work, a person might rub herself or himself with liquid deodorant to make themselves socially acceptable.

The use of incense as an air freshener was also developed by the time of Christ. Many homes burned incense to keep the air tolerable as well as keeping flies, gnats, and mosquitoes at bay. A Jewish home was usually filled with distinct fragrances because it was a necessity.

In order to control the market and keep the price up, these merchants carefully guarded their origins and secret formulas. Today we know that frankincense was extracted from a small shrub. It was highly prized and considered to be a suitable gift for a king. Therefore, it follows that it was the gift most fitting for the newborn King, and the wise men brought it to the house where the infant Jesus was.

195 AND MYRRH

MYRRH is extracted from a small tree. The bark of each tree is peeled back in several strips. Just beneath the bark, resting in the crevices of the trunk, are the gum resins which make this perfume. Slices in the bark cause the juices to run, evidently attempting to heal the wound, and these form bulges on the side of the tree. The bulges or tears harden in position during the next three or four months. Once they are firm, many of the large tears fall to the ground. Harvesters then slice off the remaining lumps and also gather those which have fallen. They are transported in special bags and before being marketed are ground into a very fine powder. Myrrh makes an excellent perfume for burning, too. Many women would stand over the burning incense and allow the aroma to permeate their clothing and hair before going out in public.

It was highly prized in Christ's day. Oh yes, both frankincense and myrrh are named in the romantic scenes pictured in the Song of Solomon . . . as you read it, you can almost smell the enchanting fragrances in these scriptural passages. And it, too, was most fitting for a gift by the Magi to the newborn King!

196 ANCIENT FOOTWEAR

ANCIENT footwear was of two types: sandals and shoes. Occasionally, some of the more wealthy people would wear socks, but sandals were usually worn on bare feet.

John the Baptist declared himself to be unworthy to tie or loosen the straps on Jesus' sandals! Removing the sandals of a guest was the job of a slave in the house. John was saying that by comparison he was lower than such people.

Ancient shoes were much like our ankle-high boots. They were usually made of soft leather with a hard sole and made from camel hide. It makes sense that people wore sandals in hot weather and shoes in cold weather, just like we do today.

Sandals and shoes play a huge role in the Bible and make a most interesting study. Shoes were to be removed at sacred occasions. Boaz, in ancient Israel, closed a deal by offering his shoes as assurance. Amos tells us that God's people had become so corrupt that a judge would rule against the poor if he was bribed with a mere pair of shoes.

When Jesus sent out His 70 disciples, He warned them not to take an extra pair of sandals so they could move quickly.

WHAT ABOUT 197 FOOT WASHING?

FOOT washing was a natural because of the wearing of sandals in this dry and dusty climate. Remember . . . no sidewalks, black topped parking lots, or roads. Abraham offered this humble gesture to the Lord when He appeared at the tent of Abraham.

If you follow this practice through the Bible you will find it has a double meaning. In the first and most common aspect, feet were washed as a sign of hospitality and comfort. What an appropriate gesture and treatment for dirty, sore feet. Those ancients had a lifestyle that we could, and perhaps should, follow.

Then there were times when this act of washing was an act of reverence and respect. When the woman washed the feet of Jesus in the home of the Pharisee, she was majoring in reverence. Abigail did much the same in showing reverence to David. The widows performed this act for believers in the Early Church.

And by washing the feet of His disciples, Jesus was showing humility and respect as a pattern for them to follow. Besides . . . there is no doubt their feet really needed to be washed before supper.

WHY STUDY THE 198 LIFE OF CHRIST?

IT IS difficult to piece together the life of a personality who lived thousands of years ago in a totally different culture and society. At best, we only have a sketchy picture. Reality is too far removed for us to see all the shades, shadows, and colors of meaning.

But remember . . . Jesus was a Jew who lived among Jews, Romans, and Greeks. The better we know about the emotions, mindsets, and lifestyles of the Jews, the better we can understand the Bible and the life of Jesus.

Jesus lived among real people, He wore the clothes, ate the food, laughed at their jokes, and sang the songs of Israel. Some of the Bible makes little sense until we can get behind the words to the real meanings. How are we able to picture the face turning red with anger or hatred; how can we hear a voice shouting out in indignation; how can we hear the whisper of tenderness; how is it possible to feel the ache of tired muscles after a day of fishing, farming, or carpentering?

In your study remember that there is no such thing as a typical Jew because their culture was moving and changing as they adopted different ways. Their culture was not static. Whatever . . . don't give up continual study. What made Jesus a real person? Again, the better we know His times the more understanding we have of His words.

JESUS LEARNED TO LET IT GO

199

CONSIDER with me the ultimate act of faith of Jesus. Was it in coming to this earth or leaving it? He had spent His entire life in preparation for the three years of training His followers in His mission. Then He had to let it go. He said, "It is finished!" Notice, He didn't say, "I am finished!" He said "IT" is finished. What was finished? His life's work. He let it go!

Do you remember the *Indiana Jones* movie scene in which he and his father have pursued the "Holy Grail" (the cup from which Jesus drank at the Last Supper)? After all kinds of adventures and mis-adventures, Indiana is at the edge of the precipice . . . and at the moment of nearly having the very grail they have been searching for. His position is so precarious on the cliff that if he retrieves the grail he will lose his balance and likely fall into the pit below. As he is about to grasp it . . . his father whispers: "Indy, Let it go." You can see the indecision . . . the thinking . . . the weighing of his opportunity. Another second passes and his father more firmly says, "Indiana, let it go!" It's a moment to be remembered as the audience collectively gasps.

This action is so un-Indiana-like, so un-American-like, so un-Hollywood-like . . . to come all this way and through all those adventures, to come to this moment and let it pass. Slowly, then it begins to dawn on the audience that this is not about the Holy Grail but about spending time together, facing death together, and building a stronger relationship.

Has Christ whispered to you about something in your life, "Let it go!" Yes . . . Jesus let it go and left His mission in the hands of others whom He had loved, trained, and prepared for the future.

WHO WERE THE MAGI?

THE "wise men" were only mentioned by Matthew in his account. Who were these mysterious strangers who sought out the child Jesus? Most likely they were members of a priestly class from Persia. They would have been skilled in astrology . . . the belief that stars affect human events. These were simply called "wise men from the East." If they had been studying the heavens . . . any unusual phenomenon would signal the birth of an important person.

It happened in about 7 B.C. and was quite near the birth of Jesus. The planets Jupiter and Saturn came close together in the constellation "Pisces" which would have been an unusually brilliant and rare occurrence. Jupiter symbolized the kingship of the world and Saturn was connected with Israel and Pisces was a sign of the earth's last days. That, according to tradition, is how it happened that the wise men came to see the special child.

There are some scholars who believe the Magi could have known about Old Testament prophecies of a coming Messiah because of the Jews who had remained behind in Persia when others had returned to Jerusalem from the Babylonian captivity.

One more thing of note . . . Matthew treats the wise men with great empathy even though astrology was condemned in the Bible as idolatry.

And, also, you must know . . . we do not know if they were only three in number! Tradition names them Caspar, Melchior, and Balthazar, and a songwriter has written "We Three Kings of Orient Are." Yes, I know there were three gifts brought — and the controversy goes on and on. Join in and take a number . . . three or more or less? Aren't these questions fun? Especially the ones that are left open and force you to make a choice.

201 JESUS WAS BOLD

I just cannot picture Jesus as a wimp in any sense of the word! His message was bold, His delivery was bold, His thinking was bold, His speaking was bold, and His actions were bold! Never once is He pictured as working through lots of committee meetings, nor did He ever ask permission, except from His Heavenly Father, before making a statement! Everything about Jesus was bold!

Just read through the Gospels with a fresh unbiased viewpoint and look for the bold. You will discover that He told bold stories, on occasion He shouted, He overturned tables and money boxes, He wept, He moaned, He cried, He prayed, He commanded, and He did not teach like some of the wimpish teachers of the law of His day.

He bombarded the minds of people with bold deeds, bold new attitudes, and bold actions that had never been seen before. His boldest message was painted in His own blood!

202 SONS OF THUNDER

TOO often we have painted the picture that all of the disciples and followers of Jesus were meek and mild — wimps. Not! Jesus nicknamed two brothers, John and James, as the "Sons of Thunder." Just what kind of people must these two have been? We do know that one time they were ready to call fire from heaven to descend on some people! Their father was Zebedee and their mother was Salome, who served Jesus in Galilee and was present at His crucifixion.

Evidently John was among the Galileans who had followed John the Baptist until they were called to follow Jesus at the beginning of His ministry. They were among the 12 men selected to become "Apostles." John became known as the disciple "whom Jesus loved" (John 13:23). The inner circle of three was composed of Peter, James, and John. James was martyred too early to have been the author of more than one book. John became one of the major pillars of the church in Jerusalem along with James and Peter.

Tradition tells us that John went to Ephesus just before the destruction of Jerusalem in A.D. 70 and later was exiled by the Romans to the island of Patmos from where he wrote "The Revelation of Jesus Christ." John, interestingly enough, was the only one of the original 12 apostles who lived long enough to have attained old age and is, according to tradition, to have died an old man at about age 96.

203 THORNS, THISTLES, AND TARES

THISTLES, tares, and thorns are abundant in dry lands like Israel . . . in fact, more than 120 different kinds grow there. Some can reach a height of near six feet (2m). Some, such as the "milk-thistle" have beautiful flowers . . . but can overrun and quickly choke out the young plants growing in a field.

Jesus told a story about the sower and the four different kinds of soils and environments. The thorns to which He referred could have been any of the 120 different varieties and would have been easily recognizable by His listeners.

The crown of thorns woven for Jesus at His crucifixion could easily have come from one of these plants. The "tares" in the story Jesus told about the wheat and the weeds are "darnel" which looks exactly like wheat in the early stages of growth.

204 THE HYSSOP PLANT

IT'S impossible for us living today in our antiseptic world to imagine the pain and suffering of crucifixion. The agony was part of the execution which could last up to three or four days. On occasion the thirst would be relieved. While hanging on the cross, Jesus was given vinegar in a sponge passed to Him on a bunch of hyssop. The hyssop is a plant which was used, especially in the Old Testament, for the sprinkling of the blood of the sacrifices. The Jews were also commanded to use it on the eve of the Passover. It is a bushy plant and is somewhat different than what is used as an herb today, even though it is called hyssop.

HEROD'S
TEMPLE

JESUS predicted that for Herod's temple"Not a single stone here will be left in its place." These words were fulfilled in A.D. 70 when the Romans set fire to the building. In order to make an area large enough for this grand temple, King Herod had built an artificial platform over the south end of the temple hill where the ground sloped away. The outer walls holding the structure still stand. The "Wailing Wall" is part of this platform.

There are two stone blocks that remain from the temple proper. The first was found more than a century ago and is preserved in a museum in Istanbul because Jerusalem was then a part of the Turkish Empire. On the face of it are some lines of carefully carved Greek. Recently, a stone piece much like it has been found in Jerusalem, this one with the letters carved out or picked out in red paint. The inscriptions threaten death to any non-Jew who passes the boundary they mark.

Josephus, the first-century Jewish historian, as well as other writers, explain that Herod's temple had four courtyards. Anyone could enter the first, which was the "Court of the Gentiles." But only Jews were allowed to walk in the inner courts. A low stone fence marked the limit of the first court with notices in Greek and Latin warning foreigners to go no farther. The two stones previously mentioned are apparently two of these.

Jesus and His disciples would have seen it when they visited the temple. Later, in the Book of the Acts, we are told of a riot provoked by Jews who thought Paul had taken a non-Jewish person past this fence. Later, Paul took this barrier as a picture of the division between God's people, the Jews, and others. He said that the work of Jesus abolished such distinctions . . . so the notice lost its purpose. All people can gain direct access to God!

JESUS IN
JERUSALEM

JESUS first visited Jerusalem as a boy and went to the Passover celebration/festival with His parents. On this trip He made His way to the Jewish teachers in the temple and communicated with them. As an adult He would have attended many of the religious festivals in the city and often taught there. Once, the sight of the moneychangers and the selling of animals in the temple courtyard called forth His angry words, "Stop making my Father's house a market-place" (John 2:16).

It was in Jerusalem that He invited all who were "thirsty" to "come to me and drink" (John 7:37). In Jerusalem He declared himself to be "the light of the world" (John 8:12); at the Pool of Bethesda He healed a man who had been sick for 38 years. He gave sight to the man born blind, telling him to wash himself in the Pool of Siloam.

When He came to Jerusalem, Jesus often stayed just over the hill at Bethany with Mary, Martha, and Lazarus. On the way there, just across the Kidron Valley from the temple, was the Garden of Gethsemane . . . where He could find a quiet place to pray.

In Jerusalem the world-shaking events of His last week on this earth took place. Here, Jesus was crucified just outside the city wall; here He rose from the grave, victorious over sin and death; and from the nearby Mount of Olives He returned to His Heavenly Father, having finished His work on earth!

NEW TESTAMENT COINS

COINAGE seems to have been introduced in the seventh century B.C. These early coins were simply pieces of metal of a standard weight and impressed with a seal. They were often named after the weights they represented. There were three different currencies used in Palestine in the time of Christ. There was the official, imperial Roman standard. There was then the provincial money minted at Antioch and Tyre with was a Greek standard. And finally, the local Jewish money which may have been minted at Caesarea.

Money for the temple, including the half-shekel tax, had to be paid in the Tyrian coinage (or the 2-drachma piece), not Roman. It's not a huge surprise that moneychangers flourished at the temple!

Money was coined in gold, silver, copper, bronze, or brass. The most common silver coins mentioned in the New Testament are the Greek "tetradrachma" and the Roman "denarius" which was an average day's wage for the common working man. So the coin which Jesus asked for would have been one of the Roman coins, likely the "denarius" which would have had engraved or stamped on it the image of Tiberius, emperor from A.D. 14 to 37.

TRADE AND COMMERCE

THE "Roman peace," since Pompey had cleared the seas of pirates, provided abundant opportunities for trade and commerce. The range of imports and exports was amazing. It's estimated that approximately 118 different kinds of luxury goods were being bought and sold here. There were trade routes by land, usually under the control of the "Nabataens" whose capital was Petra which is in modern-day Jordan.

Jewish ancient records show that there were seven different markets in the city of Jerusalem. Those who brought goods to market there were heavily taxed and those who bought were taxed, so prices were high. But most importantly, there was a brisk trade in goods required for worship at the temple — especially the animals used for sacrifices. Jesus objected to the fact that this trade went on in the temple court and cleansed it one time. However, this temple court was the only place that non-Jews could worship. Thus, the temple became the most important financial factor in Jerusalem's commerce. Every Jew was required to make payments to the temple treasury as well as other payments and sacrifices. This was one of the ways in which Jerusalem paid for luxury imports.

The rules for business deals were strictly spelled out by the rabbis and there were also market inspectors to see that they were carried out. Buyers had the right to register complaints. AND — no interest was to be charged to fellow Jews. Personal belongings could be used as security — but not an essential such as a plow, cloak, or millstones. Interesting!

KIDS' GAMES

GAMES that kids play seem to have changed little over the passing of time, except for our electronic high-tech stuff today. We know that children in Bible times had toys which made a noise — rattles and whistles. Girls played with dolls and dollhouses.

Miniature cooking pots and pans and furniture made out of pottery have been found in archeological digs. Some dolls even have jointed arms and legs with hair of beads. Some have been found with holes in their shoulders for puppet strings. Balls have been found along with wooden pull-toys.

Israelite children, like kids everywhere, also enjoyed playing "imitating" games, copying the grownups. Jesus alludes to kids playing in the marketplaces and shouting to each other as He is speaking about John the Baptist and their ministries which had come under criticism.

210 THE CHURCH OF THE TRINITY

ALL kinds of interesting monuments and churches have been built in the name of Jesus Christ by His followers. You can find one of the unique churches in Waldassen, Germany. In fact this was built on the Trinity . . . Father, Son, and Holy Spirit. It's quite easy to remember the details if you keep in mind the number "three." Of course, it is named the "Church of the Trinity," with the following details:

Three towers and three turrets, and each turret has three dormer windows. Three roofs and three openings in each roof. Three windows and three doors in each part of the structure. Three large crosses and three small crosses. Three altars and three staircases. Three doorways and three columns. Three lights and three niches. Three bays and three windows in each bay. Three statues of the Virgin Mary.

But that's not all . . . the designer of this interesting church was Georg Dientzhofer who himself was the third architect in his family. The building of this church took exactly 33 months, and 333 weeks, and 33 days. It was built at a cost of 33,333 florins and 33 kreuzer!

211 THE TRAVELING LITTER

NOT all who claimed to be followers or servants of the Lord were nice people. Consider with me the very notorious Cardinal Richelieu, who was King Louis XIII's most powerful French minister during his reign. He occupied a most extraordinary bed! The Cardinal was afflicted with headaches, hemorrhoids, boils, and some disease of the bladder. Therefore, since he couldn't get around, he had a huge litter built and he was carried by 24 bodyguards who also doubled as litter bearers. On this litter there was also a chair, a table, and a private secretary who sat on the chair and used the table. It is also reported that when the traveling bed proved too large to go through the doors of any building Richelieu wished to enter . . . he commanded his bodyguards/litter carriers to batter down the walls!

212 THE BEST READ

IT is estimated that the story of Jesus, in the Bible, is the most widely distributed book in the history of the world, and that between 1815 and today, more than two and one-half billion copies have been sold or distributed. In the year 1979 alone, over 9 million copies were sold.

The runner up spot is held by *Quotations from the Works of Mao Tse-tung,* which has been seen by more than 800 million people.

Neither of these two facts may be that startling and you probably already knew about these two books . . . but how about this one? In third place stands *The Truth That Leads to Eternal Life,* a publication of Jehovah's Witnesses who have distributed more than 100 million copies since 1968!

Another surprise is *A Message to Garcia* by Elbert Hubbard, an inspirational/motivational book, which in 1899 took the U.S.A. by storm. More than 50 million copies of this gospel book have been printed and distributed! It's no surprise that the next best-seller is the *Guinness Book of World Records,* which has sold more than 40 million copies in 23 different languages since 1955.

213 WHAT THEY DRANK

WATER was the basic liquid used in cooking but it was not very good for drinking. Water drawn from the local well or spring was usually safe enough, but water from the family cistern was far from safe for drinking. For this reason other liquids made better drinks.

There was always milk from the family goat or brought to the door by the milkman, but wine was the most common drink. At the time the grapes were picked there would be fresh grape juice, pressed straight from the bunch into a cup. But most of the juice had to be fermented so that it would keep. The first wine of the year was made from the juice extracted when the grapes were trodden in the press. A second batch was made by squeezing the remainder. Wine was often mixed with gall or myrrh to relieve pain. This was the mixture offered to Jesus at the crucifixion. Wine was also mixed with olive oil to clean and heal wounds, as in the story of the "The Good Samaritan."

Yes, wine was the normal drink for Israelites. Jesus performed His first miracle when He turned the water into wine for a wedding in Cana of Galilee. He must have consumed enough himself to have been called a "tippler" or "winebibber" by the Pharisees who may, in their vows to God, have given up drinking it. Planting vineyards and producing wine was considered to be a part of the settled-down lifestyle.

Wealthy homes in Israel usually had cellars of fine wines from all over the Mediterranean world. They were kept in narrow jars with a pointed end so they could be pushed into the earth to cool. Wine was most often stored in leather bottles or wineskins. Jesus said to put new wine into new wineskins.

214 THE MOST BEAUTIFUL CHURCH

GREAT Britain's "Salisbury Cathedral" has often been cited by many architectural experts as "England's most beautiful house of worship." It's been described as a "great chiseled diamond in a setting of emeralds."

That's not all that is unique about this church. Another aspect of the cathedral is that it is a kind of calendar chiseled out of stone. It has as many doors as there are months in the year . . . as many windows as there are days in a year . . . as many pillars as there are hours in a day . . . as many pieces of sculpture as there are minutes in an hour . . . and as many crosses for consecration as there are seconds in a minute!

215 BIRDS OF THE BIBLE

THE Bible names about 50 different kinds of birds and it's a bit difficult, from our perspective, to be positive as to the exact identity of many of them. Some of the more common were eagles, vultures, owls, ravens, doves, pigeons, partridges, quail, cranes, and sparrows.

The word "sparrow" was often used to mean any small bird suitable for eating . . . but in some places the Bible specifically refers to the "Hedge Sparrow." Larks and finches, as well as sparrows, would have been trapped to be cooked and eaten. Jesus specifically referred to the sparrow in order to emphasize how much God loves His creatures . . . especially the human kind. If He cares even for the smallest of birds, how much more will He care for you and me!

216 THE ASCENSION

THE biblical account tells us that for 40 days after Jesus rose from the dead He often visited with His disciples. Then . . . He returned to heaven. This took place on the Mount of Olives when Jesus gave His final message. Then — as they watched, they saw Him "taken up before their very eyes, and a cloud hid him from their sight" (Acts 1:9). This is what we call the "ascension."

This marked the final end of Jesus' earthly ministry but it was not the end of His work on earth. You can only imagine how intently they must have been looking up into the heavens when . . . suddenly two heavenly messengers asked them, "Men of Galilee . . ." they said, "why do you stand here looking into the sky? This same Jesus, who has been taken from you into heaven, will come back in the same way you have seen him go into heaven" (Acts. 1:11).

The rest of the New Testament makes it very clear that between Jesus' ascension and His return at the end of time He is presently with God, His Father, in the glories of heaven. He reigns over the whole universe. He represents His followers before God and has sent the Holy Spirit to help us.

217 BLOOD

THE New Testament often refers to the death of Jesus by the unique phrase, "the blood of Christ" or "the blood of Jesus." The background for this phrase is taken from the Old Testament where the word "blood" was used in a number of different and distinctive ways:

• When blood is shed, a person's life is over because: "The life is in the blood" (Lev. 17:11).

• Life is the gift of God so therefore no one has the right to shed another's blood: "Thou shalt not murder" (Rom. 13:9).

• The blood of animals was shed in sacrifice to represent the animal's life poured out in death which was a type or picture of the sacrifice Christ was to make: "Behold the Lamb of God which takes away the sins of the world" (John 1:29).

• Because life was a gift of God, the blood which was shed must not be used for food. In fact, this ruling was applied to every animal killed, whether for a sacrifice or not.

Therefore, when the New Testament uses the phrase "the blood of Christ" it refers to His ultimate sacrifice and the violent shedding of His blood on the cross which became the atonement for our sins.

THE
218 CALL

THE God of the Bible is a God who "calls" people and challenges them directly! In the Old Testament, the story of the nation of Israel begins with the "call" of Abraham and shows us how the Israelites were called to distinctly become God's people. The Israelites didn't earn the right to be His children . . . but it was because God himself "called" them to be His and follow Him.

It's just the same in the New Testament. Jesus "called" people to follow Him, to respond to His teachings, to believe in Him as the Messiah, and to become part of the family of God.

In the Early Church . . . it happened again. People were "called" to salvation, "called" to eternal life, "called" to a life of endurance, "called" to a life of peace, and "called" to specific tasks. For example, Saul was "called to be an apostle," who experienced a name change to Paul, and heeded the "call" to take the gospel of Jesus Christ to all the world.

And . . . the bottom line is simply this: God still "calls" people today with the same kind of callings!

THE
GOSPEL

IT'S such a simple concept that people have sneered at it. The word "gospel" means "good news"! This "good news," according to the Bible, is the fact that we are not cut off from God because of our sins because Jesus has come to bring forgiveness.

The "Gospel" of Mark describes itself as "the good news of Jesus Christ." It's simplicity itself . . . Jesus is the good news, or Jesus is the "gospel" himself! The facts of the "gospel" are simple: Jesus Christ died for all of our sins; He was crucified, buried, and raised to life three days later; we have forgiveness and a new eternal life because of the death and resurrection of Jesus Christ.

This "gospel" is so simple that many won't believe it to be true. It's not complex as some would like it to be. It is not a system of philosophy but the simple plan of God himself. "For all have sinned and fall short of the glory of God, and are justified freely by his grace through the redemption that came by Christ Jesus" (Rom. 3:23–24).

THE WORLD'S MOST
FAMOUS STORY?!?

WHAT story in all of human history is the most celebrated, most famous, best known, most often told, and most beloved of all? Think a moment or two before you jump to an answer.

You may not agree . . . but I nominate the events surrounding the birth of Jesus as that story! What would our world be like without the effects of the Christmas story?

This story is recorded in only two places . . . the Gospels of Matthew and Luke. They agree on the major elements of the birth of the baby Jesus in Bethlehem during the reign of King Herod the Great. This was a child conceived of the Holy Spirit and destined to become the Savior of the world. Simple and elegant. But each of these two writers give us separately detailed events that make this story even more wonderful and memorable.

Matthew's account is told more from the perspective of Joseph and shows to us his actions, designed to protect the coming child. It also shows us the part the angels played in this compelling story. The version of Luke places Mary as the central figure and is seemingly told from her perspective. Perhaps Joseph was no longer living at the time Luke wrote this gospel. It's a fact that this story has inspired writers, artists, and common folk like us with the simple beauty of God's visit to mankind in the form of the Babe born in a manger.

221   OLIVES

OLIVE oil has been called the "elixir of the gods." You can burn it, wash with it, lubricate squeaky things with it, cosmetics are based on it, diamonds polished with it, kings are anointed with it, babies are dedicated with it, the dying are anointed with it, it's loaded with vitamin E, it has no cholesterol, it's a preservative, you can eat it, it's the most versatile fruit juice ever squeezed, and boiled it's one of the more ingenious diabolical weapons of war in the ancient world.

For more than 4,000 years it has served the Mediterranean cultures as everything from medicine to money. The Israeli, Jordanian, and Syrian areas of the Mediterranean are the origin of olive cultivation and processing. The traditional milling process is to crush the whole olive, pit and all, separate the liquid from the solids, then separate the water from the oil, and finally, bottle it for use.

God said in the Old Testament, "This shall be an holy anointing oil unto me throughout your generations" (Exod. 30:31). The Mediterranean world has long considered the olive as sacred. The Bible is brimming with references to olive oil, from the parable Jesus told of the wise and foolish virgins who used olive oil as lamp oil to the story of the Good Samaritan who used oil as an unquent, to the prophet Elisha's miraculous rescue of the destitute widow who was able to use the oil to trade with. In terms of history and sacredness, oil has a deeper meaning than wine. Oil is still used to consecrate, anoint, and baptize even to this day. The word "Christ" means the "anointed one!"

222   THERE'S A TIME FOR SHOUTING

BLIND Bartimaeus was just a poor beggar before Jesus came into his life. We can only imagine how difficult his life was because of the constant humiliation as he begged for money so he could have something to eat. But Bartimaeus had at least three things working for him that produced the miracle: faith in Jesus Christ, a loud voice, and lots of gumption!

When Jesus came his way, Bartimaeus cried out for mercy at the top of his lungs. He refused to be quiet even when the disciples of Jesus attempted to calm him down. Jesus might never come that way again so he didn't want to miss the only opportunity that might be his. There's a time to shout aloud for your miracle. Jesus heard this cry of desperation and responded! Bartimaeus was a changed man because of this encounter with Jesus! No longer blind . . . now he can see!

223 THAT ALL MAY BE ONE

JUST before He went to the cross to die for our sins, Jesus prayed a very special prayer for all of us. It is called His "High Priestly Prayer" and I believe expresses one of His deepest desires for His followers, His church: ". . . that all of them may be one, Father, just as you are in me and I am in you. May they also be in us so that the world may believe that you have sent me" (John 17:21).

As you read this prayer recorded by John you will notice that five times in this entire prayer Jesus prays for unity among His followers. According to Jesus the proof of your truly following Him is how you get along with your fellow believers.

224 YOUR WORST ENEMY

THERE is a classic story about Pogo, the comic-strip possum who lived in the Okeefenokee Swamp. One day Pogo discovered the tracks of "the enemy." After gathering his friends together, they tracked "the enemy" all over the swamp until Pogo stopped long enough to make an important discovery. He noticed that the tracks of the enemy were identical to their own footprints! The truth dawned on him and he announced to his friends: "Halt! We have met the enemy and he is us!"

Jesus recognized this classic problem among humans like us. We are the worst enemy we face in life. He said to His sleeping disciples: "Watch and pray so that you will not fall into temptation. The spirit is willing, but the body is weak" (Matt. 26:41; Mark 14:38).

HIDDEN TREASURE

I have always been intrigued by glamorous stories of discovering buried or sunken treasure. Very few people in life get that opportunity.

Imagine a peasant man taking a short cut across a field. Suddenly he trips, stubs his toe, and realizes it's not a stone . . . he digs some of the dirt away and discovers that it's a chest! A real treasure chest! He carefully opens the lid and discovers it's filled with jewels, gold, and silver! He looks around to make sure nobody else has seen his discovery . . . then he covers it up. He hurries home and begins to negotiate for the purchase of this field. He knows it will be costly, for the landowner will hold him up. Imagine how worried his wife and family become when he tells them he is selling everything to buy the field. The banker attempts to talk him out of it . . . no use. He is determined! He finally makes the purchase! That spring, while plowing the field — EUREKA! He plows up the treasure chest! He takes the money and jewels to the bank for safekeeping and suddenly he has become famous! Others then realize that if they had purchased the field . . . the treasure might have been theirs, too! Do you ever think such thoughts: Where did the treasure come from in the first place?

Oh, well. Where did the above story come from? Jesus told it: "The Kingdom of Heaven is like a treasure a man discovered in a field. In his excitement, he sold everything he owned to get enough money to buy the field" (Matt. 13:44) . . . and get the treasure, too!

WHAT ABOUT YOUR MOTHER?

THERE is a rescue mission in the city of Portland, Oregon, which has a sign posted above the pulpit in their chapel which reads: "HAVE YOU WRITTEN TO YOUR MOTHER LATELY?"

Perhaps these words would be appropriate to be posted over every pulpit in every church. The way you treat your mother could well be an indicator of how much you also love God. You shouldn't neglect her.

One of the first people Jesus saw from the perspective of the cross was His weeping mother. He loved her and even in the throes of pain and anguish He did not forget her, nor her welfare into the future. As the eldest son in the family, it was His primary responsibility to see to her welfare. We can only assume that Joseph has been long gone out of this family because we never hear of him again by any of the writers except the incident at age 12 when Jesus was left behind at the Passover in Jerusalem. He turned to His trusted friend and disciple, John: "When Jesus saw his mother there, and the disciple whom he loved standing nearby, he said to his mother, 'Dear woman, here is your son,' and to the disciple, 'Here is your mother.' From that time on, this disciple took her into his home" (John 19:26–27).

IT'S WHAT IS INSIDE THAT COUNTS

THERE was a special man who was a vendor of balloons at an amusement park. Whenever business slowed down he would release one of the balloons and as it floated upward, prospective customers would notice and buy balloons. Children especially loved the balloon man. They crowded around as he walked with a huge bouquet of them tethered by their strings. He sent up all kinds of colors . . . green, blue, yellow, orange, and red.

One day a small African-American boy watched the various colored balloons bob their way skyward. Finally, he came up to the balloon man and said, "Mister, do you think if you let one of the black balloons go, it would go up in the air like all the others?"

The balloon man looked down and smiled: "Son, of course it'll go up! It's not the color of the balloon, it's what in it that makes it rise!" And with that he released the black balloon as the two of them watched it sail over the crowd.

According to Jesus . . . it's not who you are or where you have come from or how bad you have been or the circumstances that surround you that determines whether or not you will rise! It's what you have inside of you. Jesus said: "I have made you known to them, and will continue to make you known in order that the love you have for me may be in them and that I myself may be in them" (John 17:26). There you have the secret! If Christ is in you, you are on the rise! Because the Bible also says: "Greater is He that is in you than he that is in the world" (1 John 4:4).

JESUS LOVES THE LITTLE CHILDREN

THE world-renowned German sculptor Von Dannecker once worked for over two years on a marble statue of Jesus. When he thought he was finished, he asked his little girl into the studio, pointed to the statue and asked, "Who is that?"

She replied, "Oh, some great man," and ran away to continue playing. He was disappointed and knew that somehow he had failed.

He began work once more and again, about two years later, asked his little girl into the studio, pointed to the marble statue, and asked, "Who is this man?"

She looked carefully, then broke into a smile. "I know!" she exclaimed, "This man said, 'Let the little children come to me, and do not hinder them, for the kingdom of God belongs to such as these' " (Matt. 19:14). Now that is awesome!

Have you ever noticed that most often paintings, sculpture, movies, and other media always seem to depict Jesus as looking stern and serious. I don't happen to believe that He was like that . . . so much has been lost in translation. I believe that He was a person whom people loved to be with. He was a popular dinner guest and most importantly children flocked to Him. Children are astute judges of character and are not naturally drawn to stern and serious looking people.

How do I know Jesus was a happy, outgoing person? The Bible says this about Jesus, "Your God, has set you above your companions by anointing you with the oil of joy" (Ps. 45:7; Heb. 1:9). I believe that Jesus was the most joyful person who ever lived!

A POWERFUL LIFE PRINCIPLE

LOTS of things which Jesus taught run against the grain of normal human nature. After all, what seems to be more "right" than settling an account with someone who has done you wrong? A street preacher was once asked by a heckler in the crowd, "Reverend, what would you do if I came up there and punched you in the nose?"

The preacher, who happened to a large, tough-looking guy, replied: "Mister, I'd have to turn the other cheek. But after that, if I was still standing, you'd better run, because I'd be after you!" There was no further problem with that heckler . . . but on a more serious level . . . I think God would want you to keep turning cheeks and pray for your enemy while he was still hitting on you.

King Louis XII of France had so many enemies that when he took the throne, he had a list of them made up. In the presence of his court, he took a pen and marked each name with a black cross. Word of this action naturally leaked out and his enemies took flight, thinking Louis was going to have them executed. But the king called them back, telling them that he had put the cross by their name to remind him of the Cross that pardons all sinners. The king, in turn, then urged them to pray for their enemies as he was praying for his.

It's not hard to make enemies in this world. In regard to this subject Jesus said, "Love your enemies and pray for those who persecute you, that you may be sons of your Father in heaven" (Matt. 5:44–45). Your love and prayer could make a friend out of an enemy. It's a Jesus fact!

MARTYRDOM, PART I

230

THE first person martyred for the faith was Jesus Christ . . . but what of the others who were His followers? We need to be reminded of those who paid the ultimate price for being a believer.

Stephen . . . His death came about because of the fearless way in which he preached the Gospel. He died by stoning outside the city. What is not generally known is that about 2,000 Christians, along with Nicanor, one of the other seven deacons, also suffered martyrdom with the persecution about Stephen.

James the Great . . . He was James the son of Zebedee, the older brother of John and a relative of Christ. His mother, Salome, was a cousin to Mary, mother of Jesus. It was ten years following the death of Stephen that James was taken. As James was led to the place of martyrdom, his accuser was brought to seek repentance and fell down at the feet of James and begged forgiveness. He then professed himself a Christian and resolved that James should not receive the crown of martyrdom alone. So they were both beheaded at the same time.

Philip . . . He ministered in Upper Asia and suffered his death at Heliopolis in Phrygia. He was scourged, thrown into prison, and then crucified in A.D. 54.

Matthew . . . The former tax collector was missionary to Ethiopia where he suffered martyrdom, being slain with a halberd in the city of Nadabah in A.D. 60.

James the Less . . . This was the brother of Jesus who had been elected to be pastor of the church in Jerusalem. He also wrote the epistle with his name. At the age of 94 he was beaten and stoned by the Jews . . . and finally had his brains dashed out with a fuller's club.

MARTYRDOM, PART II

AND the list goes on . . . an incredible account of some who paid the cost of being a believer in Jesus Christ.

Matthias . . . Little is known about him other than he was chosen to fill the vacant place of Judas. We also know that he was stoned at Jerusalem and then beheaded.

Andrew . . . was the brother of Peter who preached the Gospel to many different Asiatic nations. It was on his arrival at Edessa that he was taken and crucified on a cross, the two ends of which were fixed transversely in the ground.

Mark . . . was born to Jewish parents of the tribe of Levi. He was dragged to pieces by the people of Alexandria, at the great celebration to Serapis, their idol, and so his life ended violently.

Jude . . . The brother of James was also commonly called Thaddeus. He was crucified at Edessa in A.D. 72.

Bartholomew . . . had translated the Gospel of Matthew into the language of India where he preached the gospel. He was at length cruelly beaten and then crucified by idolaters.

Thomas . . . also was called Didymus, preached in Parthia and India where he excited the rage of pagan priests. He was martyred by them by being thrust through with a spear.

Luke . . . The beloved physician traveled extensively with Paul and is supposed to have been hanged on an olive tree by the idolatrous priests of Greece.

Simon . . . was also surnamed "Zelotes." He preached in Africa, Mauritania, and Great Britain (where he was crucified in A.D 74).

Barnabas . . . of Cyprus but of Jewish descent, experienced death by crucifixion in A.D. 73.

This is an awesome list. Makes you stop and think!

WHAT DISCIPLE DIED A NATURAL DEATH?

ALL of Christ's disciples, including Matthais who was chosen to fill the place vacated by Judas, except one died violent deaths of martyrdom. Of these 13 . . . only 1 died a natural death! Interestingly enough, there was also an attempt made to kill him, too. Who was he? The answer is John, the "beloved disciple" who was a brother to James the Greater. The churches of Smyrna, Pergamos, Sardis, Philadelphia, Laodicea, and Thyatira were all planted or founded by him. While preaching in Ephesus he was captured and sent to Rome where it was affirmed that he was to be thrown into a cauldron of boiling oil. Miraculously, he escaped without any injury! The emperor Domitian afterwards banished him to the Isle of Patmos because he was unable to have him martyred. It was during this time, while imprisoned, that John wrote "The Revelation of Jesus Christ." Nerva, who was the successor to Domitian, recalled him from Patmos. He was the only apostle of Jesus Christ who escaped a violent death and died naturally at approximately 96 years of age.

HOW DID PETER MEET HIS DEATH?

I left him off the other listings of martyrdom because his story is most interesting. Like many of the other apostles, Peter was also condemned to death at Rome. The historian Hegesippus said that the emperor Nero had sought a reason in order to put him to death. When the Christians became aware of these plans, many pleaded with Peter to leave the city and run for his life. At length, he relented and prepared to leave. But on coming to the gate of the city he had an encounter with Jesus Christ, whom he worshipped. Then he asked, "Lord, where are you going?"

To which He answered, "I am coming again to be crucified." By this answer, Peter, who perceived this to mean that he was to be crucified, returned to the city and simply waited for the arrest. The Early Church father Jerome said that he was crucified with his head hanging down and his feet upward because Peter said he was unworthy to be crucified in the same manner as the Lord had been.

What can we say from our perspective about the martyrdoms in the Early Church? It's an amazing fact that with all these persecutions and horrible martyrdoms that the Church increased and grew. Today's Church is deeply rooted in the doctrines of the apostles and watered with the blood of the saints who have preceded us.

234 OTHER CELEBRATIONS

THE birth of Jesus Christ is celebrated annually with the festival of Christmas. But that's not the only special celebration that falls close to Christmas. Religions other than Christianity commemorate this season in their ways. In Judaism it is Hanukkak or the "Festival of Lights." In ancient Rome there was the "Saturnalia." Pre-Christian era Scandinavians enjoyed the "Feast of the Frost King." In Egypt there was the mid-winter festival in honor of their god, Horus. The Druids had an annual mistletoe-cutting ceremony. Mithraists celebrated the feast of "Sol Invictus" which represented the midwinter victory of light over the darkness. In Hinduism, the feast of "Diwali" and "Taipongal" are observed at this season.

235 GOOD KING WENCESLAS

THE origins of songs is an interesting study. For example, the Christmas carol, "Good King Wenceslas" is based on an actual historical person. Wenceslas was not a king, however, he was a tenth-century real-life duke who later became the patron saint of Czechoslovakia. Duke Wenceslas was well known for his piety, love, holiness, and compassion. He is reputed to have gone into the woods during the dead of some of those severe Bohemian winters to chop and haul wood for widows, poor people, and orphans. When asked why he did such kind acts he is reputed to have replied that he was doing what Jesus would have done if He had lived in such a cold climate.

236 HOW MANY LANGUAGES?

JOSEPH Caspar Mezzofanti, an Italian priest born in 1774, could learn a foreign language in a single day! He was once called upon to hear the confessions of two foreign criminals condemned to die on the following morning. He is reputed to have learned their language in one night and conversed with them at sunrise before their execution.

At his death, Mezzofanti was fluent in 39 languages including Chinese, Coptic, Chaldean, Gujarati, Persian, Russian, all the Romance languages, Hindi, Hebrew, Old English, Suriac, Arabic, Greek, Geez, Algonquin, and Armenian. Further, he was able to speak 11 more languages moderately well which included Welsh, Serbian, Kurdish, Bulgarian, and Angolese. And still more . . . he could understand but not speak 20 others, including some of the most obscure tongues in the world: Tibetan, Old Icelandic, Lappish, and Chippewa.

When asked where the mental capabilities came from to allow such feats of learning he was quick to acknowledge that it was a special gift given to him by the Lord Jesus Christ.

237 ALMOST OBLITERATED

ONE of the world's most famous artists, Leonardo Da Vinci, painted what is probably the best-known picture of Christ, "The Last Supper." It was almost destroyed during the Napoleonic Wars. The soldiers of Napoleon bivouacked in the chapel of Santa Maria delle Grazie in Milan, Italy, where Leonardo's "Last Supper" is painted on the chapel wall. The soldiers, bored with life in the chapel, amused themselves by using this painting for target practice. The bull's-eye was the face of Christ. That is the reason why the face of Christ is almost obliterated in the painting. It has been restored . . . but not to the original condition.

238 SOME INTERESTING CHRISTMAS FACTS

THE custom of using Christmas wreaths can be traced to the belief that the crown of thorns Christ was forced to wear when He was crucified was made of holly.

Christmas was once outlawed and illegal in England. In 1643 the Puritans outlawed all Christmas celebrations, banned the keeping of Christmas trees, and made the singing of Christmas carols a crime. The laws were in effect until the "Restoration." Also, many of the Puritans who had moved to New England adhered to many of these regulations and added some more of their own laws — such as that making a mince pie was forbidden.

In Brazil . . . Christmas is celebrated with fireworks, both public and private.

The practice of exchanging presents at Christmas originated with the Romans. Every December the ancient Romans celebrated a holiday called the "Saturnalia." During this time the people gave each other good-luck presents of fruit, sweets, pastry, or gold. Later, when the Christians began to celebrate the birth of Jesus Christ on December 25th they simply took over this tradition.

And finally . . . more than three billion Christmas cards are sent annually in the United States!

THE BLACK PLAGUE

239

IN 1347, when the "Black Plague" was raging through Europe, the citizens of Lubeck, Germany, wanting to appease the "wrath" of God, descended upon the churches and monasteries with enormous amounts of money and riches. The monks and priests inside one of the monasteries, fearful of contamination, barred their gates and would not allow any of the citizens to enter. So the persistent crowd threw valuables — coins, gold, and jewels over the walls . . . the frightened monks threw all of it back. The back-and-forth tossing continued for hours until the clerics finally gave up and allowed the riches to remain inside their walls. Within hours, piles three and four feet high arose . . . and for months following this incident, some said for years, the money and riches remained untouched.

THE APOSTLE TO THE GENTILES

240

WE need to know that Paul was not the first of the early Christians who envisioned a special evangelistic mission to the Gentiles of his day, but he was the most zealous and fanatical and became the central figure in this crusade. With his prolific writings, teachings, and preaching, he was the force that helped to resolve many of the crucial questions raised by the traditions and customs of the Jews, such as: should Gentile converts be forced to circumcise all males; must they refuse to eat pork or any other unclean animals; and did they have to refuse to have anything to do with pagans?

Paul, perhaps more than any other figure, recognized that the real issue was whether or not salvation came through following the Old Testament commandments or from the forgiveness which Jesus gives freely to all who chose to believe. According to Paul, water baptism meant the convert was free from the demands of the Old Testament law as well as being free of sins. He managed to convince the new church leaders of the Jerusalem congregation to accept new converts on this basis. Under his teachings, Jewish or Gentile were one and the same and enjoyed all the same complete privileges of being a part of the family made up of the followers of Jesus Christ.

THE DOCUMENT THAT SPLIT THE CHURCH

241

FOR more than 600 years, the popes of the Church of Rome used the *Donation of Constantine* to support their claim to being rulers of all Christendom. Constantine was the first Roman emperor to be converted to Christianity. He is said to have made the gift of half his empire, in A.D. 315, in gratitude for his religious conversion and for his miraculous cure from leprosy. *The Donation*, the document that recorded the gift, granted to the Pope of Rome spiritual authority over all the churches of Jesus Christ on the earth and temporal authority over Rome, all of Italy, and the Western World. Those who tried to overthrow it would "be burned in the lower hell and shall perish with the devil and all the impious."

This 3,000-word document became known in the 9th century and was a powerful weapon in disputes between Eastern and Western churches. This quarrel culminated in the separation of the Eastern Orthodox Church and the Church of Rome in 1054.

Ten popes cited this document until the 15th century. Then . . . Nicholas of Cusa (1401–1464), the greatest ecclesiastical scholar of his age, pointed out that Bishop Eusebius of Caesarea, Constantine's biographer, had not mentioned the emperor's gift!

Today this document is regarded as a forgery, probably made in Rome about A.D. 760. It was not even a clever one because it gave the Roman See authority over Constantinople before that city was even founded!

The French philosopher Voltaire described it as "the boldest and most magnificent forgery which deceived the world for centuries."

ROCK OF AGES

242

THE Reverend Augustus Montague Toplady was taking a walk in Somerset, England, when a sudden, violent storm forced him to take shelter in the cave or cleft of a large rock formation. The exact date is not known but is somewhere between 1762 and 1775.

While taking shelter from this storm, Toplady, then the curate in Somerset composed the words and music for one of the best-known hymns of all time: "Rock of Ages."

Of course, he was most anxious to get the words down on paper so he wouldn't forget . . . but the only piece of paper on his person was a single playing card. Do you suppose it was the "King of Hearts?"

Here's a line or two:

> Rock of Ages, cleft for me, Let me hide myself in Thee;
> Let the water and the blood,
> From Thy wounded side which flowed,
> Be of sin the double cure, Save from wrath and make me pure.

WEIRD VISIONS OF JESUS

243

IN 1983, Josephine Taylor of Constance Lake, Ontario, said that she saw the image of Jesus Christ on her bathroom floor. Taylor says that one morning she looked down and saw the image formed by dark spots on the cement floor. Edgar Sutherland, an associate of the village minister, said that the image was only worn linoleum adhesive. But about 3,000 Canadians came to see for themselves!

Thousands of people flocked to Arlene Gardner's trailer in Estill Springs, Tennessee, in 1987 to see the image of Christ on Arlene's freezer, which was on the front deck of the house. Each day after dusk, a neighbor's porch light apparently caused a bearded face to appear on the side of the freezer. Gardner also claimed to have had a dream in which Christ told her that "He connected that porch light to my freezer and turned my freezer into a TV by electricity. He made it a TV. That's how I knew He wanted this vision on television for the world to see." This family, however, refused all offers to charge viewers.

The Perez family of Taft, Texas, said that the image of Jesus appeared in the swirls of ceiling plaster in a room in their home. Petra Perez said that the image of Christ's face and "sacred heart" was best seen by kneeling and looking through a window.

Jim Armour, administrator of the Walker Medical Center in Jasper, Alabama, said that at least 10,000 people came to view what some believed to be the face of Jesus on the door of the center's recovery room. "The people who work here do believe the door is different than what it was. I believe it is different," said Armour. "We have a housekeeper who dusts that door and she says it wasn't like that before." The image was first seen by a praying relative of a motorcycle accident victim.

RESUSCITATING THE DEAD

GOD can still perform the special miracle of resuscitating the dead! He can also raise up dead or dying believers for the purpose of seeing the power of God at work in humanity.

The story of Jesus raising the dead son of the widow in Nain illustrates for us both the compassion and the response of people who were present and saw what had happened. "As he approached the town gate, a dead person was being carried out. . . ." This miracle, perhaps more than any other, also displays for us the compassion of Christ, the motivation for supernatural intervention. "When the Lord saw her, his heart went out to her and he said, 'Don't cry!' Then he went up and touched the coffin . . . and said, 'Young men, I say to you, get up!' The dead man sat up and began to talk."

Notice the response of the crowd, "They were all filled with awe and praised God" (Luke 7:12–16). The miracle and the response!

Some years later, Peter was part of the miracle of resuscitating Dorcas, also known as Tabitha, which electrified an entire city.

And yes . . . there are accounts of resuscitation of the dead happening in our world today. It can be difficult for sophisticated people like us to swallow . . . but it is for the purpose of praising God!

WHAT HOUR WAS IT?

245

HOW did the people of Israel know what exact time it was? They didn't have Greenwich time back then, you will remember. Days varied in length according to the seasons and real effective time-keeping devices didn't exist. Therefore, it is difficult to reckon precise hours or time in ancient history. Yes, I know, sundials were used but how accurate were they?

By Roman times, an hour was 1/12 of the daylight starting at sunrise and ending at sunset. You can imagine how short a winter's day was compared to a summer's day. Later, the Roman "civil" day ran from midnight to midnight.

However, specific hours of the day such as five o'clock and nine o'clock are cited in the New Testament. Three o'clock in the afternoon was called the "hour of prayer." Jesus said, "Therefore keep watch, because you do not know the day or the hour" (Matt. 24:42).

Time units such as seconds and minutes were unknown but the Roman concept of counting the hours was familiar to the Jews. A frequently repeated theme in the Gospel of John is the "hour" of Jesus' glory . . . the period between His triumphal entry into Jerusalem and His resurrection. The period between the assumption and the Second Coming is "the last hour."

HOSANNA

246

THE word "hosanna" is an interesting Hebrew word which literally means, "Save us, please!" It's taken from the phrase "Hoshiana" from the 118th Psalm. The Israelites recited this psalm and waved palm branches during the annual procession or parade at the "Festival of Booths." The Israelites had many festivals and feasts. They must have loved parties and breaks in their work schedules. And by inference . . . God loves celebrations, too, because He instituted these!

The Israelites came to associate this psalm with the coming Messiah, who they hoped would restore Israel to the glory of their golden age under Kings David and Solomon. This was the cry which was raised when the multitude greeted Jesus as He entered Jerusalem on the last Sunday before His crucifixion. The crowds expanded the phrase to: "Hosanna to the Son of David!" This is a very strong implication that they believed Jesus was the Messiah!

HYMN
SINGING

DID Jesus sing? Well, that's an easy answer and we'll get back to the answer a bit later.

A biblical "hymn" is a song written to honor God. The first mentioned song in the Bible is "The Song of Moses," which he and the Israelites sang after the triumphant crossing of the Red Sea. It begins: "I will sing to the Lord, For he has triumphed gloriously!"

The melody is a mystery . . . as is true for all the songs of the Bible. The Book of Psalms is a collection of hymns that the people recited or sang during public worship. As you read from the psalms notice their varied themes . . . jubilant praise, cries of anguished regret, asking for help, or simply praise to God. Priests sang these in the temple courtyard. Pilgrims, as they made their way to Jerusalem for any of the religious festivals, sang these as they walked.

Now here's the answer: "When they had sung a hymn, they went out to the Mount of Olives" (Matt. 26:30; Mark 14:26). Yes, Jesus was a singer! And I happen to believe that He sang the happy, upbeat Jewish music with lots of rhythm and hand clapping! Hymn singing was an expression of joy!

Perhaps the most famous hymn in the New Testament is the "Magnificat," which was Mary's song of praise, and the first line begins like this: "My soul magnifies the Lord" (Luke 1:46). A happy hymn? Yes, as sung by this young teenaged prospective mother!

HYPOCRITES!

THE word, "hypocrite" really has two different biblical meanings. In the Old Testament the term refers to someone who is "opposed to God," or simply "godless." In the New Testament the word is used to describe "someone who pretends to be a better person than they really are." Jesus berated the "hypocrites" who pray and fast, or at least pretend that they do so they can seek praise from others. He accused the scribes and Pharisees of hypocrisy by saying they do not practice what they preach. On one occasion He called them "whitewashed tombs, which on the outside look beautiful, but inside they are full of the bones of the dead and of all kinds of filth" (Matt. 23:27). Wow! Strong, picturesque, descriptive language . . . you did not have to ask what Jesus meant. Hypocrites of any shape or form were soundly denounced by Him!

249 INSECTS

DO you ever wonder what the ancients did to deal with bugs without the sprays, repellants, and technology of today? Some of those ancient bugs were useful, such as the honeybee, silkworms, and lowly maggot, which eliminated decaying matter. But let's face it . . . a pest today was a pest back then, too! Locusts could destroy crops and they were very common in the Near East. Fleas were the carriers of bubonic plague and other diseases which were deadly to people and animals.

In the Old Testament, Israelites were forbidden to eat insects except, "those that have jointed legs above their feet" (Lev. 11:21). These would be locusts, crickets, and grasshoppers.

Jesus, in one of His more picturesque and humorous sayings, pointed out that the Pharisees did everything they could to avoid swallowing even one unclean insect, "You blind guides! You strain out a gnat but swallow a camel" (Matt. 23:24). It was their custom to strain their drinking water through a cloth to insure no bugs. I just happen to think that His crowd on that day howled, laughed, and slapped their knees upon hearing this. (My opinion, you understand as to the crowd reaction. Why can't we lighten up a bit more in our living . . . Jesus sure did!)

250 TO KISS OR NOT TO KISS

IN the Near Eastern culture of biblical times, the kiss was a gesture of love, friendship, respect, or worship. Then there was the kiss between lovers, the erotic expression of love as written in the opening verses of the Song of Solomon: "Let him kiss me with the kisses of his mouth." Kissing didn't always have a sexual connotation.

The Old Testament prophet Samuel kissed Saul when he anointed him to be the first king in Israel. It was common for relatives to kiss as a greeting or parting goodbye. Then, too, a kiss signified pardon as in the story Jesus told about the prodigal son who returns to his father's house to be welcomed home with a kiss. The kiss also showed respect by the kissing of the hands or feet of a leader.

The kiss was also used as deception . . . as when Joab stabbed his rival Amasa because he caught him off guard with a kiss. Perhaps the most famous kiss in all of history was administered by Judas to Jesus in the moment of betrayal. And the early Christians of the first church greeted each other with a "holy kiss" which was to indicate the love that filled this organism. So the question is still . . . to kiss or not to kiss? Some do and some don't.

251 HOW MANY IS A "LEGION"?

AT the time of Jesus, the emperor Augustus had ordered the reorganization of his army into "legions" of troops. A legion was composed of about 4,500 to 6,000 men, made up of the finest of Roman soldiers. The legion was built upon "centuries" (thus, the centurion) of 100 men each, which were then grouped into "cohorts" of 600 men each. So a legion was composed of 10 cohorts. The Roman army at its peak under Augustus numbered 28 legions. It is doubted that more than a few "centuries" were stationed in Israel at the time of Christ. The famed legions didn't appear in the Holy Land until about A.D. 66 when the Jews rebelled against their oppressors.

When Jesus had been arrested and was being defended by Peter with his sword, He said, "Do you think I cannot call on my Father, and he will at once put at my disposal more than twelve legions of angels?" (Matt. 26:53).

252 LEPROSY

THIS was a disease which struck terror into the hearts of all who contracted it. The biblical reference to leprosy likely included a wide variety of skin diseases from eczema to psoriasis. Modern day leprosy or "Hansen's disease" is accompanied by running sores, white patches, and loss of appendages. This is a disease which attacks the nerves . . . with no feeling in a hand or fingers it's easy to see how they could be injured and eventually worn away with use.

In Bible times, suspected lepers were quarantined for seven days and then examined by a priest. If the condition continued, they were quarantined for another seven days. Then, if still afflicted, they were cast out of their community. If they were healed, they could be restored by ceremonies during an eight-day period. As the final act of restoration, the healed person was daubed with oil and the blood of a sacrificial lamb on the right ear lobe, right thumb, and right big toe.

To avoid contact with healthy people, lepers were to call out "Unclean, unclean" when anyone came near them. They were reduced to being outcasts and beggars. Think of being cast out from your own family and away from loved ones. Jesus, however, did not consider lepers to be unclean. He touched them and healed them without hesitation, and commanded His followers to do the same.

253 THE MUSTARD SEED

THE mustard seed of the Bible may have referred to the species called "black mustard" or the technical name of "Brassica nigra." Mustard seeds were cultivated for their oil or were ground into powder and used for eating or medicinal purposes. This tiny mustard seed was then mistakenly believed to be the smallest seed of all the plants. Once planted, it quickly grows into an annual plant which may reach as much as six feet in height.

Jesus, to illustrate how quickly God's kingdom would grow, told the parable of the mustard seed growing large enough to become a tree in which birds could nest. He also used the mustard seed to illustrate how much faith was needed: "If you have faith as small as a mustard seed, you can say to this mountain, 'Move from here to there,' and it will move. Nothing will be impossible for you" (Matt. 17:20).

254 OINTMENTS

LIVING in the semi-arid, hot, dry climate of the Holy Land, men and women alike would rub olive oil on their skin as a moisturizer. No Avon products back there. Also, perfume makers would use this same oil as a base for making fragrant ointments. They would boil the oil and add their secret blend of root powders, bark powders, tree resins, and other spices. Myrrh, frankincense, cinnamon, and aloe were additives commonly used to make these scented oils. With such blendings they were able to turn a fine-grade olive oil into a jar of ointment easily worth a common laborer's yearly wage.

To preserve them, they were often sealed in small alabaster jars. The owner would not break the seal until ready to use. It would have been such an ointment that a "woman who had lived a sinful life . . . brought an alabaster jar of perfume and as she stood behind him at his feet weeping, she began to wet his feet with her tears. Then she wiped them with her hair, kissed them and poured perfume on them" (Luke 7:37–38).

255 PENTECOST

THIS ancient Jewish festival of "Pentecost" took its name from the Greek meaning "fifty." It was celebrated 50 days following the offering of the barley harvest on the second day of Passover. It took place seven weeks or a week of weeks, plus one day, after the barley offering, so it came to be known as the "Festival of Weeks."

As the Jewish people celebrated Pentecost it was a happy time of rejoicing which commemorated the wheat harvest. It was one of their three annual festivals when every able-bodied male was required to appear at the temple or main sanctuary. There, each was to present at least two loaves of bread made from the newly harvested grain along with other offerings which were to be made. It was a huge gathering marked by joy.

For the first Christians of the first church, Pentecost took on a whole new meaning of significance. The account can be read in the "Acts of the Apostles" when 120 disciples gathered in an Upper Room following Jesus' death and resurrection. When day had arrived, "Suddenly from heaven there came a sound like the rush of violent wind and sat on each of them." Then the account continues that each of them began speaking in another tongue, which they had not learned (Acts 2:2–4). It was a supernatural visitation of the Holy Spirit and the beginning of a whole new era. Jesus had commanded His followers to wait in Jerusalem until this outpouring from heaven was experienced. This was the descent of the Holy Spirit upon those believers and this phenomenon is still happening today! Jesus had previously told them that when He went away He would be sending the "Comforter," the Holy Spirit, to dwell within them to lead and guide them in His absence.

SOME INTERESTING BIBLE FACTS

THE following is generally agreed upon by most theologians . . . however, some statements are subject to debate. Read on and join in the debate.

• The number of books in the Hebrew Bible is 24. These are traditionally under three headings: the Torah or "the Law," Prophets, and Writings.

• The number of books in the Protestant versions of the Old Testament are 39.

• The number of books in the Catholic version of the Old Testament is also 39, plus 7 books of the Apocrypha.

• The Bible was not a single book, but a collection of scrolls and/ or a stack of volumes until the 4th century.

• Sometime in the 16th century, the Bible was divided into the chapters and verses we use today.

• The number of chapters in the Old Testament is 929, the number of verses is 23,314, and the number of words is 593,493 — give or take, depending upon the version you might be reading.

• The number of books in the New Testament is 27; chapters, 260; verses, 7,959; and words, 181,253.

• The Bible's longest verse is Esther 8:9 with 90 words describing the Persian Empire.

• The most recently written book is the Gospel of John dating from about A.D. 100.

• The name "Yahweh" or "Lord" appears 855 times in the entire Bible.

• The name "Jesus" appears 700 times in the four Gospels and Acts but fewer than 70 times in the Epistles. The name "Christ" was written 60 times in the Gospels and Acts, and 240 times in the Epistles and the Revelation of Jesus Christ.

THE STUFF OF WHICH LEGENDS ARE MADE

AREN'T we all interested in antiquities? Especially anything that can be traced back to the time of Christ or some object He may have used while here on earth.

Two of these most famous relics of Christendom do exist mainly in the human imagination. Time has enhanced and embellished these items. For example, by the 4th century it was widely believed that the very cross on which Jesus had been crucified had been found in Jerusalem. And there are at least three different legends about St. Helena, who identified the cross by restoring a corpse back to life with its touch. And there is a fourth version relating how the empress Protonica, after seeing Peter perform miracles, found the original cross in the first century.

Then . . . there is the "Holy Grail." This is thought to be the chalice or cup of the Eucharist, or the Last Supper, from which Jesus would have drunk. Or it is the dish of the paschal Passover lamb used by Jesus at the Last Supper. This cup or dish was the subject of much medieval poetry and writings. There are many versions of the story describing in great detail the search for the "Holy Grail" by King Arthur and his Knights of the Round Table.

SOME OF THE STORY BEHIND THE BIBLE

TODAY . . . the "Old Testament" is the Christian/Protestant term for the Hebrew Bible. It was originally transmitted orally, and some or most of it had been written down by the time of King David. For the Jews, the most sacred part of the Bible is the "Torah" or "The Law" or the "Pentateuch." These are the first five books of the Old Testament or the "Books of Moses."

Sometime in the 3rd century B.C., the Torah was translated into the Greek language, the most commonly used language of that day, and this translation is known as the "Septuagint" which is the Latin word for "seventy." The Septuagint refers to the 70 scholars who supposedly worked on the translation. In this version, the word "covenant" is translated as "testament."

Therefore . . . in the 27 books of the Christian scriptures, Jesus Christ established a new covenant which continued the covenant between God and Abraham as well as the covenant of Moses at Mt. Sinai. These 27 books form the "New Testament" or "New Covenant" of Jesus Christ.

More than 300 years following the life of Christ, St. Jerome translated what is considered to be the definitive "Latin" version of the Scriptures. This is the basis for the Catholic Bible and was known as the Latin "Vulgate" version. Absolutely fascinating!

HOW MANY "ANNUNCIATIONS"?

YOU cannot read it without being moved. It's the story of the announcement to Mary by the angel Gabriel that she would give birth to Jesus Christ. This scene has captured people everywhere and has stamped the spiritual lives of countless people. The angel went to her and said, "Greetings, you who are highly favored! The Lord is with you" (Luke 1:28). An "annunciation" is an angelic visit to a human being. Mary's reply to this angelic visitor is the example for all who will also submit in obedience to the Lord, "I am the Lord's servant," Mary answered. "May it be to me as you have said" (Luke 1:38).

This visit of Gabriel to Mary is called "The Annunciation." However, there were two more angelic annunciations surrounding the birth of Jesus. One of these happened six months previous to this one when an angelic visitor told the aged priest Zechariah, who was a relative to Mary by marriage, that there would be a miraculous birth in his home. He and his wife were old and childless and this annunciation so astounded him that he questioned the angel. A sign was given to him . . . he would be unable to speak until the predicted event took place!

The third annunciation is only recorded by Matthew and concerns Joseph. When Joseph discovered that Mary was pregnant, naturally there was concern. His reaction was commendable. So an angelic visitor, who is not named, told him the whole story. Interestingly, Gabriel is identified in the first two but not in this third appearing. And there is nothing in Matthew's account about Gabriel's visit to Mary . . . Matthew focuses on Joseph while Luke focuses on Mary and barely even mentions Joseph.

THE SEARCH FOR
THE REAL CROSS

THE New Testament is silent on the subject of what might have happened to the cross on which Jesus was crucified. It was not until A.D. 350 that St. Cyril of Jerusalem said that the Cross had now come into the possession of the Church. Many pieces had been scattered throughout the Roman Empire to be placed in any number of churches.

Supposed pieces of the cross have been widely distributed throughout the Christian world and are said to survive in a number of "reliquaries," which are very elaborately decorated boxes or containers built in the shape of a cross. These were made of ivory; wood with gold overlays; or bronze with intricate carvings, and sometimes encrusted with gemstones, built to preserve the contents from the elements.

The Bible, of course, doesn't mention what happened to the cross used to crucify Christ. Although the centurion understood immediately who Jesus really was, it would have been unlikely that anyone would have thought to dismantle the cross and really, the thought of it being reduced to a souvenir is hard to imagine. There is an interesting story in the Book of Jude in which we are told that Michael, the angel, contended with Satan for the body of Moses after the great prophet died. We don't know the details, but it seems possible that Satan wanted to preserve the body as a relic of worship (like Lenin's body in the former Soviet Union). The fact is, no one knows where Moses is buried, and no one knows what happened to the cross.

THE
APOCRYPHA

THIS is a name given by the ancient scholar-writer-Church-father Jerome to a number of books or scrolls which in the Septuagint version are included among the canonical books of the Bible. However, these do not belong to the "Sacred Canon" of the biblical books. The term itself, "apocrypha," means "hidden" or "concealed" books. This term strictly refers to the 14 books written after the Old Testament canon was closed. They are without question of historical and literary value but have been rejected as part of the canon because:

• They are full of historical and geographical inaccuracies as well as a number of anachronisms.

• They teach doctrines which are false and encourage practices which are in conflict with the rest of the Bible.

• They resort to a literary style which is not in keeping with the rest of the Bible. They are artificial.

• They lack the distinctive elements which give genuine Scripture their divine character.

There are 14 of these Old Testament-era books and more than 100 which have not been claimed by the New Testament church. Some may have appeared before the second century but most of them are of a much later date. None of these has ever received the sanction of any ecclesiastical council. These writings about the life and times of Christ have been rejected because of the above problems.

SOME APOCRYPHAL STORIES OF JESUS

AS you can imagine . . . as early as the second century A.D., many stories were circulated about the childhood of Jesus. One such source for these many stories was a writing called "The Infancy Gospel of Thomas."

According to this "Infancy Gospel," Jesus was purported to have practiced a full range of His miraculous powers. For example, He could make clay sparrows by a stream . . . then clap His hands and they would fly away. If any other child quarreled, fought, or even bumped into Him, Jesus might strike him dead — only later to raise the child back to life again. When Jesus was working in the carpenter shop, if Joseph happened to cut a board too short, Jesus could stretch it to the right length. Another story relates the time when a teacher attempted to begin Jesus' education by starting with the alphabet . . . Jesus in turn explained to him the full meaning of the letters.

One of the most popular stories was the anecdote popular in the Middle Ages which relates how Jesus, when fleeing to Egypt with Mary and Joseph, hid himself and His parents behind a fully grown wheat field which sprang up instantly at Jesus' touch.

What do we do with such "legends"? It is likely we should ignore them because of the problems with the "apocryphal" type of books.

THE HIDDEN MEANING OF JESUS' NAME

THE name "Jesus" was very common in the first century and was usually tagged with "of Nazareth" or "son of Joseph" which was used to make the distinction between one Jesus or another.

Now here's where it becomes interesting. The name "Jesus" comes from the Greek form of the Hebrew name "Joshua" which means "Yahweh is salvation." The angel predicted to Joseph that "he will save his people from their sins" (Matt. 1:21). These words were the confirmation of something highly unusual. If the name "Jesus," or more literally Joshua, means "Yahweh is the source of salvation," then the angel is saying that Jesus himself will assume this activity which was previously assigned to God alone!

And you should also know that long before the Christian era, Jews had banned anybody pronouncing the four consonants "YHWH" because this was the most sacred name of God as it was revealed to Moses. Interestingly . . . a secret pronunciation of this name may have been given by Jesus to His disciples which confirmed the meaning of the divine name as "He who is," or more literally, perhaps, "He who causes to be." The Gospels substitute the Greek "Kyrios" or "Lord" for "YHWH" which followed the practice of the Septuagint, which was translated in the third century B.C.

Jesus said to God that "I have made known to them your name." And the New Testament writers write of activities done "in the name of Jesus." Such activities were prayer, baptism, exorcism, receiving a child, giving a cup of cold water, and healings. It was an identification with the power, authority, and glory that is associated with Jesus!

ZEALOTS

WOULD you be willing to both die or to kill for your religious beliefs? If so, you would have qualified to be a member of the "Zealots." Their name comes from the Hebrews words for "zeal" and "jealous." Principally, they refused to tolerate any foreign influence which polluted their religion or controlled their government policies. These zealots were more than willing to risk their lives in their cause of serving God and restoring their nation.

Historically, the term "zealot" was used in two ways: to describe their official organization and to explain the attitude of any particular person or group of people which might or might not have been part of the group. The "Zealot" party came into most prominence during the time of Christ, as a resistance movement against Rome. This movement was almost crushed in A.D. 70 when the Romans invaded Jerusalem and destroyed Israel. Today, we best remember the Zealots for their final stand at Masada, which finally ended in May of A.D. 74 with a mass suicide.

The most famous "Zealot" in the New Testament is Simon the Zealot who became one of the original 12 disciples of Christ. We can only assume that he was a former member, for it would not have been possible, in good conscience, to belong to Christ and the party at the same time.

JESUS WAS NOT THE ONLY CLAIMED MESSIAH!

JESUS was not the first nor was He the last person who claimed to be the Messiah and or God's anointed! The Jews desperately desired a deliverer who would restore them back to the glory days they enjoyed under the reign of King David and King Solomon.

As background . . . understand that at the time of Christ they had suffered more than a thousand years of capture, exile, divisions, and enemy occupation. As a result, most of them were holding on to the Old Testament Scriptures which promised a Messiah who they believed would deliver them from their problems in a political sense.

The culture of His day was ripe for rumors and theories concerning the coming Messiah. Diverse opinions were held then, just as they are today, among the Jews about the Messiah. This happened to be one of those recurring themes in the ministry of Jesus. When Andrew went to bring his brother Peter to Christ, the first thing he told him was: "We have THE Messiah!" The Jews who attended the "Feast of Dedication" asked Jesus bluntly if He was the Messiah! When Jesus was on earth . . . this hope was at its highest fevered pitch.

History does record a few of the false Messiahs. Theudas attracted a large following and he asked them to join him as he parted the Jordan as Moses had the Red Sea. The Jordan did not part . . . but his crowd did. There was an Egyptian "Messiah" who gathered a huge crowd on the Mount of Olives when he told them they would witness the walls of Jerusalem collapse at his command. The walls didn't move. Another promised in A.D. 70, in the final days as the Romans were destroying Jerusalem, that the 6,000 gathered to him would be delivered directly into heaven. There is only one TRUE MESSIAH determined by His works!

MUSICAL INSTRUMENTS

TO really understand the Jews of Bible times, as well as Jesus, we need to see them as people who loved music. It was not a "spectator" type of music . . . many played, danced, and sang. Just about any kind of an occasion was reason enough to make music together. For example, you remember the ruler who had the sick, and then dead, daughter who came to ask Jesus for help. "When Jesus entered the ruler's house and saw the flute players and the noisy crowd . . ." (Matt. 9:23). What were the instruments?

Pipe . . . This was a wind instrument made of wood and had holes for pitch and note control. It was the ancient ancestor of our clarinet and because of its high tones it was ideal for funerals or weddings.

Lyre . . . David played this wood-based, stringed instrument which had 3 to 12 strings. "Kinnor" is the Hebrew word for it.

Flute . . . This was similar to the pipe and was made from wood or bone. It was a favorite of shepherds and was not normally used in temple worship.

Trumpet . . . It had a straight tube with a bell-shaped end and was most often made of copper or silver. It had no valves. At least two silver trumpets were required for any temple service and as many as 120 were used at a time.

Shofar . . . This was blown in the synagogues. It was a curved instrument made of ram's horn. It was the shofar that was blown when the walls of Jericho fell.

Harp . . . Strings were stretched over a jar or skin bottle with 10 to 20 strings and it could be made of wood or metal.

Timbrel . . . We know it today as the tamborine, a handheld drum made of skin stretched over a wooden hoop.

Cymbals . . . Made of brass and just like ours today!

267 DANCING

AS you can imagine . . . with so much rhythmic music being played in Israel, the average Jew had trouble standing still! Add to this the tendency of the Jew to be expressive and freely express joy and sadness and you can easily see how they danced and why they danced!

David danced before the Lord in the Old Testament. Jesus talked about children and dancing in the streets. He also told the story about the return of the Prodigal Son and of the dancing guests at the homecoming party. The form of their dancing is not really known, but likely, as with most folk dancing, men and women danced separately.

268 PROSELYTES

IT was possible, and many Gentiles converted to Judaism, but the results were not always as promised, nor ideal. Many Jews would be suspicious of these proselytes and added all kinds of burdensome senseless religious baggage on these poor unsuspecting newcomers.

Jesus accused the Pharisees of making life difficult with these words: "They tie up heavy loads and put them on men's shoulders, but they themselves are not willing to lift a finger to move them" (Matt. 23:4). Strong words, but He continued on a bit later and made it even more specific: "Woe to you, teachers of the law and Pharisees, you hypocrites! You travel over land and sea to win a single convert, and when he becomes one, you make him twice as much a son of hell as you are" (Matt. 23:15). What a strong indictment!

What specifically did they do? Some converts were rejected because of their background or the method of conversion and were considered to be genetically blemished. They didn't consider them qualified for any kind of Jewish leadership positions. They were counted as bastards. They falsely assumed that all heathen or Gentile women engaged in prostitution, therefore, according to their thinking, no Gentile child could be sure as to who their father was. So they were treated as fatherless people.

In theory and according to the law, the convert was to be welcomed and treated as if they had been born into Judaism. Many proselytes didn't fully understand the implications of becoming a Jew.

The Jews were not strangers to prejudice because they had a broad experience both as victims and perpetrators of bigotry. One of the purposes of Christ's ministry was to set them free of their prejudices.

THE CAPITAL PUNISHMENT OF STONING

269

LAW and order, in the best sense of the word, were very high priorities for the culture and society of Israel. Laws were formulated so the population could live at peace and the lawless minority punished and held in check.

There were several forms of capital punishment including execution by stoning, sword, or burning. Stoning was the most widely prescribed in ancient Israel. There was a long list of crimes to be punished by stoning — adultery, infant sacrifice, blasphemy, witchcraft, rejection of parents, violation of the Sabbath, and treason. The executioners would always include several members of the community and the witnesses throwing the stones.

Jesus saved a woman caught in the very act of adultery from being stoned by a mob who thought they had Him in another trap. He wrote on the ground and then said, "If any one of you is without sin, let him be the first to throw a stone at her" (John 8:7).

WINNOWING

270

WINNOWING was always a part of the grain harvest in Israel. The purpose was to separate the grain from the chaff; a simple process because the grain was heavier than chaff. It was done by tossing the mixture into the air when the wind was blowing. The wind would blow the chaff away but the grain would fall back to the ground.

They used a simple six-pronged type of pitchfork or a scoop shovel carved out of wood. John the Baptist pictured Jesus as using a winnowing fork in order to separate the grain from the chaff — believers from unbelievers: "His winnowing fork is in his hand, and he will clear his threshing floor, gathering his wheat into the barn and burning up the chaff with unquenchable fire" (Matt. 3:12).

JESUS' ATTITUDE
TO THE POOR

THIS is one of those major recurring themes in the ministry of Jesus. He always showed great compassion on the poor. He never made a single derogatory remark about them or their condition . . . neither did He blame them for their situation.

He did say, "The poor you will always have with you, and you can help them any time you want. But you will not always have me" (Mark 14:7). This did not change His view, however.

His compassion for the poor was part of His credentials for being the true Messiah. He told us to invite the poor rather than the rich to our feasts and festivals. After Christ had that very special dinner with the little short man, Zacchaeus demonstrated the reality of his repentance by giving half of his goods to the poor and Jesus didn't intervene but approved.

Jesus chose a life of relative poverty in this life so that we could gain. After all . . . just think — all of the riches of heaven were His before He came to this earth and after He left this earth.

THE FIRST
LADY MARTYR

NERO was the first infamous emperor who began the persecutions of the Christians. He was primarily responsible for the first wave of cruelty but he was not the only emperor who indulged in such sport. The second wave was under Domitian, the third under Trajan, the fourth under Marcus Aurelius Antoninus, and so forth. There were ten different waves of primitive persecutions of the first church. Men, women, and children were martyred . . . all without having done harm to the Roman Empire.

There were many women killed, but it seems that the first identifiable woman martyr was Felicitatis, an illustrious Roman lady of a well-known family. She was a devout follower of Jesus Christ — a Christian in every sense of the word. She was the mother of seven sons who had also been educated and were avid followers of Christ.

Januarius, her eldest, was scourged and then crushed to death beneath heavy weights. Felix and Philip, the next two had their brains dashed out with clubs. Silvanus, her fourth son, was murdered by being thrown over a cliff. And finally, her three younger sons, Alexander, Vitalis, and Martial were beheaded. Following the beheading of her three youngest, she too was beheaded by the same sword for living an exemplary Christian lifestyle. It makes a person think . . . what would we do if faced with death because we were committed followers of Christ?

WHAT ARE THE WORLD'S OLDEST CITIES?

273

IT is generally believed that tops on this short list would be the city of Jericho in Israel. Archaelogists believe it was inhabited approximately 6,000 years ago. The runner-up is Jerusalem, founded in 3,000 B.C. There are other cities of note in this list . . . Zurich in Switzerland and Kirkuk in Iraq. Damascus, the capital of Syria, has also been continuously inhabited since about 2,500 B.C. There is a special surprise on this list: Lisbon, Portugal, is said to have started around 2,000 B.C., long before many Asian cities.

Of course, the history of Jerusalem is intertwined with the life and history of Jesus Christ. And Jericho is identified with the Israelites conquering it and becoming inhabitants of the Promised Land.

WHY WAS JESUS CRUCIFIED?

274

IN order to maintain some kind of peace in Israel, the high priests were held responsible by the Roman procurators. In turn, the high priests believed that by appeasing the Romans and helping them do away with any of the rebellious Jewish patriots that they could gain some kind of a "peaceful" benefit for their people.

Today, we don't think much of such an unholy alliance. We tend to think in terms of traitors as we look at the Sadducees and priests in their conniving with their Roman captors. However, it made sense back then as it did serve a useful national purpose . . . it did help maintain some kind of relative peace in this far-flung province from Rome. It allowed some sort of practical governing to take place. Were it not for this unholy alliance, it seems that the political conditions would have been much worse.

John, in his Gospel, reports that the Jewish national figures believed that the death of one man — Jesus Christ — might avert political disaster for the entire nation. As He came to Jerusalem the last time . . . He came to bring His nation into a relationship with God yet lost his life because of their fear that He might lead the nation into an uprising which would lead to ultimate destruction.

275 JESUS SAID "YES"!

THINK about it — Jesus often said "yes"! "Yes," I will be a guest at your wedding feast. "Yes," I will show you where my house is. "Yes," I will come to your house for dinner. "Yes," I will heal your daughter who is now dead. "Yes," I will pray for you. "Yes," I will pick up and bless your little children. "Yes," I am going away but I will send you another comforter. "Yes," I will go and prepare a place for you . . . you can also come and spend eternity with me. "Yes," I will go to the cross and pay the ultimate price for your salvation. "Yes," you can follow Me and be My disciple. "Yes," you can count on Me to answer your prayer. "Yes . . . yes!" On the other hand . . . how many times did He say "no" to any person or request?

Jesus said, "Yes"!

276 THE ROMAN ATTITUDE TOWARD CHRIST

HISTORY tells us that at first the empire saw Christians as nothing more nor less than a nuisance. Perhaps this is the reason why Nero faced little or no resistance in his persecution and killing of some of them. You also need to know that Roman law did protect the freedoms of Christians . . . however, there was no one of any consequence or import to defend this tiny sect of Judaism and this left them vulnerable. So any emperor who bordered on insanity would have found the Christians to be easy victims, people who would provide diversion and sport for the empire.

There really were some specific reasons for their utter disregard for Christians and Christianity:

• The Christians were foreign, Jewish, and far removed. So, why take something seriously that was so different from them?

• Then, there was the Christian refusal to worship more than one

God. This led to the thinking that the Christians were atheistic because of their one God. They refused to worship Caesar.

• Christianity also fell prey to all kinds of nasty rumors and gossip. Rumors of cannibalism and offensive sexual practices were just two that were easily believed by suspicious Roman pagans.

• The Early Church was not loyal to the empire. After all, they were circulating stories in reference to a kingdom and a returning king. This really did antagonize the Roman emperors and other authorities.

And . . . it likely never occurred to the Romans that a simple carpenter from Galilee would be a real threat to their power. Jesus had no ambitions to overthrow Roman rule, but many of His followers did want to revolt. Pilate, in mockery, had written on the cross: "Jesus of Nazareth, the King of the Jews!"

THE FALL OF ISRAEL

277

THE fires of rebellion against the rule of Rome climbed high during the reign of Pilate and rose again to an even higher pitch during the governorship of Felix and refused to die. There were pockets of rebels who finally caused great concern to King Herod Agrippa II and the Roman government.

Finally, in A.D. 67 and 68, Vespasian, under the command of Emperor Nero, recaptured Galilee and Samaria who were in rebellion . . . and then marched on Jerusalem. The death of Nero brought Vespasian back to Rome where he became the next emperor. Then . . . after he had taken firm control of the empire, he sent his son Titus to finish off the conquering of Jerusalem. It was in A.D. 70 that Jerusalem fell, even though there were some outposts such as the Masada where the fanatical patriots fought on for three more years. Israel, the land of Jesus, did not fully recover from this disastrous war until it became a nation by fiat of the United Nations in 1948. Historically, it's been a tough road for the chosen people of God.

TEMPTATIONS

278

THE Bible tells us only two different temptation stories . . . the temptation of the first man and woman, and the temptation of

Christ in the wilderness where He fasted for 40 days. The first temptation led to the fall of man . . . the second led to the ultimate downfall of Satan.

Interestingly, all of the other human temptations in history have to do with these two original stories of temptation. Either we are tempted in Adam, in our fleshly bodies, or we are tempted in Christ, in a spiritual sense.

Bonhoeffer concluded this thought by writing: "Either the Adam in me is tempted . . . in which case we fall. Or the Christ in us is tempted . . . in which case Satan is bound to fall."

JESUS REVEALS HIS MISSION

279

JESUS, on the Sabbath, went into the synagogue in Nazareth, where He had been brought up, and in those familiar surroundings read a passage from the scroll of Isaiah: "The Spirit of the Lord is on me, because he has anointed me to preach good news to the poor. He has sent me to proclaim freedom for the prisoners and recovery of sight for the blind, to release the oppressed, to proclaim the year of the Lord's favor" (Luke 4:18).

He rolled the scroll back up and handed it to the "hazzan" or attendant and sat down. This must have been one of those special hushed moments, as Luke tells us that all eyes were on Him. Then Jesus, with all of their attention, says, "Today this scripture is fulfilled in your hearing!" Luke also records their reaction, one of amazement.

And here at this point, the story turns with the question: Isn't this Joseph's son?" Here is a question of the validity of Jesus' mission in life. Jesus didn't answer them directly but told them two proverbs and then told them two stories about Elijah and Elisha.

The crowd became enraged. They forced Him out of the synagogue and attempted to throw Him over a nearby cliff so as to kill Him. Not a nice time nor nice people. Oh, yes, the Bible tells us that He simply walked through the angry crowd! How did He do it? Did He become invisible? Did He have such power that nobody could touch Him?

This incident, as much as any other, shows to us the contradictory reception Jesus encountered in His life and ministry.

DID JOHN REALLY EAT LOCUSTS?

280

WHILE he lived in the wilderness, John the Baptist enjoyed a diet of "locusts and wild honey" (Matt. 3:4; Mark 1:6). Did he really have insect lunches?

Among the vegetation of the Holy Land, the carob, or as it is more commonly called, the "locust" tree, can be found. This locust tree produces pods which have on the inside a dark, sweet syrup which is quite edible. These flat, horn-shaped pods can grow up to as long as a foot and were often ground up and fed to livestock.

Jesus, in telling the story of the prodigal, said, "He longed to fill his stomach with the pods that the pigs were eating, but no one gave him anything" (Luke 15:16). Often, it was the poor people who would eat the sweet, ripe pods. So . . . perhaps John supplemented his meal of locusts with these pods.

FOLLOWING JESUS' FOOTSTEPS

281

SINCE the beginning of the Church, it has been traditional for Christian pilgrims to travel to the Holy Land to visit the places where Jesus preached, healed, taught, suffered, and died. And yes, even to walk where He walked.

In the early 4th century, the emperor Constantine and his mother, Helena, set out to make Jerusalem one of the most important, if not *the* most important, cities of Christianity by building churches in and around the city. Most of these churches or shrines have been destroyed by those who conquered Jerusalem in the centuries following. However, even today, many have been restored.

Perhaps the most famous of these sanctuaries is the "Basilica of the Holy Sepulchre," which many believed was built on the site of the place where Jesus was buried. Also, according to tradition, this marks the site where Helena was to have found the "true" cross of His crucifixion. Today, it contains a reconstruction of the tomb of Jesus.

Another route of great significance is the "Via Dolorosa" which is marked by 14 special tablets indicating the "14 Stations of the Cross."

ACCORDING TO THE GOSPEL OF THOMAS

In December 1945 two peasants from the village of Nag Hammadi in southern Egypt stumbled across a cache of pottery jars containing 52 ancient manuscripts, which were bound into 13 books! This find had been buried sometime in the 4th century and is one of the most important manuscript discoveries of our time. One of these books is *The Gospel of Thomas*. It has many parallels to the Gospels of the New Testament . . . Matthew, Mark, Luke, and John.

This "Gospel" is a collection of sayings, proverbs, and parables attributed to Jesus. It includes 11 parables also recorded in the four Gospels. It's from about the same time as the Synoptic Gospels. It opens with these words: "These are the secret sayings which the living Jesus spoke and which Didymus Judas Thomas wrote down. . . . Whoever finds the interpretation of these sayings will not experience death."

Jesus is primarily depicted as a wisdom teacher, one who reveals the kingdom of God. Elsewhere in this intriguing book are a number of passages which have no parallels in Scripture. Here is one such writing: "Jesus said, 'If you bring forth what is within you, what you bring forth will save you. If you do not bring forth what is within you, what you do not bring forth will destroy you.' "

And of further interest . . . this "Gospel of Thomas" is not the only discovery of a new gospel. There are 11 more which have also been found, but none of these are considered to be on an equal standing with the canon of biblical Scriptures.

A GRUESOME MURDER

ONE of the most famous stories found in the Gospel written by Mark is the account of a banquet held by King Herod to celebrate his birthday. While the merriment was going on . . . John the Baptist was still imprisoned. In the great hall one thing led to another . . . food, merriment, entertainment, music, and drinking. Then, Herod's step-daughter performed her infamous dance which so pleased the king that he foolishly promised her that she could have whatever she wished. She asked her mother what to ask for and Mom said, "The head of John the Baptist" (Mark 6:24). Herod was sorry for his rash promise but because of pride and because the crowd had heard his promise, he did it.

This is a scene from the Bible which has been immortalized in literature, theater, and opera . . . John's head delivered to the girl on a platter while the guests looked on. How did this happen? The followers of John believed the reason for his arrest was his denunciation of Herod's marriage to Herodias. She had been formerly married to his brother Philip. This was the reason for the loss of his head which was instigated by the deceitful and vengeful Herodias.

The historian Josephus adds that at this time Herod was also married to the daughter of Aretas, the king of Nabatea. Later, Aretas went to war with Herod to seek revenge because of his daughter and sought for her repudiation. When Herod's army was defeated, many Jews interpreted the defeat as God's punishment for his treatment of John.

The implication of including this story by Mark was a foreshadowing of the death of Jesus. The prophet who excited the masses met his end at the hands of a cruel ruler.

WHAT ABOUT CHRISTIAN SYMBOLS?

WHERE did they come from? We see Jesus often shown as a "lamb," which likely came from the "Passover Lamb" of the Exodus of the children of Israel out of Egypt. Then, too, the Gospel of John speaks of Jesus as the "Lamb of God" which takes away the sins of the world.

How, then, did the symbol of the "fish" come into use? The first Christians ate bread and fish at their communion meals. Abercius, a 2nd-century bishop in Asia Minor, wrote of eating fish at the holy meal just like the feeding of the 5,000 by Jesus. Also, the newly baptized Christians were referred to as "little fish" because they were born again in the waters of baptism. The symbol of the fish almost became the universal symbol instead of the cross for Christianity. The Greek word for "fish" is "Ichthus" which formed an acrostic for the phrase meaning, "Jesus Christ, Son of God, Savior."

The "dove" came into use because a dove appeared at the baptism of Jesus symbolizing the Holy Spirit. The dove also announced to Noah the end of the flood. And because of this, the dove also symbolized faith.

You will often see "grapevines" used by a number of artists. These were representations which symbolized Jesus and the relationship of the Church to Him. You remember that He said "I am the vine; you are the branches" (John 15:5).

285 PRAYER AND THE CONSTITUTION

AMERICAN history is replete with stories of how church and state are intertwined in the development of our nation. In 1787 the Constitutional Convention convened in Philadelphia in order to form an agreement on how to put together an effective form of government. It was deadlocked because the 13 former colonies could not come to any sort of agreement. When the deadlock became heated and appeared too great for any human wisdom or human power to break, the 81-year-old Benjamin Franklin rose to his feet to speak. He eloquently said that all of his life he was convinced that the Bible was right when it said: "Unless the Lord builds the house, its builders labor in vain" (Ps. 127:1). Then . . . dramatically, he moved that the delegates would begin the next day's meeting with a prayer meeting which was to be led by a Philadelphia clergyman. The motion carried.

The rest is well-known history. The morning began with prayer led by the clergyman who implored for unity, direction, and the will of God to be done in the name of Jesus! This event marked the turning point. The turnaround was dramatic and legislative progress was made until our document, "The Constitution of the United States," came into being. In fact, this prayer time was of such help that Congress to this day still observes the precedent set by Benjamin Franklin.

286 ARRESTED BY THE LIGHT

SAUL was a very agitated man who was leading a delegation into Damascus a year or so following the death of Jesus. Somehow, "Saul of Tarsus" had managed to convince the High Priest in Jerusalem that all of those new Christians should be brought to trial and even done away with. This must have been quite an operation to put together. He carried letters to the synagogues as a proof of his authority to do such a thing. It seems that Saul was acting on his own and this was not an organized attack by others of the Pharisees.

What action had set Saul off on this crusade? Likely the stoning of Stephen, the first martyr, and the message he had preached which incited the crowd to stone the young man. Saul approved of this death.

The next event is most interesting . . . he saw a "great light" which knocked him to the ground. Then the voice, "Saul, Saul, why do you persecute me?" He must have felt sheer terror but he managed to ask, "Who are you?" And the reply: "I am Jesus, whom you are persecuting" (Acts 9:4–5).

After he had managed to get to his feet . . . he discovered he was blind! He had to be led by the hand into the city of Damascus where he couldn't eat for three days. He simply must have sat, not knowing what to do. Then a man named Ananias, reluctantly, fearfully, touched him. When he touched the blinded man, something like scales fell from his eyes and he regained his sight.

The rest of the story is well known. Saul had his name changed to Paul and became a flaming evangelist for the cause of Jesus. He left his mark by writing most of the Epistles found in the New Testament, a traveler whose journeys took him all around the then-known world.

287 PASSOVER

IF you are Jewish, the "Passover" is supreme in importance! You cannot read anything about Jesus without coming across reference to the "Passover." What is it and where did it come from?

God told Moses, as the Israelites were preparing for their Exodus and the last night in Egypt, to slaughter a lamb and mark their doors with its blood. As the last of the plagues of deliverance God would send a death angel to kill the firstborn of the Egyptians, animals as well as humans. But if the angel of death saw the blood on the doors of the Israelites, he would "pass over" their houses and spare their firstborn. Further . . . as a lasting memorial of this miraculous deliverance, God commanded the Israelites to observe this feast unto the Lord for all generations.

On the 15th day of the Jewish month of "Nisan" which corresponds to our March or April, Jews the world over still commemorate the "Exodus" out of Egypt. It is also called the "Feast of Unleavened Bread."

Passover, today, is observed always at home in a very special first-night ceremony called the "Seder." The slaughter of the "paschal lamb" is symbolized by having a shank bone of a lamb to display; the tears of slavery are symbolized by a dish of salt water; the mortar that the slaves were forced to use for Pharaoh's building projects is symbolized by the sweet paste of apples, nuts, and raisins, called "haroset"; and the flight from bondage by the "matzot," bread or unleavened bread. Throughout the observance of the "Seder," the Passover "Haggadah," a book of prayers and benedictions which recount the events of the Passover, is read aloud by and for family members. Jesus is often symbolically referred to as the "Passover Lamb."

THE STORY BEHIND
288 THE WORD "ISRAEL"

IT'S interesting that this word is surrounded by mystery. The first usage in the Bible takes place in the first book of the Bible, Genesis. And here is the mystery . . . we don't really know the exact meaning of this word. It may mean, and has been translated as, any of the following: "he who fights for God" or "he whom God fights" or "he whom God rules" or "the upright one of God" or "God is upright."

Historically, when the kingdom of Israel was divided in 922 B.C., the northern kingdom retained the name "Israel" and the southern one was called "Judah." This land was bordered by the Mediterranean Sea on the west and on the east by the Jordan River. This land is also called "Eretz Israel" or the "Land of Israel."

Interestingly . . . one of the names ascribed to Jesus is that of "The Lion of the Tribe of Judah" or simply "The Lion of Judah."

CLAY
289 MUDPACKS

WHY did Jesus make clay mudpacks for a blind man who came for healing? If you recall some of His other miracles which are written about in the Gospels, normally He spoke a command of healing and people were healed or He touched them and they were healed. But . . . mudpacks? Clay mudpacks? Kind of messy to our way of thinking . . . spittle and clay! Unsanitary, too! Why?

In my opinion, it was because this man needed help to receive his miracle. He was part of the miracle. He had to go to the Pool of Siloam and wash. He, through his act of obedience, was a vital part in the receiving of his sight. And what an investigation this miracle set off among the Pharisees. They questioned the man who was formerly blind until they finally threw him out. The bottom line in this story is told by the blind man: "One thing I do know. I was blind but now I see!" (John 9:25).

WHY ARE WE CALLED "CHRISTIANS?"

290

AS you read through the New Testament, you will quickly discover that the followers of Christ described themselves as "brothers," "saints," "disciples," or "the Way." It's believed that these were first called "Christians" so as to differentiate them from the Jews . . . also it's believed that the title carried with it some element of ridicule.

This term was coined in the Greco-Roman city of Antioch. It combines the Greek word "Christos" with the Latin ending, "-ianus" in order to make up a word meaning those "that belong to Christ." It's highly unlikely that the Jews used the word, because "Christ" means "the Messiah." They referred to this breakaway group as "the sect of the Nazarenes."

The word "Christian" only appears three times in the New Testament. It originated outside of the church circle . . . but soon the Christians adopted it for themselves. In the 2nd century a person could be executed for simply being a Christian because the Romans developed prejudice against all such people.

CENSUS TAKING

291

IN the ancient world, just like in our modern world, a census of the population was generally held for the purposes of taxing the folks or as a registration for military service. So what has changed?

The first biblical census was taken by Moses of his people at Mt. Sinai, but to forestall the anger of God, all who were registered were forced to pay taxes to support the sanctuary! This same census excluded all the Levites from military duty. A census was considered sinful because it did imply this was done by a secular society governed by humans instead of a confederation that put it's total trust in God.

There were reprisals following a census ordered by King David . . . a plague devastated the land. In the 5th century B.C. a count was taken of all who returned from the Babylonian captivity. In the New Testament, Gamaliel speaks of an uprising by Judas the Galilean at the time of another census, which was likely for the reason of preparing another new tax levy.

But of most importance was the census based on the decree of Caesar that "all the world should be registered." This census required that Joseph would travel to his ancestral home in Bethlehem . . . so Jesus was born in the city of David, which had been prophesied by the Old Testament prophet Micah.

292 BREAD

IN the ancient world, bread was considered to be the staff of life and no Jewish meal was complete without it. Usually the father in the household would offer up thanks . . . then the first act would be to "break" the bread and pass pieces around to all seated at the table before anyone would start eating. Bread was such an everyday necessity that it became an idiom for all other types of necessities.

When Jesus taught His disciples how to pray He included this request: "Give us this day our daily bread" (Matt. 6:11). It was a daily task for every woman to bake bread. It was made from wheat or barley flour, some salt, water, and leavening or yeast. They would often keep some of the old dough in order to make the new rise.

Unleavened bread was to be eaten during the celebration of Passover as a reminder to the Jews that their ancestors didn't even have time to allow the bread to rise when they left Egypt in the Exodus. This bread would be baked on hot stones or in an oven, and would end up being a round flat loaf about half an inch thick and about a foot in diameter . . . and it would keep forever, unlike leavened bread.

Jesus selected bread as an element in observing the Last Supper: "And he took bread, gave thanks and broke it, and gave it to them, saying, 'This is my body given for you; do this in remembrance of me'" (Luke 22:19). Why bread? I think it was so that whenever they ate a meal they would think of Him!

WHAT LANGUAGE DID JESUS SPEAK?

IF you are a Bible scholar, you are aware that three languages were most commonly written and spoken during biblical times — Hebrew, Greek, and Aramaic. Which of these would have been the language of the day in which Christ lived?

Aramaic is an ancient Semitic language which originated among the Aramaeans who were desert nomads who eventually settled in Syria during the 2nd millennium B.C. By the 8th century B.C. it became the main language of commerce and diplomacy in the Near East.

While the Jews were exiled in Babylon they spoke in Aramaic but wrote sacred texts in Hebrew. Some parts of the Old Testament Books of Daniel and Ezra were written in Aramaic. Some of the New Testament words such as "Golgotha" came from Aramaic. It is most likely that Jesus spoke in one of the Aramaic dialects even though the New Testament was written in Greek. Aramaic is still spoken in some parts of the Near East today.

PARABLES

PARABLES are metaphorical stories which illustrate a truth or teach a lesson. Parables are more than clever stories which were central to the teachings of Jesus. It was His chosen style of communicating the gospel — these provided hooks upon which truth could be hung. Sometimes the meanings were hidden to the casual listener, others made the listener think through to the truth, and some were to be understood only by His followers.

How important was the use of parables to Jesus? Here's how much: "He did not say anything to them without using a parable. But when he was alone with his own disciples, he explained everything" (Mark 4:34). It was the most exciting method of communicating truth in His day . . . and it still works today.

Depending on how you count them, there are about 40 parables in the Gospels which Jesus told. These were stories drawn from everyday life designed to entertain and pull the listener into His arena of thought. He used them for teaching eternal truths. For example, He told the parable of the creditors and debtors to one named Simon and concluded with a question: "Now which of them will love him more?" (Luke 7:42).

Jesus knew and used the power of parables to open the minds of His hearers. And centuries later, to our day, His teachings are still being spread through the use of these stories, these parables. In fact, much of their teachings have found their way into regular usage among our society today. Everybody knows about the "Prodigal Son," for example.

THE PROSTITUTE IS AN ANCESTOR

295

MOST of us, it seems, have someone in our ancestry of whom we are not so proud. Yes, I refer to the proverbial "black sheep" lodged in the family tree. Let's explore this a bit further in regards to the life of Christ.

Prostitution apparently was an accepted institution in biblical lands but was considered to be degrading. Israelites were forbidden to make prostitutes of their daughters and there were lots of biblical warnings for young men to stay away from such women. A priest was forbidden to marry a prostitute and the daughter of a priest who became one was to be burned to death as a punishment.

The best-known Old Testament prostitute was Rahab, who was really held in high esteem because she saved the spies sent out by Joshua to check on Jericho. The bottom line is that the Gospel of Matthew lists Rahab as a direct ancestor of King David and Jesus!

WHO CARRIED A PURSE?

296

IN the society of the biblical Near East, a "purse" was a small leather pouch in which money was carried . . . much like today. Except that it's been taken to a new high in design and utility today. Well, back to our question.

When Jesus sent out the group of 70 He gave specific instructions to "carry no purse" (Luke 10:4). Why? Because He was telling them to have faith that God would provide for them and that they shouldn't put their trust in their money. A hard lesson to learn, even today.

Another time, Jesus said, "But now if you have a purse, take it, and also a bag and if you don't have a sword, sell your cloak and buy one"

(Luke 22:36). This time, He is telling His followers to be prepared!

Probably the most infamous purse was the "common purse" which held the communal monies of Jesus and His disciples . . . but was in the hands of Judas.

Nothing is said about ladies carrying a purse.

297 WAS JESUS A REAL "RABBI"?

THE word "Rabbi" is taken from the Hebrew "rab" meaning the "Great One," and later came to mean "teacher" or "master." It was usually used in reference to a Pharisee or religious scholar who had served an apprenticeship under an older teacher. This term didn't refer to a specific person or an "ordained" person. It was a title to be earned through study. It was more a title given out of respect. It was not formally earned, it was informally bestowed upon those who were respected for the knowledge they had attained.

The disciples and others often addressed Jesus as "Rabbi," and it was a title which He didn't reject. John the Baptist was also called Rabbi. But Jesus criticized the scribes and Pharisees for taking this title upon themselves because they wanted special treatment. Jesus warned His disciples to never accept this title for themselves, warning that "all who exalt themselves will be humbled" (Matt. 23:8–12).

298 THE REFINER

THE last Old Testament prophet, Malachi, prophesied this about the coming Messiah: "For he will be like a refiner's fire. . . . He will sit as a refiner and purifier of silver; he will purify" (Mal. 3:2–3).

The "refiner" was a highly skilled craftsman who separated the impurities out of metals. When silver was mined it was mixed with lead taken from the "ore galena." The refiner would extract the pure silver by melting the lead and silver mixture in a special clay crucible and would blow hot air on it from bellows. The crucible, which would be porous, would absorb the lead so that only the pure metal remained. Then it would be further refined by mixing it with another alloy of lead, and under heat the lead would absorb these impurities as they oxidized.

THE SIGNIFICANCE OF
THE NUMBER SEVEN

THE number "SEVEN" of all numbers has great religious significance and can be found hundreds of times in the Bible. God created the world in six days and rested on the SEVENTH. Noah took SEVEN pairs of every "clean" animal with him into the ark. Passover, the Festival of Weeks, and the Festival of Booths were SEVEN-day festivals. Every SEVENTH year was to be a Sabbath year. Every 50th year, SEVEN times SEVEN plus one, was the year of Jubilee.

Mark records in his Gospel that Jesus fed the multitude with SEVEN loaves and a few small fish and had SEVEN baskets full leftover. When Peter asked Jesus if he should forgive as many as SEVEN times, Jesus said: "I tell you, not SEVEN times, but SEVENTY times SEVEN" (Matt. 18:22). The number is used in the Book of the Revelation of Jesus Christ . . . there are SEVEN churches, SEVEN stars, SEVEN lamp stands, SEVEN angels, SEVEN trumpets, and SEVEN seal judgments.

SAVED BY THE
CHAPLAIN

ONE of the long-surviving myths, or fallacies, is that people who survived their execution would later be reprieved. There have been some cases where equipment has failed or that the victim recovered but there is no law of any kind that made this obligatory in the United States or Great Britain.

Nevertheless, where the death sentence was lawful, there was a sense of humanity that often resulted in mercy being shown for those criminals who survived their death sentences. Perhaps the most famous of all was that of the English murderer John Lee. He is still remembered as "the man they couldn't hang." Three times, as he stood on the scaffold in 1885, the trap door under his feet didn't open, although each time it worked perfectly during the tests.

It was later thought that a warped board was responsible and the weight of the prison chaplain, appointed by the church of Jesus Christ, who was present only at the actual attempted executions, caused it to bend and jam the trap. After the third unsuccessful attempt to hang him, Lee's sentence was commuted to life imprisonment on humanitarian grounds. He was later released, emigrated to the United States, and died in his sleep in 1933.

THE BEST ROLE MODEL FOR MEN

301

DO this exercise with me . . . try to picture Jesus and what comes into your mind? Doesn't your mind automatically shift to that famous, ever-present portrait of Jesus showing Him as a long-haired, effeminate, wimpish individual? Right? Right! Then, too, Hollywood persists in picturing Him as never quite being in touch with reality.

The real Jesus . . . the real model for true manhood is more than these distorted images! Words such as caring, compassionate, loving, strong, kind, unselfish, and pure do describe Jesus. However, there was one major overriding characteristic of His life that is most important: *His sense of purpose!* This showed up as early as age 12 with Him in the temple. Already He was a man with a purpose, a man with a mission.

Jesus knew where He was going and persevered in the face of all kinds of obstacles. The importance of His mission outweighed all other factors. We can see it in His final cry: "It is finished!" He didn't say, "I am finished." This was not a final whimper of defeat but a triumphant shout of victory! He had set His face like a flint and carried it out. Men are made for a cause which is larger than themselves . . . and the cause of Christ is eternal — it never dies! To be really fulfilled as a man demands a calling with a single purpose.

THE REAL LIFE AND DEATH OF JESUS

302

MANY of us attend churches that are modern, comfortable, on the cutting edge of technology, and sterile. The vast majority of our churches are far removed from the real life situations that Jesus encountered. Jesus was not crucified in a cathedral between two lighted candles set in beautifully made candlesticks! He was crucified on a cross and between two thieves . . . on a town garbage dump and at a crossroads so cosmopolitan that they had to write His title in Hebrew, Latin, and Greek. He was crucified at the kind of a place where the rednecks talked smut . . . where thieves cursed all who came by and where soldiers gambled. That is what He was about, where He died, and what He died for.

HOW DID JESUS TREAT WOMEN AND WHY?

303

HIS treatment of women was certainly very different from the practices of His day. Mary sat at His feet . . . a place reserved for disciples, *male* disciples at that. It seems that other women traveled with His group and helped finance the ministry. One time a woman was commended by Him for crashing an all-male party to make a spectacle of herself. He chose women to be the first to share a witness of His resurrection in a culture where women were not considered competent to testify in court! What kind of lessons can be learned from Jesus' response to women and their response to Him?

From these women it's easy to see how important it is to focus on Jesus. Both men and women who were drawn to Him were drawn to His person. The men, however, quickly got caught up in jostling for position and power. The women maintained their focus of meeting the needs of their beloved Master.

What can we learn from how Jesus treated women? He came to tear down the walls of prejudice and gender. He came to a world and society which was marked by its utter contempt for women and broke the power of that contempt by His example and His teaching. This was a breath of fresh air from heaven . . . this was a sign of the true kingdom . . . this was part of the works of Jesus to destroy the works of the devil, and contempt for women was surely one of those works which came out of the pit of hell.

HOW MANY MARTYRS IN HISTORY?

304

DAVID Barrett is a well-known missions researcher who, among other things, collects data on Christian martyrs. His thorough investigations have led him to currently estimate that an average of 160,000 Christians are being killed for their faith in Jesus Christ every year! Not in ancient history but in current history! And about 150 foreign missionaries are murdered every year!

Barrett says: "For every killing of a Western missionary or a high-profile Christian leader that captures international attention, there are a thousand anonymous Christians who die virtually unnoticed, except by God."

So how many followers of Christ have died for their faith since the first martyr, Stephen? Barrett's best estimation places that at about 50 million believers to the present. Of such martyrdom, Barrett also writes: "The evidence of the centuries is that evangelization proceeds very fast when there are Christians prepared to die for their faith."

305 WHAT'S OFFENSIVE?

WARNER Sallman painted one of the best known of all the portraits of Jesus. He said when he had finished this labor of love that his intent was to attract people to the Savior he knew and loved.

In May of 1995 the Supreme Court ruled that it was too offensive for the Bloomingdale High School to hang this picture in their hallway. This Michigan school began having a problem with the picture in 1992 when Eric Pensinger was a senior, an agnostic who found the painting offensive so he asked for help from the American Civil Liberties Union. The Supreme Court upheld the lower court's decision that "the portrait advances religion." Sallman's goal was accomplished . . . but one high school senior found this goal offensive. The portrait had been hanging in the same spot for 30 years with no previous complaints . . . but when one kid found it offensive, down it came.

306 THE CHRISTO-CENTRIC PRINCIPLE

THIS principle simply states that the entire written Word of God is centered in Jesus Christ. Consider with me that this is the only Book giving the past, present, and future of mankind . . . but mankind is not the theme of the Book. Further, it is the only Book to give the past, present, and future of Satan, the nations, and the Church.

The very living embodiment of the Bible is Christ. He is the perfect example of the perfect Man! The same things that are said of the Living Word can also be said of the written Word. The life of the Bible is Christ. Wherever the Word of God is preached, taught, and received, Jesus Christ will act upon the human heart.

The biblical viewpoint is that of Christ. It is the history of the first man, Adam, and the second Adam, Christ. The first man put the second man to death. And we can conclude that if you look, every page of the Bible speaks of Christ or points toward Christ.

SOME OF THE NAMES OF CHRIST . . . PART I

307

THE names ascribed to Christ are many and varied. In fact, if you study each book of the Bible you will find Him in type, symbol, or in the name of some characteristic of His. Authors and writers have attempted to describe Him in many ways. The following are a few you can garner from reading the Bible:

Creator, Seed of Woman, Lamb of God, Passover Lamb, High Priest, Star out of Jacob, Prophet, Captain of the Lord's Hosts, Messenger of Jehovah, Kinsman Redeemer, Despised King, Rejected King, Lord of Heaven and Earth, Risen Redeemer, Returning Redeemer, Blessed Man, Son of God, Son of Man, the Crucified One, Risen One, Coming One, Reigning One, Leader of Praise, Wisdom, Forgotten Wise Man, My Beloved, Everlasting God, Prince of Peace, Lily of the Valley, Bright and Morning Star, Rose of Sharon, Stronghold in the Day of Wrath, Anchor of our Faith, Judgment, Cleansing, Smitten Shepherd, the Branch, Sun of Righteousness, King of the Jews, Servant of Jehovah, Perfect Son of Man, the Ascended Lord, Our Righteousness, First-fruits from among the Dead, End of the Law, Our Armor, Supplier of Every Need, the Preeminent One, Returning Lord, Mediator, Bestower of Crowns, Suffering Substitute, Our Righteousness, Man of Sorrows, the Throne Sitter, Smiting Stone, David's Greater King, Lord of Bounty, Rescuer of Israel, Deliverer upon Mount Zion, Buried and Risen Savior, Great God, Savior, the Father's Partner, the Rest of Faith, Fulfiller of Types, Lord of the Sabaoth, and Theme of Old Testament Prophecy.

SOME OF THE NAMES OF CHRIST . . . PART II

308

LOOKING at Jesus Christ and the many aspects of who He was and who He is to us today is much like studying the many facets of a diamond. There is great comfort to be derived from the names of Christ — they describe His attributes, His ministry, and His person. Let's continue this interesting study:

The Long Suffering Savior, Word of Life, Target of the Antichrist, Personification of Truth, The Believer's Security, Messiah, the Babe of Bethlehem, Bright and Morning Star, Messenger, Mediator, Lord of Mercy, Bread of Heaven, Bread of Life, the Way, the Truth, vhe Life, Light of the World, Master, Manna of Heaven, the Lamb, Honey in the Rock, Rock of Ages, the Rock Hewn out of the Mountain, vhe Lord of Glory, the Door, the Vine, the Fountain of Life, the First-born Son, the Elder Brother, the Living Water, Day Star, Counselor, Mighty God, Prince of Peace, the Chief Cornerstone, Carpenter's Son, Jesus of Nazareth, Bread of the Presence, Lifter of my Head, the Lamb of God Which Taketh Away the Sins of the World, Balm in Gilead, the Living Word, Forever Living One, the Eternal God, Everlasting from Everlasting, the Lion of the Tribe of Judah, Shepherd, the Testimony, Teacher, Rabbi, the Living Tabernacle, the Rock of Your Refuge, the Lord of Glory, the Great I Am, the Suffering Savior, Servant King, the Anointed One, Giver of Life, River of Life, I Am, the Resurrection, and finally, *the KING of kings and LORD of lords!!*

THE BIBLE'S DULLEST READING

WHO enjoys reading a genealogy? I must confess that I would not normally turn there for inspiration. But there is exciting truth to be found in the two genealogies of Jesus.

Matthew's genealogy starts with Abraham and is most interesting. It includes 42 names but there are some omitted from this by God because of sin in that line. From Abraham we follow the line to David, Solomon, and Rehoboam. Under Rehoboam the nation was divided into the northern and southern kingdoms. Further down the line we come to Jehoiakim and his son Jehoiakin. How could Jehoiakin be childless? This didn't mean that he had no children but that his sons were cursed as far as this line was concerned. Not a single son of his would sit on the throne, although they had the right to it.

Joseph was a son of David and this is what the angel called him. He had the title to the throne of David because Joseph was a descendant of Jeconiah. All of Jeconiah's sons had a title to the throne, however none of them could sit on it. Joseph was of the line of David. Apparently God's promise must come to nothing. This must have given the devil great joy for he must have thought he had succeeded in breaking this lineage. For even if Joseph did have a son, that son could not use his title because he, too, would have been a son of Jeconiah.

Back to Zedekiah . . . the judgment said that Coniah's sons would not reign. However, when Nebuchadnezzar besieged Jerusalem, he appointed Zedekiah as king and Zedekiah was Coniah's uncle, brother of Jehoikim, the father.

Now that I have you properly confused . . . the bottom line is simply that Matthew's genealogy, which shows the lineage of Jesus, is considered to be the "legal" line of Jesus.

THE OTHER DULLEST PAGE IN THE BIBLE

310

LUKE'S genealogy has 77 names in it and corresponds to Matthew's line from Abraham to David but then makes a change. Nathan was an elder brother of Solomon and had the same mother and should have been on the throne instead of Solomon. Apparently Nathan didn't object. Absalom tried to take the throne but Nathan's mouth was sealed, perhaps for the same reason that the lion's mouths were closed when Daniel was in the den. God closed it!

Heli and Joseph were both sons of David, but Joseph had the title to the throne. However the title did him no good because he couldn't use it. Heli had a daughter named Mary, a distant cousin to Joseph. These two became engaged. Here is the working out of the two different genealogies. This is where it gets exciting! God's curse on Jeconiah is nullified by the other line.

An engagement in the Near East was considered to be sacred. It was usually about a year in length and could not be broken without a divorce. Those who were engaged were considered man and wife. Today, Mary is honored but in that day she was not. Joseph was a just man and wanted to do what was right. When Mary was pregnant before their marriage, there were three choices for Joseph: 1) He could make her a public example and by the law of Moses she would be stoned. 2) He could give her a private bill of divorcement. 3) He could marry her and legitimize the child. Joseph chose to give her a bill of divorcement . . . until God sent an angel with a special message. He then chose to marry her so that Jesus was born in wedlock in the eyes of the law. So now . . . do you understand it a bit better as to the reason for two different genealogies?

SON OF JOSEPH
311 OR SON OF GOD?

WHILE the puzzle of why there were two different genealogies is still on our mind . . . let's return to these genealogies and explore another truth. Was Jesus the son of Joseph or the Son of God?

Neither genealogy says that Joseph "begat" Jesus. Jesus was not the child of Joseph, but He was the son of Joseph in the eyes of the law. Joseph was the legal father of Jesus. Jesus was the literal son of Nathan and the legal son of Solomon so He received the title to the throne of David. Jesus, the legal son of Joseph, was heir to the title from Jeconiah, but He was not the son of Jeconiah.

Suppose that another son of Joseph wanted to claim the throne . . . Jesus had the title. Joseph had the title, but had no child. Therefore, if Jesus did not rise from the dead then the Bible would not be true. Jesus had a Father in heaven who begat Him and a legal father on earth. He had all the rights of the first-born. He had the right to the throne through Joseph legally, and through Mary He had the right and could rule because He was not of the seed of Jeconiah. No other son of Joseph could have sat on the throne. There was only one person in the whole universe of God to whom the throne could rightfully come and that was Jesus! He had the blood of David through Mary.

Suppose someone should dispute Solomon's right to the throne and demand the throne through Nathan's name . . . Jesus still meets that claim! How the devil and all his imps had fought the line of Solomon and attempted to destroy it. He didn't know that Jesus was not coming through that line at all!

WHEN IT ALL DEPENDED
312 UPON A BABY

THOSE ancient kings were a bloody and insecure lot of men, by and large. When a new king ascended to the throne . . . usually the first act was to have all other heirs or claimants to the throne murdered. These were the times when it was not healthy to be a part of the king's family. This is what happened a number of times in the line and lineage of Jesus. In fact, there was one time when the entire line depended upon one small baby — Joash.

Here's the background. Jehoshophat was in the regular line. Jehoram killed all his brothers so that he and his sons were all that were left with a claim to the throne. But the Arabians came and killed all of the sons except Ahaziah. Then when Ahaziah was killed, Athaliah, nice lady that she was, killed all of the rest of the sons, she thought. Little baby boy Joash, however, escaped. So there was a period of time when he was the only one in that lineage.

Later, when the time came, that little king who had been hidden in the house of God where he escaped death, came forth to take the throne of the kingdom. It's a picture of the hidden king who will some day come from the house of God to rule this world. I hope you have caught some of the deeper meanings in the genealogies of Jesus. There is more to it than simply the proof of the humanity of Jesus.

THE PROGRESSIVE MENTION PRINCIPLE

313

THIS is the principle by which God makes the revelation of any given truth increasingly clear as the Bible proceeds to the finish. You find the Word to be progressive . . . as it is studied, more added details reveal the truth at hand. Now there are many such examples of this concept in practice. But let's take a look at this growth of truth as it relates to some of the predictions of the coming Messiah.

• When sin entered the world in the Garden of Eden, God gave the promise that the "seed of the woman" would bruise the head of the serpent. This is the first mention of Christ's coming.

• Time passes . . . then comes the man Abraham, with whom God makes a covenant: "All nations will be blessed through you" (Gal. 3:8). We now know that the "bruiser" is a descendant from the man Abraham . . . not just any family of the earth.

• The next detail is that of Abraham's two sons . . . Isaac is the chosen one.

• Isaac then has two sons and the promise is definitely made to Jacob.

• Jacob has 12 sons, but this time the promise is limited to only Judah.

• Judah becomes a great tribe numbering thousands. Now where do we look? The family of King David is selected.

• Not only the family of David . . . but it is prophesied in the town of Bethlehem.

• Zechariah tells us that he will ride into the city of Jerusalem.

• Malachi tells that the forerunner will be John the Baptist.

• The Psalmist promises that not a bone shall be broken.

• To Isaiah is revealed God's part in Christ's death.

And this is the "progressive mention principle" in action in Christ.

THE NUMBER "THREE" AND JESUS

THE study of numbers in the Bible is very interesting . . . a sort of spiritual mathematics. With "THREE" we come to the number of union, approval, co-ordination, completeness, and perfection. This is the number of the Trinity. THREE persons in One God . . . Father, Son, and Holy Spirit . . . THREE members of Divine perfection.

The resurrection of our Lord on the THIRD day speaks of divine power. Jonah was THREE days and nights in the great fish as a sign of Christ's burial and resurrection.

Christ was crucified at the THIRD hour. The inscription over His head was written in THREE languages suggesting the completeness of man's rejection of Christ. On the THIRD day, following His burial, He rose from the dead.

THREE persons were raised from the dead by Christ: Jairus' daughter, the widow's son, and Lazarus. This shows the completeness of His divine power in every stage of human existence, for the daughter of Jairus was 12 years old, just a girl; the widow's son of Nain was of adult age, a young man; and Lazarus was full grown, an old man.

There are THREE offices of Christ which show His perfection: Prophet, Priest, and King. The completeness of His Shepherd care is seen in these three titles: the Good, the Chief, and the Great Shepherd.

The perfection of Christ in His temptation is show in His THREE-fold use of "It is written!"

THREE times the Heavenly Father spoke from heaven to His Son, showing His pleasure in the Son's obedience and the completeness in carrying out the mission for which He came.

HE HAD A SENSE OF DESTINY

DO you live with a sense of destiny? Do you have the feeling that you were destined to be doing something more or different than what you are doing at the present? Jesus never hesitated in His life purpose — His destiny, if you please. He once said: "I know where I came from and I know where I am going" (John 8:14). I don't know if at that point He knew every detail He would be living or facing . . . but He was positive about this mission in life.

There were times when His life was threatened . . . such as in the storm on the Sea of Galilee. He slept calmly. Why? I think it was because He knew it was not yet time for Him to die — there was more to His life. When He was turned over to the authorities who had the power of life and death over Him, He said, "You could have no power over me unless it was given to you from on high" (John 19:11). In other words, if they were to take any action against Him, it had to be part of the larger plan. This destiny, this mission, was like a magnet that pulled Jesus toward the culmination of His life and work.

MANAGEMENT PRINCIPLES OF JESUS

STOP in at any bookstore and you can wander through shelves of books on management principles. There's one on Attila the Hun, another about swimming with the sharks, and more about looking out for number one, and on and on.

The all-time, greatest management entrepreneur who has ever lived is Jesus Christ! How can I say that? Quite easily. Just consider what He accomplished in 3 short years! The evidence is in and the jury has ruled — the organization founded by Jesus is the most successful of all time by any standard you want to use. What are the standards you choose for evaluation? Longevity? Two thousand years and still counting! Wealth? It is simply beyond calculation! Numbers? Just try to count up all His followers from His day to our day! Loyalty of His followers? Millions have given their lives for His cause! Distribution? It is worldwide and expanding! Diversification? Think of how His followers have integrated His principles into just about every kind of enterprise known to mankind!

Therefore . . . I declare that Jesus Christ reigns supreme as the greatest manager, entrepreneur, CEO, innovator, organizer, and leader that this world has ever known! If you really want to make your life and your enterprise successful in every sense of the word . . . study, learn, and apply the life and management principles of Christ!

JESUS AND DEMOCRATIC LEADERSHIP

317

THIS thought may be news to you, but Jesus did not run a democratic type of organization! Not once, not any place in the Gospel accounts did He call for a vote on the next course of action. He was in charge! He was a positive leader! He did not waver from the course set before Him. He based His leadership authority on the Bible and on the mandate He was given by His Heavenly Father. But even He submitted to a "higher" authority. "Father, if you are willing, take this cup from me; yet not my will, but yours be done" (Luke 22:42).

In our business world, "non-authoritarian" leadership is the concept being touted. But Jesus knew better and so do many of today's business leaders. No really successful business or organization is built or maintained without someone being the ultimate final authority. Just ask any of the great corporate leaders of our time. Did you have any doubt who was boss when Iaccoca was CEO at Chrysler; or Watson at IBM; or Perot at EDS; or Buffet at Berkshire Hathaway? And did you ever have any doubt as to who ran Wal-Mart? You bet . . . Sam Walton did! Participatory leadership can be okay in some situations . . . but only if there is a real, final authority in charge. Jesus showed us how to do this.

UNEQUAL RESULTS

318

TRUE success is a multiplier! It doesn't divide . . . it makes more for everybody. When the effects of your efforts are multiplied, success serves God by benefiting others. In creating life, God made the system in such a way that the results are lopsided . . . always biased in favor of more life.

Jesus told an interesting story in which most of the farmer's efforts were wasted. The minority of the seed produced the majority of the harvest. It is the universal law of "Disproportionate Rewards" in action. Here's a line from this story: "Still other seed fell on good soil, where it produced a crop . . . a hundred, sixty or thirty times what was sown" (Matt. 13:8).

Let's do some simple math on Jesus' parable of the sower: 25 percent was eaten by the birds, 25 percent didn't sprout, 25 percent was choked out by the weeds, and only 25 percent produced a crop. Yet even the productive 25 percent varied in production. All of the harvest came from the minority of the seed . . . but most of it came from a minority of the minority! Of this productive seed a portion produced 30 grains per plant (15 percent of the total harvest), some produced 60 grains per plant (32 percent), and the last portion produced 100 grains per plant (53 percent). Notice that 53 percent of the harvest came from only 8 percent of the seed!

There's a line from a song which says, "Little is much when God is in it." Don't give up, keep on planting!

TYPES OF CHRIST

319

A "type" is a divinely appointed illustration of some biblical truth. Sir Robert Anderson said: "The typology of the Old Testament is the very alphabet of the language in which the doctrine of the New Testament is written; and as many of our great theologians are admittedly ignorant of typology, we need not feel surprised if they are not always the safest exponents of the doctrines."

Our English word "type" is taken from the Greek word "tupos" which occurs 16 times in the New Testament. The Greek word is unique in original meaning: it's the effect of a blow, making an impression or stamping, marking, a pattern, a form, or setting a mold.

How does it work out? For example, the "Passover Lamb" is typical of Christ, a divinely ordained picture or pattern. The "brazen serpent" is another type of Christ which pointed out the ministry or work of Jesus in healing. Every Old Testament sacrifice is "typical" or a type of Christ in some aspect. The heavenly "manna" is a type of Christ . . . manna came down from heaven, Christ is the Bread of Life which came down from heaven. The Old Testament "Holy Festivals" are another type of Christ. The "tabernacle" erected in the wilderness contains all kinds of pictures of the Christ which was to come . . . the tabernacle was where God dwelt and it was made of material things. The New Testament tabernacle is where God dwells but is made of flesh and blood.

I hope that your interest in "types" and "typology" has been piqued and that you will spend some time in further study. It's most fascinating and will give you biblical insights that will be of benefit to you.

WHO OR WHAT IS A JEW?

320

A "Jew" is any person, male or female, who descended from the biblical Israelites or is a convert to and practices Judiasm. The word originally was taken or derived from the southern kingdom of Judah. It first described who the Judean citizen was. But that changed following the Babylonian captivity and exile in 587 B.C. The term was then applied to all Israelites including any who could trace their descent from this ethnic or religious group without regard to race.

The usage we see in the Bible of the term "Jew" is often used in contrast to "Gentile," or all who are non-Jewish. Of course, Jesus was a Jew as were most of His early followers.

DID JESUS WEAR A ROLEX WATCH?

321

GREAT question! Well . . . what do you think? Would Jesus have worn a "Rolex" if it had been available?

Tradition and custom tell us that in biblical times both men and women of all social classes wore jewelry. Archaeologists' digs have uncovered all kinds of jewelry. The conclusion is that both sexes wore earrings, necklaces, chains, brooches, bracelets, beads, ankle bracelets, and signet rings which were also used to seal documents and were also a sign of authority. The only piece of jewelry exclusive to women were the nose rings (and I'm not going to touch that!).

Most jewelry was made of bronze or ivory, but the rich afforded gold and silver. Interestingly, high priests and royalty wore semi-precious and precious stones often set in a gold or silver filigree. So . . . what do you think? Would Jesus have worn jewelry or a "Rolex" if it had been available to Him? It's doubtful.

THE JUDGMENT SEAT

322

IN the Roman Empire, a "judgment seat" was most often a raised bench or platform on which the judge, magistrate, or other official sat with their counselors to deliberate or judge on cases brought before him. It was seen in public places. "When Pilate heard this, he brought Jesus out and sat down on the judge's seat at a place known as the Stone Pavement (which in Aramaic is Gabbatha)" (John 19:13).

It was to this judgment seat that Pilate's wife sent word to him to have nothing to do with Jesus, the innocent man (Matt. 27:19). The apostle Paul in his letter to the Romans says that "We will all stand before God's judgment seat" where "each of us will give an account of himself to God" (Rom. 10–12).

THE DETERRENT TO FLOGGING

323

THERE are many beliefs of mariners that have become legends. In fact, faced with the perils and the mysteries of the oceans, sailors have adopted beliefs from anywhere and in anything that seems to work. Some animals, birds, names, and even actions that normally would be harmless — such as whistling — can be dire omens at sea.

One of the stranger of these beliefs comes out of the 18th century when and where it was a common punishment for a sailor, being found drunk while on duty, to be given 24 or more lashes with a whip. Old sailors who were experienced hands at cheating authority had some words of advice for newcomers: "Get a crucifix of Jesus Christ tattooed on your back." Why? It was believed that the bosun's mate would flinch from laying his whip onto the face of Christ . . . and also that the lash itself would cringe away from the blows on Christ's body or face.

DID JESUS EVER SEE SNOW?

324

ISRAEL is a moderate, dry climate that can be quite hot. But does it ever snow in Israel? Rarely! The Bible does specifically mention snow on a few occasions. However, snow was common enough in the northern mountainous regions that the Lord asked a rhetorical question of the prophet Jeremiah: "Does the snow of Lebanon ever vanish from its rocky slopes?" In other translations is says, "Does the snow of Lebanon leave the crags of Sirion?" (Jer. 18:14). Sirion is Mount Hermon with an elevation of more than 9,200 feet and is snowcapped year around! So did Jesus ever see snow? Play in snow? Shovel snow? If He came near to Mount Hermon, He at least saw it and possibly during His lifetime it might have snowed.

Snow also served as a beautiful metaphor for cleanliness, whiteness, and divine glory . . . such as when the angel appeared at the empty tomb wearing clothing described as being "white as snow."

WHAT THEY REALLY SAID ABOUT HIM

325

RENAN, the Frenchman said: "In Jesus is condensed all that is good and exalted in nature."

Thomas Paine, the noted infidel said: "The morality that He preached has not been exceeded by any."

Rousseau stated: "If the life and death of Socrates were those of a martyr, the life and death of Jesus Christ were those of a God."

Disraeli, the Jew, acknowledged the fact that: "Jesus has conquered Europe and has changed its name to Christendom."

Thomas Jefferson, said: "Jesus Christ has given to us the most sublime and benevolent code of morals ever offered to man."

David Strauss, theologian and biblical critic, wrote: "Jesus remains the highest model of religion within the reach of our thoughts. No perfect piety is possible without His presence in the heart."

WHERE IS THE "PINNACLE"?

326

AFTER Jesus had been baptized in the River Jordan He was sent into the wilderness for 40 days. While there, one of the temptations to which the devil subjected Him was to transport Him to the Jerusalem temple's "pinnacle." He was challenged to throw himself down from this pinnacle and allow God to save Him.

Scholars don't know just where this highest point of the temple was located since the Romans in A.D. 70 destroyed the temple and no plans have survived. However, there are many scholars who argue that the "pinnacle" was the southeast corner of the great wall which surrounds the temple area. This corner overlooks the Kidron valley and had a magnificent panoramic view. There was a drop of many feet to the ground below.

HOW MUCH WINE?

THE Gospel of John opens or begins the ministry of Jesus with an interesting story. It seems that almost immediately after Jesus had returned from the Jordan River and the wilderness temptations that He and His mother were the invited guests at a wedding in the village of Cana.

The host ran of out of wine for the party . . . which would have been a social tragedy. Weddings lasted about seven days and it was a matter of pride for the host to provide lots of food and drink for the guests for the duration. This hardly seems the kind of incident which would call for a supernatural miracle. Yet, we're drawn into this story with the remarks of Mary to Jesus: "They have no more wine." His response is remarkable. He doesn't answer her directly but with: "Dear woman, why do you involve me?" Jesus replied, "My time has not yet come."

Then her reaction is equally interesting . . . she doesn't say anything more to Him but turns to the servants and says: "Do whatever he tells you!" What is she expecting from Him? What did He mean about his "time"? What did she know about Him that we are not told in this story? Is this not a strange request? And a strange response?

He asks them to fill six stone jars with water. Each of these are believed to have contained about 20 gallons . . . about 120 gallons in all. A sample is taken to the host and indeed it is first class . . . better than what they had run out of!

How did it happen? Why did it happen? John concludes and answers: "This, the first of his miraculous signs, Jesus performed in Cana of Galilee. He thus revealed his glory, and his disciples put their faith in him" (John 2:11).

John didn't answer our specific questions . . . but added to our sense of mystery and awe.

WHO REALLY WAS
328 PONTIUS PILATE?

HISTORICALLY, there are very few references to Pontius Pilate outside of the New Testament record. He was the procurator in Judea for about ten years. He is only mentioned in passing by the Roman historian Tacitus, with this quote: "The execution of Christus, author of that sect, by the procurator Pontius Pilate in the reign of Tiberius."

For a much more complete account we must refer to the Jewish historian Josephus, who gives us three incidents which occurred during his rule. Once, Pilate deliberately offended the Jews by sending soldiers into Jerusalem who were carrying images of the Roman emperor, but had to recall them because of an angry mob demonstrating in the streets. Next, he attempted to win their favor by improving the water supply of Jerusalem — but again managed to outrage the Jews when he tried to use funds from the temple for the project. As a result of this action there was more rioting in the streets with several citizens being killed because Pilate's soldiers disobeyed his orders to use batons rather than swords.

Finally, Pilate was ordered by his superior, Lucius Vitellius, to return to Rome to answer questions about why his soldiers ambushed and killed a number of religious fanatics in the area of Samaria. According to Josephus, he was tried and condemned to exile in France where he committed suicide during the reign of Caligula.

It is also interesting that the New Testament authors seemed to be somewhat sympathetic toward Pilate. This thinking went so far that some of the Early Church fathers even thought of him as being a closet Christian because of his conscience following the trial of Christ.

THE MAN WHO
329 CARRIED THE CROSS

"SIMON of Cyrene" was a Hellenistic Jew born at Cyrene, on the north coast of Africa. He happened to have been in Jerusalem at the time of the crucifixion of Jesus . . . either as one of the many who came to attend the feast celebration or perhaps as one of the newer settlers from Africa to settle in Jerusalem. However he happened to be at this exact spot at this exact time is secondary. He was forced into the service of carrying the cross, likely the heavy cross piece, when

Jesus was weakened so that He couldn't carry it any farther.

Mark, in his Gospel, describes him as the father of Rufus and Alexander. Likely this was the Rufus known to the Roman Christians.

Frank Harris wrote the play *The King of the Jews,* and in it strongly hints that Simon was enroute from his fields in the countryside to apply for a job as a temple doorkeeper when he was pressed into service by the soldiers on the way to the place of Jesus' crucifixion. It's an interesting dialogue between Simon and his wife, Hushim. Find the play and read it for further insight surrounding this story.

WHAT ABOUT THE MISSING YEARS?

WHAT really happened during those 30 years between His birth and the time when His earthly ministry began? Have you ever wondered about how His personality developed? Or how His interests, passions, and education came about? Did He have any foibles? How did He become the person He was? We are frustrated by the silence . . . biographers have also been frustrated by the enigma of these missing years. There is only one story in one of the Gospel accounts to say anything during these three decades. Nothing is said, other than this, about the spiritual intellectual, emotional, or social development of this foundational world figure.

Three Gospels give us NO specific information at all. Both the Gospels of Mark and John begin with Jesus as an adult who is launching His ministry. Matthew tells us about His birth and then goes directly to adulthood. All we can do is speculate that they were not interested in the childhood years or they didn't have any information about those years. Only the Gospel of Luke gives us one tiny glimpse, at age 12, to the boy Jesus. It happened at the Feast of Passover. According to the Laws of Exodus, every Jewish male was expected to make three trips to the temple in Jerusalem annually. Being age 12, Jesus would have been considered a "Son of the Law" and expected to make His appearance at the temple feasts. Could this have been His first such journey to the Holy City since His appearance in the temple for presentation and circumcision?

From this incident, we can only conclude that at the early age of 12 He was already absorbed in the study of the Bible and could carry on a knowledgeable conversation with professional scholars of the temple.

BURIAL CUSTOMS IN ISRAEL

331

THE dead from wealthy families were customarily put to rest in the family burial place which had likely been in use for generations. This could be in a selected cave or tomb carved into soft rock. Criminals were usually put into a trench grave where the poor were also disposed of. But Jesus did not receive the burial of a criminal. And there was another problem . . . the family burial place of Jesus' family would not have been near Jerusalem. So a follower, Joseph of Arimathea, arranged to bury Jesus in his own unused tomb in a garden near Golgotha.

Such tombs were cut out of a rock formation and usually had more than a single chamber. They were cut in such a way as to have a ledge on which the deceased would be placed to rest. No coffins were used. The entrance was blocked by a stone which had been cut to fit the opening to the outside. This was to protect the corpse from jackals and other wild animals or grave robbers.

The dead were buried quickly, as Jesus was, because the Jews did not embalm the deceased and bodies decomposed rapidly in the heat, creating a health hazard. It was customary for the corpse to be washed, anointed with spices, wrapped in linen, and lovingly laid on the prepared ledge in the tomb.

THE MAN WHO COULD NOT BELIEVE

332

THOMAS is that man! He will always be remembered as the man who could not believe. He is, in fact, so well remembered that the phrase "doubting Thomas" is still in use today. When Jesus had died on the cross and when it seemed as though all the dreams of His followers had been dashed . . . it appears as though Thomas desired to be left alone. So when Jesus made His first appearance in the closed room where the disciples had gathered, Thomas was not there, for whatever reason. He, then in turn refused to believe the good news from the other disciples that Jesus was truly alive again. He said he could only believe if he saw, touched, and handled the risen Lord. Thomas had to see before he could believe! How many of us are in this category?

THE GREAT IMPOSTER

JUST about everybody wants to be somebody. However, Ferdinand Waldo Demara went further . . . he wanted to be everybody! Demara is one of the great impostors of all time and successfully posed as a theologian, psychologist, doctor of philosophy, prison officer, teacher, and surgeon.

In 1941 he deserted from the U.S. Army, used the name of Dr. Robert Linton French, a doctor of philosophy, and joined a Trappist monastery in Kentucky. He introduced himself as a man sick of war and wanting the peace of a religious order. He submitted to all of their disciplines . . . except he began to steal food and then was sent to work in their vineyards where he and another monk ate grapes and let their vows of silence go by. Their sins were discovered and Demara left.

Most impostors are exposed by their faults but Demara's downfalls came as a result of his brilliance and intelligence.

In 1952, in the middle of his most spectacular acts, he had used the credentials of a doctor to get a commission as surgeon-lieutenant in the Royal Canadian Navy during the Korean War. His first task as medical officer aboard the HMCS *Cayuga* was to pull a tooth from the captain. Demara, who had never pulled a tooth, sat up all night studying a book on dentistry. The next morning he gave the captain a shot of novocaine and removed the tooth. He later set up a clinic in South Korea to help with medical care and other assistance. The story was written up and he was exposed as an imposter.

Demara, in turn became a psychologist, teacher, and prison officer . . . until exposed as a fraud. He was asked why and replied, "Rascality, pure rascality." In the end, he claimed to become a follower of Jesus Christ and became an ordained minister!

WHO IS THE PATIENT?

MOTHER Teresa was widely acclaimed for her work among the poor of Calcutta and was awarded the Nobel Peace Prize in 1979. She exemplified a life and ministry of compassion to others, portraying the truest way of serving Jesus Christ. The following is a portion of a prayer she prayed on a daily basis:

DEAREST LORD, may I see you today and every day in the person of your sick, and whilst nursing them minister to you. Though you hide yourself behind the unattractive disguise of the irritable, the exacting, the unreasonable, may I still recognize you and say, "Jesus, my patient, how sweet it is to serve you."

Lord, give me this seeing faith, then my work will never be monotonous. I will ever find joy in humoring the fancies and gratifying the wishes of all sufferers.

Lord, increase my faith, bless my effort and work, now and forevermore. AMEN.

THE LIFE OF JESUS

335

JUST think about it . . . the life of Jesus was brief, particularly His public life of approximately three short years. This short life was lived out in a remote province of the powerful Roman Empire some 2,000 years ago. What we know of this life is almost entirely from the accounts recorded in the four Gospels: Matthew, Mark, Luke, and John. There are also a few references in the Acts of the Apostles and some from the various Epistles. Yet . . . more has been written about this man Jesus than any other person in all of human history. The events and teachings of His life are better known to more people than are those of any other person who has ever lived.

There is no physical description of Jesus any place in the biblical writings. None of His chroniclers said anything about His appearance. No other person in history has inspired so many artists to attempt to recreate the happenings of His life. No one else can claim to have left behind the rich artistic legacy that He did.

What we are doing here, as have so many others, is to attempt to celebrate once more the greatest life ever lived in human history!

REDEMPTION

336

TO "redeem" something or someone is to buy it or them back. The picture that most clearly illustrates this concept is of a slave being "ransomed" in order to be set free. Mankind is said to be a "slave to sin." There is helplessness here — even if we want to give up committing sin, we cannot do it in our own power. Therefore, we find ourselves slaves to sin.

Jesus said that He came "to give his life to redeem many people." By His life, death, and resurrection, Jesus paid the price or ransom that would set us free! Therefore, Christians are "the redeemed" of today! We are just like the Israelites who were kept in bondage and slavery until they were "redeemed" out of the slavery of Egypt. One thing about a "redeemed" person is that he or she is a free person! Therefore, we should walk and live as being free!

MESSENGERS FROM GOD

337

THE word "angel" comes from a Greek word meaning "messenger." When delivering a message from God, angels assume a form which can be seen — they become visible. During the ministry of Jesus, no angels were needed as messengers, because Jesus himself brought the message from God for all who would hear it.

According to the biblical account, angels were created by God as moral beings . . . capable of choosing between good and evil. When the wicked angels rebelled, following the leadership of the angel Satan, they were defeated and thrown out of heaven by the archangel Michael and other loyal angels. The Bible tells us that one-third of the angels fell. But, unlike humans who can sin and be forgiven, the rebellious angels cannot be redeemed.

Only two angels are mentioned by name in the Bible — Gabriel and Michael. The Apocrypha names Raphael. And there are other non-biblical Jewish writings which name Uriel.

In the Bible there are suggestions as to a distinct hierarchy of angels with the archangels being at the top. The exact number of archangels are varied, but in the Book of the Revelation the number is seven. Some Early Church teachings held that angelic beings were also grouped in nine groups or choirs: angels, archangels, cherubim, seraphim, virtues, powers, principalities, dominions, and thrones. Gabriel, which means "hero of God," is mentioned four times in the Bible.

Angels, for believers, have been a source of comfort. In this Christian era, many have claimed that everyone has been assigned a "guardian angel." It's believed by many that angels come at the hour of death in order to lead the soul to heaven.

THE JEWISH BETROTHAL

338

MUCH speculation has surrounded the "betrothal" of Mary to Joseph. When you know a bit more about this custom, you can be even more amazed at the reaction of Joseph to the news that Mary was pregnant. "Betrothal" or "engagement," according to Jewish custom, was to last about a year. It carried most of the rights and obligations of marriage. For example, if Joseph had died during his betrothal to Mary, Mary would have been legally considered his widow. Any child born to this couple during betrothal was considered to be illegitimate. And there's more . . . any unfaithful bride-to-be who became pregnant during this period could have been stoned to death for committing adultery!

But Joseph, because of his kindness, was more than willing to end their betrothal quietly while shielding Mary from public ridicule or the legal punishment of death by stoning. This putting her away quietly was out of the question following the visit of the angel to Joseph.

Many legends have sprung up about Joseph. The primary one is that he was much older than Mary. The Bible doesn't allude to that fact at all. Once again, according to Jewish custom, girls were betrothed at about age 12 or soon after; the boys were usually age 18 or so.

The arrangements were almost always made by the boy's father who negotiated or arranged the betrothal with the prospective bride's father. There was always a price or dowry to be paid. And I'm sorry to tell you romantics this . . . romantic love was not a reason for betrothal — it could be considered, but very rarely was betrothal and marriage based on true love. Love was to develop as the marriage progressed!

JESUS WANTS TO SHARE WITH OTHERS

339

APPARENTLY, as we read the Gospel accounts . . . Jesus did not like to eat alone! When He talked about a great banquet, He used the term "whosoever will may come." Think of the many times

He invited others to eat with Him. The last time was on the shores of the lake when He invited them to come and eat some charcoal-broiled fish, already prepared. He invited us all to share in the coming Marriage Supper of the Lamb. His last request on this earth centered around the fact that He wanted all of His followers to join Him in heaven. He even invited the thief who was being crucified with Him to meet Him in paradise. He wanted to take as many people as possible with Him to enjoy heaven for eternity!

THE ORIGINS OF WATER BAPTISM

340

FROM the beginning of Christianity, water baptism has been a rite of initiation or testimony to the public of the inner conversion. There are at least four opinions as to the origins of this practice: (1) To the ancient Jews, ritual washings symbolized moral cleansing. These Jews also demanded baptism for their converts along with circumcision for males. (2) The Essenes at Qumran had a purification rite of baptism in flowing water and a cold water ritual bath which was to take place every day at the fifth hour (about 11:00 a.m.). (3) This ritual was practiced by John the Baptist for all his converts. He may have taken this practice from the Essenes. (4) Of course, Jesus was baptized by John. Following the Day of Pentecost, the disciples of Jesus baptized all new converts "in the name of Jesus." From these beginnings it has been one of the most important rituals of Christianity.

THE NUMBER 12 IS SIGNIFICANT

341

NUMBERS in the Bible are always an interesting study . . . but not all are meant to be taken literally nor should more importance be read into them beyond their notation. On the other hand, numbers are often used as symbols that are sacred. The number "12" is especially significant: Jesus chose 12 apostles, there were 12 tribes of Israel, and there were 12 minor prophets in biblical canon. The night sky was divided into the 12 signs of the zodiac by the Chinese. The Babylonian numerical system was based on 12 rather than multiples of 10 which is the basis of our decimal system today. Other ancient cultures divided the year into 12 months and the day into 12 hours.

The number 12 combines with other numbers that were and are considered sacred. It's the sum of 5 plus 7 and the product of 3 times 4. The Old Testament uses multiples of the number 12 such as in the 24 different classes of Levites and priests. King David had 24,000 servants assigned to him. The vision of John, as revealed in the Revelation of Jesus Christ, makes much use of the number 12 . . . the special servants during the Great Tribulation will number 144,000, 12,000 from each tribe. The New Jerusalem has 12 foundations of jewels and 12 gates of pearl. Then in the center of this city stands the tree of life which bears 12 different kinds of fruit which is for the healing of the nations.

342 DID A WHALE REALLY SWALLOW JONAH?

JONAH is an interesting biblical book. Even though it is located among the 17 Old Testament prophetical books it contains no prophecies except for this: "Yet forty days, and Nineveh shall be overthrown." Further, Jonah doesn't look like any of the Hebrew prophets and nowhere is he referred to as a prophet or depicted as a prophet like Amos, Isaiah, or Jeremiah. He was an unprophetic-like character. The story is a prophetic narrative unlike any other.

But is this a true story? Did the "great fish" swallow Jonah or not? Was it a whale or a "great fish?"

The most authentic endorsement of the truth of this story is the observation that Jesus refers to this story. "For as Jonah was three days and three nights in the belly of a huge fish, so the Son of Man will be three days and three nights in the heart of the earth" (Matt. 12:40). Jesus didn't question the validity but simply stated that as Jonah was three days and three nights in the belly of a huge fish, so He would be in the earth. If Jesus endorsed it . . . then it must be a true story. The huge fish did swallow Jonah!

343 SAMARITANS

WHO were they and where did they come from? When Samaria, the capital of the northern kingdom of Israel, was conquered by the Assyrians in 721 B.C. and the people were carried away and forced into slavery, other Jews felt it was God's punishment. They were sure of it because there had been the practice of idolatry, witchcraft, and sorcery going on in the area. In Jesus' day, anybody living in the area was known as a "Samaritan." A likely explanation is that the Samaritans were the descendants of the Israelites who had escaped deportation by the Assyrians and intermarried with non-Jewish people who had also settled in this area.

The Jews, pure Jews, looked down and hated the Samaritans as contemptible heretics and outcasts. In the Gospel accounts there were times when Jesus was not treated with hospitality in Samaria. So you can imagine what a stir this must have caused when Jesus used a Samaritan as the hero in the parable we have called "The Good Samaritan." Also, it was a woman at the well, another Samaritan, whom He encountered, to the surprise of His disciples.

THE FOX

344

HEROD the Great is remembered as the tyrant who ordered the death of all the infant boys in his realm following the birth of Christ. Herod "Antipas" was the most gifted of his sons and inherited only a part of his father's kingdom at his death. Even though he was not Jewish, Antipas managed to rule for 43 years as the tetrarch of Jewish Galilee. He kept the peace while respecting the religious beliefs of his subjects. He was present in Jerusalem at the time of the arrest and trial of Jesus. This would have been an indication that he, too, celebrated the Passover with his pilgrimage to the Holy City. Jesus called him "that fox."

He was ambitious and loved luxury. He built the gorgeous seaside town of Tiberias as his capital but none of the religious Jews would move there because during construction they had uncovered an ancient cemetery, which made the site impure to practicing Jews. Antipas was then forced to populate this new capital with foreigners and people of the lower classes. In the meantime, he was a rising star in the Roman Empire because of his skill as a loyal diplomat.

His downfall started when he fell in love with Herodias, who was both his niece and sister-in-law. His wife became enraged and escaped home to her father, the Nabatean king, who came after his philandering son-in-law and handed him a disastrous military defeat.

Herodias, you remember, asked for the head of John the Baptist. She was responsible for his final, fateful error. Jealous that her brother Agrippa had been elevated to kingship, she urged Antipas to go with her to Rome to ask Caligula for a crown. The emperor was convinced by Agrippa that Antipas was a traitor and banished him to Gaul in A.D. 39 along with Herodias.

FISHING NETS

345

AS for fishing nets among the Israelites, we really have no direct information. However, it is quite likely that they were much like those of the Egyptians. There were two kinds . . . the drag net with floats on the top and weights on the bottom edge. It could be let down by boat while those who pulled it were on the shore. In lake fishing the net was cast from and then drawn into the boat except in the case of a very large catch when the net was dragged after the boat to shore.

A smaller net was used to fish in shallow water. It could be laid on the bottom between two poles that were held by the fisherman who would lift the net up catching the fish swimming over it . . . or it could be cast over a swimming fish or school to be dragged to shore.

It's quite likely it was the former that produced a miraculous catch that was almost beyond the capability of the fishing disciples to land. This was the kind of net which Jesus told them to throw or cast on the other side of the boat after they had fished all night and caught nothing. Perhaps we need to also throw our nets on the other side. Give it a try! Do as Jesus told you!

EVENTS OF THE FINAL WEEK

346

ALMOST one-third of the Gospel accounts are taken up with the final events leading to the execution of Jesus. There is more detail available to us than about any other week of His life. This week is also called the "Holy Week" and is celebrated with solemnity throughout the world. Let's just take a very brief walk through this week.

Six days before the Passover, while enjoying a quiet supper in

Bethany, Mary, the sister of Lazarus, anointed the feet of Jesus with a very costly perfume/ointment and dried them with her hair. It was almost as if done in preparation for His burial.

The next day Jesus rode into Jerusalem in triumph. We call it "Palm Sunday." The crowd was made up of pilgrims to the Holy City, as well as residents, who expectantly greeted Him as the promised Messiah in the hopes He would seize political power and lead the rebellion against Rome. Instead He preached His message of a heavenly kingdom, which challenged the Jewish religious establishment.

These leaders then enlisted the aid of Judas to arrest Jesus while at prayer and away from the crowd in the Garden of Gethsemane. This followed the Last Supper, or the Passover meal, with His disciples.

The trial began with false witnesses enlisted to testify against Him, and the religious authorities were able to quickly get the death sentence from the Roman procurator, Pontius Pilate.

Finally . . . this week ended with the excruciating, humiliating death on the Cross. This was followed His disciples fleeing in despair. His opponents gloated with the satisfaction that this radical, fanatical, upstart rabbi from Nazareth had been finally eliminated! Sunday, however, began a new day!!

WHICH TEMPLE?

347

OBVIOUSLY the temple was the center of religious life for the Jews. It played an important role in the ministry of Jesus. For example, the Bible says that "Jesus entered Jerusalem (on Palm Sunday) and went to the temple. He looked around at everything, but since it was already late, he went out to Bethany with the Twelve" (Mark 11:11). This particular temple was the temple renovated, enlarged, and beautified by Herod the Great. It was new architecturally, but religiously it was still the Temple of Zerubbabel which was rebuilt following the return of the Jews from Babylonian captivity. The six centuries between this return from exile and the destruction of Jerusalem by Titus in A.D. 70 are known in Jewish history as the age of the "Second Temple."

The temple which Solomon built had stood on this site for more than 350 years before it was destroyed by the Babylonians in 587 B.C. About 70 years later a new temple was built, and when dedicated on

March 12, 515 B.C., some of the old people who remembered Solomon's Temple said it was a poor imitation of the original temple.

So the temple to which Jesus went was a rebuilt, second temple and not the original. The first contact with the temple we have record of was in infancy when He was taken there for the ceremony of purification and praised by Simeon and Anna as the coming "Deliverer" of the Jews!

HOW MANY TEMPLES?

348

THERE were three different temples in the history of Israel. The first was built by King Solomon in 970 B.C. This was the finest of the temples and was destroyed by the Babylonians in 586 B.C.

The second was built by Zerubbabel and dedicated in 514 B.C. and was destroyed by the Seleucids in 197 B.C. Then there was the temple built by Herod in the first century B.C. This was the temple visited by Jesus in His earthly ministry. This third temple was destroyed by Titus and the Roman hordes in A.D. 70.

One of the most waited for and promised facts of future Bible prophecy will be the rebuilding of the temple! Perhaps in our lifetime!

THE GREATEST PERSECUTION

349

WHEN the Roman emperor Diocletian took the throne he divided the empire into two parts . . . East and West, and appointed two "senior" emperors and two "juniors," the caesars. He became "augustus" of the East and his aim was to reform the government and the military. In A.D. 298, as these reforms were being undertaken, he became outraged when Christian members of his court made the sign of the cross during the "taking of omens." The omens were not good so Diocletian began a purge of all Christian courtiers and Christian soldiers.

He and others blamed the empire's economic troubles on the Christians in A.D. 303 so he set down the first of four edicts which were designed to eliminate all Christians. The first decree banned all religious gatherings and called for the destruction of churches and books, and took away the civil rights of Christians. A second decree called for the jailing and imprisonment of all Christian clergy. The third provided for their release if they were willing to offer pagan sacrifices but condemned to death if they refused. The fourth was a blanket demand that "all the people" offer pagan sacrifice with the alternatives being death or slavery in hard labor.

This became the most far-reaching and most destructive of all the great persecutions again the Church of Jesus Christ under the Roman Empire. Nero was bad but Diocletian was worse.

350 THE SANHEDRIN

THE Jewish people honored the wisdom and experience of their elderly. Tradition was important to them and they depended upon their elders to keep them in line. This was an attitude which gave Israel strength and long-term stability. Sometimes it also made the Jew resistant to change.

The term "elder" was a title of dignity in both Old and New Testaments. An elder was looked to for direction, for knowledge, for wisdom, and for leadership. The 70 people Moses appointed to assist in governing Israel were "elders" who received the outpouring of the Spirit.

After Israel had settled down in the Promised Land of Canaan, each city appointed "elders" to help govern. After the monarchy of Saul, David, and Solomon was established, "elders" still functioned as a legislative body. As you follow the turbulent history of Israel, you will be impressed with the fact that the elders were the cohesive force in helping the nation survive.

When Jesus was doing His ministering in Israel, the "elders" were operating as a legislative, religious body called the "Sanhedrin." They ruled from the city of Jerusalem and held sway over all religious matters in Israel. Also, the Romans had granted to them some areas of civil government . . . but not the granting of a death penalty.

351 WOULD JESUS HAVE EATEN MEAT?

THE dietary laws of the Bible as given in the law of Moses, were very strict concerning meat. Oxen, cattle, sheep, and goats were considered "clean" animals because of their split hooves and they chewed a cud and were suitable for sacrifice and human consumption. Pigs, camels, rabbits, birds of prey, and rock badgers were considered to be unclean and not to be eaten or sacrificed.

Customarily, the Israelites didn't eat very much meat, except on some feast days. When they did cook a calf, lamb, or kid it was usually for guests or to celebrate a special occasion such as the return of the prodigal son in the parable which Jesus told.

So . . . did Jesus eat meat? I think we can say that He did on special occasions when He may have been the special guest in a home.

THE FIRST CRUSADE

352

THE Moslem "infidels" had captured Palestine in the year of A.D. 969. When the word finally reached Rome in 1095 that the Church of the Holy Sepulcher had been ransacked, Pope Urban II called for the faithful to pick up arms. To motivate them, he promised a number of things which God-fearing Christians could not easily ignore.

The deal was this: Any and all crusaders would receive complete remission from any punishment due to them because of their sins. They would also be released from any suffering through purgatory, and further — on the authority of the pope — would be allowed to enter heaven immediately after their death.

The results were that this First Crusade was a smashing success. The "Christians" took back Jerusalem in July of 1099 and promptly massacred every last Moslem and Jew they found there in the name of Jesus Christ.

JESUS' DISCIPLES

353

PETER'S name always is the first to appear in the Bible listings of Jesus' disciples. Simon (Peter) is taken from the Hebrew "Symeon." The Greek name "Peter" means "rock" or "stone." Andrew, who was Peter's brother, and Philip are the only other disciples with distinctly Greek names. Four of the other disciples' names are Greek in form but of Semitic origin: Bartholomew, Matthew, Thomas, and Thaddaeus. There is some uncertainty about Thaddaeus . . . instead of him, Luke includes Judas who is "not Judas Iscariot."

James and John, the sons of Zebedee, were called "Boanerges" by Jesus, which means "Sons of Thunder." These two might have been thundery in temperament or the holders of strong apocalyptic views since they were more than willing to call down fire from heaven on an unfriendly Samaritan village. The three who were present at the great moments of Jesus' life were Peter, James, and John.

James is to be distinguished from the disciple called "James the younger." Little is known of this disciple.

There was another Simon known as "Simon the Cananean" but Luke also calls him "Simon the Zealot."

Judas Iscariot is usually named last in the listing of disciples most likely because of his betrayal of Christ. But you must give him credit . . . he held a privileged position as treasurer of the 12.

STATIONS OF THE CROSS

THERE are 14 stations of the cross, according to church traditions. The whole series is also known as the "via Calvaria" or the "via Crucis." Each of these stations represents some aspect in the passage of Jesus from Pilate's Judgment Hall to Mount Calvary. At each of these stations, the faithful are expected to kneel and offer up a prayer in memory of that particular event. They are as follows:

1. Jesus is condemned to death.
2. Jesus is made to carry His own cross.
3. Jesus falls the first time under the weight of His cross.
4. Jesus meets His weeping mother.
5. Simon the Cyrenean helps Jesus carry the cross.
6. Veronica wipes the face of Jesus.
7. Jesus falls the second time.
8. Jesus speaks to the daughters of Jerusalem.
9. Jesus falls the third time.
10. Jesus is stripped of His garments.
11. Jesus is nailed to the cross.
12. Jesus dies on the cross.
13. Jesus is taken down from the cross.
14. Jesus is placed in the sepulchre.

TWO VERSIONS OF
THE LORD'S PRAYER

355

THE Lord's Prayer is recorded by Matthew and Luke in their Gospel accounts . . . but differ from each other. Many phrases which Jesus used have parallels in other Jewish religious writings . . . yet as Jesus prayed it, it forms a new and original whole prayer.

Luke's version begins simply with "Father. . . ." This is the word representative of the Aramaic "Abba," an intimate way of addressing the Heavenly Father. In our translation it would be like saying, "Daddy, God." You should also note, Jesus encouraged His followers to use this term when addressing God.

Matthew's version is more adapted to the kinds of prayers heard in a Jewish synagogue. Matthew's opening is "Our Father," or "Abinu" in Hebrew, which was the usual Jewish description of "the one in the heavens." Matthew also adds, "Your will be done on earth as it is in heaven."

Maybe this would be a good moment to take your own Bible down and read the two different versions. You will find them in Matthew 6:9–13 and Luke 11:2–4.

JESUS
BAR-ABBAS

356

THE Gospels tell us that Pontius Pilate attempted to save the life of Jesus by following a custom that allowed a prisoner to be set free at the celebration of the Passover. Instead . . . the crowd shouted for Barabbas to be set free. He was a man described as a bandit who had also been part of a rebellion as well as having committed murder. The word translated "bandit" is also the same one used by the Jewish historian Josephus, for "Zealot." Have you picked up on the irony? Barabbas, a freedom-fighter, is released and the one who is innocent of such activities was not.

There is other speculation surrounding this man. It's believed that he led an attempted coup as he and his followers stormed the citadel. The story has a difficulty in that only the Roman emperor could have released a prisoner condemned to death and it also unlikely that any responsible leader would have released a notorious nationalist.

Further . . . there is much curiosity in the man's name. One text originally is to have read "Jesus Bar-Abbas." We can only presume that the "Jesus" was removed from the manuscripts which Matthew wrote because it would be offensive to give such a sacred name to such a notorious character. One further oddity: "Bar-Abbas" means "Son of the Father." It's interesting that Jesus Christ also was the "Son of the Father."

357 BIBLICAL AUTHENTICITY

THE Bible is unique among all the works of literature. It was written over a 1,600 year period in 66 books by 40 different and diverse authors. Two of these authors were half-brothers of Jesus who didn't believe His claims until after His death and resurrection. The Bible was written in such diverse settings as palaces and dungeons. It was written in different places . . . on three different continents . . . Asia, Africa, and Europe. It was written in three different languages . . . Hebrew, Aramaic, and Greek.

When you consider such diversity and the fact that few of these authors had access to each other or to each other's writings, there is a total consistency in the facts presented and in the theology written. Not one of these authors criticizes the writings of any other. There are no dissenting opinions among these authors and their writings. It truly is an amazing compilation of truth.

The New Testament primarily tells the story of the "new covenant" between God and the people of God. It centers on the life, teachings, miracles, death, and resurrection of Jesus. Jesus is presented as the "Messiah" of the world.

Interestingly, though there are stories about His life, nothing is said about His physical appearance. This record is dependable as history. The British scholar F.F. Bruce wrote: "There is no body of ancient literature in the world that enjoys such a wealth of good textual attestation as the New Testament."

358 THE POWER OF THE SPIRIT

AS you read through the Bible, you cannot help but note the many different references to the Spirit: the Spirit of God, the

Spirit of the Lord, the Holy Spirit, the Third Person of the Trinity, the Teacher, the Holy Ghost, or the Comforter. In the Old Testament there are many examples of leadership strength and wisdom given through the power of the Spirit. Prophetic insight was given under the Spirit's influence.

Jesus is depicted in the Gospels as receiving the Spirit at His baptism as the Spirit descended in the form of a dove. Early in His ministry He said, "The Spirit of the Lord is upon me." The works that He performed, the wisdom of His teachings, and the good which He did are attributed to the workings of the Spirit through Him.

But the ministry of the Spirit didn't end with Him, because He promised that when He left He would send the "Comforter" who would also teach and guide His followers. You can follow this enduement with power through the Book of the Acts of the Apostles of Jesus Christ.

GROWTH OF THE
EARLY CHURCH

JESUS left behind Him a well-trained community of believers who had also been brought up in the Jewish faith . . . a mixture of some Jews and Greeks with some other proselytes. It was a remarkable beginning with 120 filled with the Holy Spirit on the Day of Pentecost. Then the first Jerusalem Christians held their possessions in common, worshiped regularly in the temple and met in private homes for prayers and the breaking of bread.

In contrast to the world around them . . . they cared for the poor, needy, and widows. It was a remarkable testimony to the change which had taken place within. Yes, they had some tensions and conflicts between them but this was an outstanding fellowship. They exemplified everything that the Church was intended to become.

Christianity spread rapidly through Syria, Asia Minor, Rome, and Greece. By the 2nd century the Church was a strong presence in North Africa, India, and Egypt.

It's been said that two important things triggered this remarkable growth: the quality of life and the quality of death. The lifestyle and the dying of the martyrs or "witnesses" was of such renown that the early Christian theologian Tertullian wrote: "The blood of Christians is seed."

TWO GREAT THEMES

THE Old Testament is the very foundation of our Western civilization. From this has come the beginnings of the Judaeo-Christian heritage. From this we can trace the moral and spiritual basis for the peoples of Europe, the Americas, and wherever the Bible has been taught, cherished, and followed. It's a huge panoramic sweep of great biblical people of history such as Abraham, Moses, David, the prophets, and the judges that have been the forerunners of human consciousness by way of examples. The events described here . . . the flood, building of the Tower of Babel, and conflicts between kingdoms are all the building blocks of our own society, judicial systems, literature, and religious traditions.

The New Testament is primarily the story of Jesus and the Church which He founded. He is the central figure in all of human history. This story, His story, is at the same time beautiful, awesome, sometimes terrible, dramatic, at times shocking, but always fascinating!

SAINT PETER'S FISH

EVEN today the Sea of Galilee is stocked with a wide variety of edible fish. One of the tastiest is the "Tilapia galilea" or "Saint Peter's fish." According to Matthew's account, Jesus told Peter to take a coin from the mouth of a fish in order to pay the temple tax. Legend has it that the fish was a "Tilapia galilea" and that Peter left his fingerprints as markings that identify the species today.

Speaking of fishing on the Sea of Galilee, in Christ's day different types of nets were used. A small circular net was cast from shore or shallow water and hauled in with a catch. Peter and Andrew were casting from shore when Jesus called them. A dragnet was drawn between two boats or between a single boat on water and a fisherman walking along the shore. Luke tells us that James and John were Peter's partners, therefore it was likely they owned one or more boats and probably used a dragnet.

After making their catch, the fish were sorted and some were discarded because they were forbidden by Jewish dietary laws. The others were cleaned and sold. Then there was the job of continually mending their nets, which James and John were doing when Jesus called them and Simon and Andrew to follow Him and become "fishers of men" (Matt. 4:18–21; Mark 1:16–17).

AN ENEMY REPORTS

362

THE Early Church was under close scrutiny by the Roman Empire. They were alarmed about what this new group or sect would do to their authority. The growth was to be watched and some emperors wanted to completely destroy the followers of Jesus Christ. But not all the reports about those early Christians were of a negative sort. The following was written from the Roman governor Pliny, to the emperor Trajan about A.D. 113:

> They were in the habit of meeting on a certain fixed day before it was light, when they sang an anthem to Christ as God, and bound themselves by a solemn oath not to commit any wicked deed, but to abstain from all fraud, theft and adultery, never to break their word, or deny a trust when called upon to honor it; after which it was their custom to separate and then meet again to partake of food, but food of an ordinary and innocent kind (Pliny, Letters X.96).

CREEDS AND HYMNS OF THE CHURCH

363

THE New Testament Church of Jesus Christ was a community of believers which held to some very basic truths such as the "apostles teachings" or "the true teaching" or "true words." Many of these are contained in New Testament writings but others were used in worship, in the writing of hymns, and the repeating of their creeds.

Some of these were short and simple: "Jesus is Lord" was the foundational, basic one used by all of them. But especially it was used by new converts and was the affirmation most looked for as a confession of faith. Some of their creeds were longer but also pithy and to the point: "There is one God, and there is one mediator between God and men, the man Christ Jesus," or another stated, "One Lord, one faith, one baptism."

Paul the Apostle, in his second letter to Timothy, penned such a statement of faith, which is in the form of a hymn. It most likely would have been sung at a service of baptism:

> He appeared in human form,
> Was shown to be right by the Spirit
> And seen by angels.
> He was preached among the nations,
> Was believed in throughout the world,
> And was taken up to heaven.

WHAT WOULD YOU DO?

364

A number of years ago, a noted group of educators and philosophers had gathered in a clubroom in a prominent London hotel. The conversation took a surprising turn during a discussion of some of the most illustrious figures of the past. One of those present suddenly asked: "Gentlemen, what would we do if Milton were to enter this room?"

"Ah," replied one of the members in the circle, "we would give him such an ovation as should compensate for the late recognition that was not accorded to him by the people of his day."

"And if Shakespeare entered?" asked another.

"We would arise and crown him master of the phrase," was the answer from another.

"And if Einstein were to enter?" asked somebody else.

"Applaud and congratulate him on the achievements made possible because of his theories."

"And if Jesus Christ were to enter?" one more asked.

"I think," said Charles Lamb, following an intense silence, "we would all fall on our faces."

A FINAL TRIBUTE

365

SOCRATES philosophized for 40 years, Plato for 50, Aristotle for 40, and Jesus Christ for only 3! Yet those 3 years infinitely transcend in influence the combined 130 years of the teachings of Socrates, Plato, and Aristotle.

Jesus painted no pictures nor created no art work, yet the works of Raphael, Michelangelo, and da Vinci received their inspiration from Him. Jesus wrote no poetry nor prose, yet Dante, Milton, and scores of others were inspired by Him. Jesus composed no music, yet Haydn, Handel, Beethoven, Bach, and Mendelssohn reached their highest level of perfection in compositions when written to His praise.

Every area of human achievement and greatness has been incomparably enriched by the humble carpenter of Nazareth. His most unique and wonderful contribution to humanity is the changing of the human soul. Not philosophy, art, literature, nor music can do that. Only Jesus can break the power of sin and set the captive free! The world admires Him from afar but all need to invite Him in to be a personal Savior.

This final tribute has been written by Phillips Brooks and is a most eloquent and fitting conclusion to this compilation of facts about Jesus Christ. It is entitled . . .

ONE SOLITARY LIFE

I am far within the mark when I say that all the armies that ever marched, and all the navies that ever were built, and all the parliaments that ever sat, and all the kings that ever reigned, put together, have not affected the life of man upon this earth as powerfully as has that one solitary life . . . the LIFE OF CHRIST!

Perhaps your interest in Jesus Christ has been raised and you would like to do further research or reading about His life. The following are suggestions and recommendations of books you might want to consider:

BROWN, RAYMOND E. *The Birth of the Messiah.* Garden City, NY: Image Books, 1979.

BAMMEL, E. and C.F.D. MOULE. *Jesus and the Politics of His Day.* Cambridge, UK: Cambridge University Press, 1984.

BRINER, BOB. *The Management Methods of Jesus.* Nashville, TN: Thomas Nelson Publishers, 1996.

BRUCE, F.F. *Jesus and Paul, Places They Knew.* Nashville, TN: Thomas Nelson Publishers, 1983.

BRUCE, FREDERICK F. *New Testament History.* London: Thomas Nelson Publishers, 1969; New York: Doubleday, 1971.

DANIEL-ROPS, HENRI. *Jesus and His Times.* New York: E.P. Dutton & Co., Inc., 1956.

DODD, C.H. *The Founder of Christianity.* London: Collins, 1971.

GUIGNEBERT, CHARLES. *The Jewish World in the Time of Jesus.* New Hyde Park, NY: University Books, Inc., 1959.

HENGEL, MARTIN. *Crucifixion.* London: SCM Press, 1977.

JONES, LAURIE BETH. *Jesus CEO.* New York: Hyperion, 1995.

KEATING, THOMAS. *The Mystery of Christ.* Amity, NY: Amity House, 1987.

KEMPIS, THOMAS A. *Of the Imitation of Christ.* New York: Holt, Rinehart and Winston, Inc.

LOCKYER, HERBERT. *All About God in Christ.* Peabody, MA: Hendrickson Publishers, Inc., 1995.

MONTEFIORE, HUGH. *Jesus Across the Centuries.* London: SCM Press, 1983.

PAX, WOLFGANG E. *In the Footsteps of Jesus.* Leon Amiel Publisher, 1976.

PELIKAN, JAROSLAV. *Jesus Through the Centuries.* New Haven, CT: Yale University Press, 1985.

READER'S DIGEST. *Jesus and His Times.* Pleasantville, NY: Reader's Digest Association, Inc., 1992.

WATSON, DAVID, and SIMON JENKINS. *Jesus Then and Now.* Herts, England: Lion Publishing, Lella Productions, 1983.

WHISTON, WILLIAM, translator. *The Life and Works of Flavius Josephus.* New York: Holt, Rinehart and Winston.

WILSON, IAN. *Jesus The Evidence.* London, UK: Weidenfeld & Nicolson, 1984; New York: Harper & Row, 1984.